Cuisinart Air Fryer Oven Cookbook for Beginners

800 Affordable, Delicious and Super Crisp Recipes for Cooking Easier, Faster, And More Enjoyable for You and Your Family!

Menye Bardan

© Copyright 2020 Menye Bardan - All Rights Reserved.

In no way is it legal to reproduce, duplicate, or transmit any part of this document by either electronic means or in printed format. Recording of this publication is strictly prohibited, and any storage of this material is not allowed unless with written permission from the publisher. All rights reserved.

The information provided herein is stated to be truthful and consistent, in that any liability, regarding inattention or otherwise, by any usage or abuse of any policies, processes, or directions contained within is the solitary and complete responsibility of the recipient reader. Under no circumstances will any legal liability or blame be held against the publisher for any reparation, damages, or monetary loss due to the information herein, either directly or indirectly.

Respective authors own all copyrights not held by the publisher.

Legal Notice:

This book is copyright protected. This is only for personal use. You cannot amend, distribute, sell, use, quote or paraphrase any part of the content within this book without the consent of the author or copyright owner. Legal action will be pursued if this is breached.

Disclaimer Notice:

Please note the information contained within this document is for educational and entertainment purposes only. Every attempt has been made to provide accurate, up-to-date and reliable, complete information. No warranties of any kind are expressed or implied. Readers acknowledge that the author is not engaging in the rendering of legal, financial, medical or professional advice.

By reading this document, the reader agrees that under no circumstances are we responsible for any losses, direct or indirect, which are incurred as a result of the use of information contained within this document, including, but not limited to, errors, omissions, or inaccuracies.

Table of Contents

Introduction 8
Chapter 1: Cuisinart Air Fryer Toaster Oven Basics 9
    What is Cuisinart Air Fryer Toaster Oven? 9
    Features of Cuisinart Art Air Fryer Toaster Oven 9
    Cooking Functions 10
    Benefits of Using Cuisinart Air Fryer Toaster Oven 11
    Tips 12
Chapter 2: Breakfast & Brunch 13
    Breakfast Oatmeal Cake 13
    Banana Oat Muffins 13
    Easy Cheese Egg Casserole 13
    Quick & Easy Granola 14
    Delicious Baked Eggs 14
    Apple Cinnamon Oat Muffins 14
    Healthy Baked Oatmeal 15
    Easy Apple Pie Baked Oatmeal 15
    Mushroom Spinach Egg Muffins 16
    Crunchy Vanilla Granola 16
    Nutritious Egg Breakfast Muffins 16
    Soft Banana Oat Muffins 17
    Healthy Breakfast Cookies 17
    Banana Coconut Muffins 18
    Delicious Broccoli Quiche 18
    Tator Tots Casserole 19
    Simple Apple Crisp 19
    Cheesy Hash Brown Casserole 19
    Egg Ham Casserole 20
    Hashbrown Breakfast Casserole 20
    Easy Egg Bites 21
    Flavorful Zucchini Frittata 21
    Mushroom Sausage Breakfast Bake 21
    Delicious Baked Omelet 22
    Spicy Egg Casserole 22
    Moist Banana Breakfast Bread 23
    Hearty Sweet Potato Baked Oatmeal ... 23
    Mediterranean Spinach Frittata 24
    Broccoli Asparagus Frittata 24
    Perfect Sausage-Hash Brown Casserole 24
    Perfect Chicken Casserole 25
    Potato Egg Casserole 25
    Crustless Breakfast Quiche 26
    Perfect Potato Casserole 26
    Delicious Pumpkin Bread 26
    Healthy Bran Muffins 27
    Carrot Banana Bread 27
    Protein Packed Breakfast Casserole 28
    Easy Cheesy Breakfast Casserole 28
    Delicious French Eggs 28
    Basil Dill Egg Muffins 29
    Easy Zucchini Frittata 29
    Berry Breakfast Oatmeal 30
    Bacon Bread Egg Casserole 30
    Jalapeno Corn Egg Bake 30
    Sweet Pineapple Oatmeal 31
    Breakfast Sweet Potato Hash 31
    Nutritious Cinnamon Oat Muffins 32
    Baked Peanut Butter Oatmeal 32
    Cinnamon Sweet Potatoes 32
    Breakfast Potatoes 33
    Sweet Potato Chickpeas Hash 33
    Poppy Seed Muffins 33
    Healthy Oatmeal Bars 34
    Whole Wheat Carrot Bread 34
    Zucchini Breakfast Bread 34
    Choco Chip Banana Bread 35
    Flavorful Pumpkin Bread 35
    Lemon Blueberry Bread 36
    Moist Orange Bread Loaf 36
    Kale Egg Muffins 36
    Chicken Breakfast Muffins 37
    Spinach Zucchini Egg Muffins 37
    Spinach Egg Bites 38
    Omelet Egg Muffins 38
    Easy Breakfast Bake 38
    Zucchini Breakfast Casserole 39
    Easy Egg Quiche 39
    Baked Breakfast Quiche 39
    Ham Egg Muffins 40
Chapter 3: Poultry 41
    Juicy Baked Chicken Breast 41
    Baked Spinach Cheese Chicken 41
    Green Chili Chicken Noodle Casserole 41
    Baked Chicken Noodle Casserole 42
    Simple & Healthy Baked Chicken Breasts 42
    Flavorful Lemon Pepper Chicken 43
    Delicious Tender Chicken Breasts 43
    Potato Garlic Chicken 43
    Italian Veggie Chicken 44
    Easy Smothered Chicken 44
    Baked Fajita Chicken 44

Juicy & Tender Chicken Breast	45
Juicy Balsamic Chicken	45
Pesto Chicken	46
Cheesy Bacon Chicken	46
Juicy Baked Chicken Wings	46
Bacon Broccoli Chicken	47
Easy Creamy Chicken	47
Easy Baked Chicken Drumsticks	47
Crispy Cajun Chicken Breast	48
Honey Garlic Chicken Wings	48
Tasty Turkey Meatballs	48
Delicious Turkey Cutlets	49
Herb Turkey Tenderloin	49
Juicy Chicken Patties	50
Parmesan Baked Chicken Pasta	50
Ranch Chicken Thighs	50
Bacon Ranch Chicken	51
Flavors Cheesy Chicken Breasts	51
Mexican Salsa Chicken	51
Baked Lemon Pepper Chicken	52
Easy Pesto Chicken	52
Cheesy Chicken Casserole	52
Chicken Pasta Broccoli Casserole	53
Mustard Chicken Breasts	53
Tasty Chicken Tenders	54
Baked Chicken Fritters	54
Chicken Burger Patties	54
Meatballs	55
Turkey Meatballs	55
Zucchini Chicken Meatballs	56
Garlic Chicken	56
Greek Chicken Paillard	56
Olive Caper Chicken	57
Tasty Lemon Chicken	57
Baked Italian Lemon Chicken	57
Meatballs	58
Meatballs	58
Spinach Turkey Meatballs	59
Lemon Mustard Chicken	59
Baked Zucchini Chicken Tenders	59
Roasted Pepper Chicken Thighs	60
Chicken with Vegetables	60
Mustard Chicken Thighs	61
Coconut Chicken Tenders	61
Crispy Crusted Chicken	61
Cracker Apple Chicken	62
Air Fry Chicken Drumsticks	62
Honey Chicken Wings	62
Crispy Chicken Nuggets	63
Ranch Chicken Wings	63
Sweet & Spicy Chicken Wings	63
Garlic Butter Wings	64
Garlic Chicken Wings	64
Simple Jerk Chicken Wings	65
Sriracha Chicken Wings	65
Easy BBQ Chicken Drumsticks	65
Air Fryer Chicken Tenders	66
Greek Chicken Breast	66
Meatballs	66
Chapter 4: Beef, Pork & Lamb	**68**
Perfect Beef Hash brown Bake	68
Spicy Meatballs	68
Juicy & Tender Pork Chops	68
Ranch Pork Chops	69
Pesto Pork Chops	69
Pork Chops with Potatoes	69
Meatballs	70
Crunchy Parmesan Pork Chops	70
Delicious Pork Belly	70
Cheesy Pork Chops	71
Baked Pork Ribs	71
Herb Beef Tips	72
Meatballs	72
Meatballs	72
Meatloaf	73
Delicious Lamb Patties	73
Meatballs	74
Tender Pork Tenderloin	74
Easy Pork Chops	74
Baked Sweet & Tangy Pork Chops	75
Curried Beef Patties	75
Tender Baked Pork Chops	75
Cripsy Crusted Pork Chops	76
Easy Ranch Pork Chops	76
Meatballs	76
Pork Burger Patties	77
Parmesan Herb Meatballs	77
Meatballs	78
Crispy Cracker Crusted Pork Chops	78
Meatballs	78
Cheesy Baked Burger Patties	79
Meatballs	79
Baked Beef & Broccoli	79
Meatballs	80
Meatloaf	80
Jalapeno Basil Lamb Patties	80
Meatballs	81
Meatloaf	81
Pork Chops with Potatoes	82
Herb Pork Tenderloin	82

Paprika Pork Tenderloin	82
Garlic Pork Roast	83
Baked Pork Tenderloin	83
Rosemary Pork Chops	83
Stuffed Pork Chops	84
Crispy Crusted Pork Chops	84
Spiced Pork Chops	84
Meatballs	85
Meatballs	85
Goat Cheese Meatballs	86
Quick Baked Pork Patties	86
Asian Meatballs	86
Cajun Burger Patties	87
Asian Pork Shoulder	87
Tasty Breaded Pork Chops	87
Air Fryer Herb Pork Chops	88
Steak Seasoned Pork Chops	88
Parmesan Cajun Pork Chops	89
Pork Belly Strips	89
Easy Pork Bites	89
Juicy Pork Loin	90
Honey Garlic Pork Chops	90
Air Fryer Juicy Pork Chops	90
Meatballs	91
Delicious Air Fryer Kebabs	91
Tasty Steak Tips	91
Meatballs	92
Simple Burger Patties	92
Ranch Beef Patties	92
Flavorful Sirloin Steak	93

Chapter 5: Fish & Seafood 94

Tender & Juicy Cajun Cod	94
Lemon Butter Shrimp	94
Spicy Lemon Garlic Tilapia	94
Cajun Red Snapper	95
Perfect Baked Cod	95
Flavorful Baked Halibut	95
Healthy Haddock	96
Delicious Baked Basa	96
Baked Pesto Salmon	96
Paprika Basil Baked Basa	97
Delicious Shrimp Casserole	97
Easy Blackened Shrimp	97
Old Bay Shrimp	98
Spicy Baked Shrimp	98
Baked Scallops	98
Blackened Mahi Mahi	99
Herb Baked Catfish Fillets	99
Moist & Juicy Baked Cod	100
Parmesan Salmon & Asparagus	100

Baked Spinach Tilapia	100
Paprika Cod	101
Salmon Beans & Mushrooms	101
Baked Tilapia	101
Easy Baked Fish Fillet	102
Italian Salmon	102
Flavorful Herb Salmon	102
Spicy Halibut	103
Air Fryer Spicy Shrimp	103
Thyme Rosemary Shrimp	103
Easy Shrimp Fajitas	104
Tasty Lemon Pepper Basa	104
Baked Buttery Shrimp	104
Orange Fish Fillets	105
Baked Garlic Paprika Halibut	105
Spicy Catfish	105
Baked Lemon Swordfish	106
Baked Garlic Tilapia	106
Sweet & Spicy Lime Salmon	107
Spicy Lemon Cod	107
Rosemary Garlic Shrimp	107
Tomato Garlic Shrimp	108
Delicious Crab Cakes	108
Quick Tuna Patties	108
Simple Salmon Patties	109
Herb Fish Fillets	109
Marinated Salmon	109
Honey Glazed Salmon	110
Air Fry Prawns	110
Tasty Parmesan Shrimp	110
Dill Salmon Patties	111
Air Fry Tuna Patties	111
Dijon Salmon Fillets	111
Old Bay Seasoned Scallops	112
Lemon Pepper White Fish Fillets	112
Basil Tomato Salmon	112
Greek Cod with Asparagus	113
Italian Cod	113
Spinach Scallops	113
Miso White Fish Fillets	114
Perfect Crab Cakes	114

Chapter 6: Vegetables & Side Dishes 115

Baked Vegetables	115
Cheese Herb Zucchini	115
Healthy Spinach Muffins	115
Honey Corn Muffins	116
Delicious Mac and Cheese	116
Jalapeno Bread	117
Healthy Barley Bread	117
Rice Broccoli Casserole	117

Cinnamon Sweet Potatoes 118
Herb Cheese Sweet Potatoes............. 118
Baked Paprika Sweet Potatoes 119
Cheesy Broccoli Rice........................... 119
Creamy Broccoli Casserole 119
Baked Apple Sweet Potatoes 120
Mac & Cheese..................................... 120
Dijon Zucchini Patties......................... 120
Baked Asparagus 121
Baked Potatoes & Carrots 121
Spicy Brussels Sprouts........................ 122
Cheddar Broccoli Fritters 122
Baked Cauliflower & Mushrooms...... 122
Baked Cauliflower & Tomatoes 123
Parmesan Baked Asparagus................ 123
Baked Cauliflower & Pepper 123
Baked Broccoli 124
Baked Eggplant Pepper & Mushrooms
.... 124
Baked Garlic Mushrooms 124
Herb Balsamic Mushrooms................. 125
Parmesan Zucchini.............................. 125
Baked Italian Vegetables 125
Broccoli Olives Tomatoes 126
Baked Artichoke Hearts 126
Healthy Asparagus Potatoes 127
Easy Broccoli Bread............................ 127
Baked Lemon Broccoli........................ 127
Baked Root Vegetables 128
Cheesy Squash Casserole 128
Cheddar Cheese Cauliflower Casserole
.... 128
Baked Honey Carrots......................... 129
Paprika Potatoes 129
Baked Potatoes Eggplant.................... 129
Baked Sweet Potatoes........................ 130
Baked Ratatouille 130
Baked Turnip & Sweet Potato........... 130
Scalloped Potatoes.............................. 131
Delicious Baked Potatoes 131
Simple Baked Potatoes....................... 131
Air Fry Broccoli Florets...................... 132
Air-Fried Herb Mushrooms 132
Lemon Garlic Brussels Sprouts.......... 132
Air Fryer Corn.................................... 133
Air Fried Eggplant Cubes 133
Healthy Green Beans 133
Ranch Potatoes................................... 134
Air Fry Garlic Baby Potatoes............. 134
Brussels Sprouts & Sweet Potatoes.... 134
Tasty Hassel Back Potatoes 135
Spicy Brussels Sprouts........................ 135
Chili Lime Sweet Potatoes 135
Tasty Butternut Squash...................... 136

Chapter 7: Snacks & Appetizers............137
Jalapeno Spinach Dip 137
Flavorful Crab Dip.............................. 137
Spicy Brussels Sprouts........................ 137
Baked Almonds 138
Cheesy Spinach Dip............................ 138
Cheese Garlic Dip............................... 138
Tasty Ricotta Dip................................ 139
Cheesy Onion Dip............................... 139
Easy Cheese Dip 139
Spicy Cauliflower Florets.................... 140
Delicious Jalapeno Poppers................ 140
Air Fryer Walnuts 140
Garlic Cauliflower Florets................... 141
Cheesy Brussels Sprouts..................... 141
Air Fryer Spicy Chickpeas 141
Sweet Cinnamon Chickpeas............... 142
Easy Sweet Potato Fries 142
Salsa Cheese Dip................................. 142
Perfect Ranch Potatoes 143
Tasty Potato Wedges 143
Delicious Cauliflower Hummus 143
Air Fryer Mixed Nuts.......................... 144
Air Fry Olives 144
Sweet Potato Croquettes................... 144
Healthy Carrot Fries 145
Artichoke Cashews Spinach Dip 145
Easy Air Fryer Tofu 145
Tasty Broccoli Fritters........................ 146
Healthy Baked Pecans........................ 146
Vegetables Balls.................................. 146
Margherita Pizza 147
Rosemary Roasted Almonds.............. 147
Parmesan Green Beans 148
Tasty Cauliflower Tots 148
Cheesy Sweet Pepper Poppers 148
Easy Bacon Bites................................ 149
Tasty Jalapeno Poppers 149
Spicy Crab Dip.................................... 149
Chestnuts Spinach Dip....................... 150
Cheesy Beef Dip.................................. 150
Cajun Sweet Potato Tots................... 150
Crack Dip.. 151
Tasty Sweet Potato Fries................... 151
Parmesan Zucchini Fries.................... 151
Air Fryer Pepperoni Chips.................. 152

Crispy Eggplant Bites	152
Bacon Cheese Jalapeno Poppers	152
Air Fryer Cabbage Chips	153
Healthy Broccoli Tots	153
Kale Chips	153
Easy Bacon Jalapeno Poppers	154
BBQ Chicken Wings	154
Vegetable Kebabs	154
Shrimp Kebabs	155
Tofu Steaks	155
Healthy Lemon Tofu	155
Broccoli Nuggets	156
Yummy Turkey Jalapeno Poppers	156
Arugula Artichoke Dip	156
Crab Stuffed Mushrooms	157
Creamy Chicken Dip	157
Air Fryer Paprika Almonds	157
Zucchini Coconut Bites	158
Coconut Broccoli Pop-Corn	158
Cheese Artichoke Spinach Dip	158
Spicy Chicken Wings	159
Habanero Chicken Wings	159
Cheddar Dill Mushrooms	159
Air Fryer Nuts	160
Air Fryer Radish Chips	160

Chapter 8: Desserts 161

Delicious Raspberry Cobbler	161
Orange Almond Muffins	161
Easy Almond Butter Pumpkin Spice Cookies	161
Moist Pound Cake	162
Banana Butter Brownie	162
Peanut Butter Muffins	162
Baked Apple Slices	163
Vanilla Peanut Butter Cake	163
Strawberry Cobbler	163
Moist Chocolate Brownies	164
Yummy Scalloped Pineapple	164
Vanilla Lemon Cupcakes	165
Walnut Carrot Cake	165
Baked Peaches	165
Cinnamon Apple Crisp	166
Apple Cake	166
Almond Cranberry Muffins	167
Vanilla Butter Cake	167
Coconut Butter Apple Bars	167
Easy Blueberry Muffins	168
Tasty Almond Macaroons	168
Moist Baked Donuts	168
Eggless Brownies	169
Vanilla Banana Brownies	169
Choco Cookies	170
Chocolate Chip Cookies	170
Oatmeal Cake	170
Delicious Banana Cake	171
Chocolate Cake	171
Almond Blueberry Bars	172
Healthy Sesame Bars	172
Coconut Pumpkin Bars	172
Almond Peanut Butter Bars	173
Delicious Lemon Bars	173
Easy Egg Custard	174
Flavors Pumpkin Custard	174
Almond Butter Cookies	174
Tasty Pumpkin Cookies	175
Almond Pecan Cookies	175
Butter Cookies	175
Tasty Brownie Cookies	176
Tasty Gingersnap Cookies	176
Simple Lemon Pie	177
Flavorful Coconut Cake	177
Easy Lemon Cheesecake	177
Lemon Butter Cake	178
Cream Cheese Butter Cake	178
Easy Ricotta Cake	179
Strawberry Muffins	179
Mini Brownie Muffins	179

Chapter 9: 30-Day Meal Plan 181
Conclusion 183

Introduction

The Cuisinart air fryer toaster oven is one of the multifunctional kitchen appliances that perform an operation like air fry, oven, and toaster. It requires very little fat and oil to cook your food. It circulates hot air to cook your food quickly and gives you even cooking results. The quick hot air circulation mechanisms not only cook your food faster but also improve the taste and texture of your food. The Cuisinart oven allows you to cook almost everything in a single appliance. Using the Cuisinart oven you can cook vegetables, meat, fish, poultry, seafood, fruits, desert, and more. The combination of cooking like bake-convection and quick heat up mechanism makes it a faster and reliable cooking appliance.

The Cuisinart air fryer toaster oven has a versatile cooking appliance which broils, air fry, toast, bake, and reheat your foods. The oven circulates hot air into the cooking chamber to cook food faster and evenly without any cold spot. The Cuisinart oven comes with large enough space which is capable to handle a large number of foods like chicken, small size pizzas, and more. The main advantage of cuisine air fryer oven is that it saves more than 80 % of oil while frying your food without compromising food taste and texture.

The Cuisinart air fryer toaster oven book includes healthy and delicious recipes range from breakfast to desserts. The recipes written in this cookbook are easily understandable form and written with their perfect preparation and cooking time. All the recipes are unique and at end of each recipe written with their nutritional value information. The nutritional value information helps you to know about your daily calorie intake. The cookbook also comes with a 30-day meal plan which helps you to decide the quantities of food you need. Meal planning will also help you to reduce the food wastage and your grocery bills. There is lots of cookbook available in the market and online store on this topic, thanks for choosing my cookbook. I hope you enjoy and love the recipes written in this cookbook.

Chapter 1: Cuisinart Air Fryer Toaster Oven Basics

What is Cuisinart Air Fryer Toaster Oven?

The Cuisinart air fryer toaster oven is an innovative and advanced cooking appliance used to perform different cooking techniques. As its name indicates that, it works as an oven toaster and air fryer these three different cooking techniques make it a unique cooking appliance.

The Cuisinart air fryer toaster oven is working on 1800 watt and it is made up of a sturdy stainless steel body that gives sleek look to your Cuisinart oven. It is one of the multifunctional cooking appliances not only Air fry your food but also performs different operations like broil, toast, bake and warm, etc. Due to large capacity, you can toast 6 bread slices at a time, roast 4 pounds of chicken, and bake a 12-inch pizza.

It allows you to cook lots of different dishes like meat, poultry, fish, desserts, vegetables, and fruits. It runs on hot air circulation techniques in which hot air is circulating into the cooking chamber with the help of a convection fan situated at the top side of the oven. Using this technique Cuisinart air fryer toaster oven cooks your food faster and evenly from all the sides. It fries your favourite French fries, chicken wings, and shrimp with very little oil or no oil. It is one of the healthier ways to prepare your favourite food faster.

Features of Cuisinart Art Air Fryer Toaster Oven

The Cuisinart air fryer toaster oven is loaded with various features that make your daily cooking easiest, fastest, and safest way. These features are:

- Power LED indicator

The power light is illuminated continuously when the oven is in use. Continuous light illuminates indicates that when the oven is in use the exterior wall of the oven gets very hot.

- On/Oven Timer Dial

The timer dial is used to set the desire cooking time as per your recipe needs. The timer range is set in between 1 minute to 1 hour. When the timer is finished the oven is turned off. You cannot use the timer dial while using the toast function.

- Temperature Dial

The temperature dial helps you to set the desire temperature setting as per your recipe needs. The dial temperature range starts in between 150°F to 450°F.

- Function Dial

The function dial is used to select desire cooking functions from warm, broil, toast, bake, and air fry.

- On/ Toast Timer dial

This function allows you to select the desire toast shade from light, medium to dark. First set the function dialer at toast position then select the desired shade from the toasting dial. When the desire cooking cycle is completed the oven is power off automatically.

- Light Button

Using this button you can switch on the oven interior light to see the cooking process when the oven door is closed.

- Pull Crumb Tray

The Crumb tray is situated at the front bottom side of the oven. You can pull it out to easily clean for crumbs, bits, and pieces of foods fallen during baking or grilling

- Air Fryer Basket

It is recommended that while using the air fryer function you can use the air fryer basket seated into baking pan/drip tray to avoid the mess created during the air frying process.

- Baking Pan/ Drip Tray

As per your convenience, you can use it while you are roasting or baking your food. You can also use it while air frying your food to prevent spills residues.

- Safety Auto OFF Door Switch

The Cuisinart air fryer toaster oven is equipped with a safety auto-off door switch which automatically shuts off the oven power supply if the oven door is opened.

- Cord Storage

At the backside of the oven, cord storage is given to store excess cord to keep your kitchen countertop clean and neat.

Cooking Functions

The Cuisinart air fryer toaster oven comes with 5 different cooking functions these functions include:

1. Warm

This function is used to keep your food warm until it to be served. You can also reheat your leftover food or frozen food using this function. It keeps your food warm and makes your air fried food crisp again.

To use this function set your oven rack at rack 2 position. Then set the temperature dial at the warm position and function dial at warm. Select the desired time for warming your food using a timer dial. While the warming cycle is going on the power led illuminates and when the warming cycle has been completed the oven is automatically power off itself.

2. Broil Convection Broil

This function is used to broil your favourite burgers, melting cheese, and toppings spread over sandwiches. The combination of broil and convection gives a nice brown texture to your favourite meat and fish from all the sides.

While using this function first place the air fryer rack over a baking pan and set it into the rack to the position. Then set the function dial at broil convection position and temperature dial position to Toast/Broil position. Select the desire cooking time to start the actual broiling process. After finishing the cooking cycle the oven is automatically power off itself.

3. Toast

Using this function you can toast your favourite sandwich, bread, and warmed up your waffle.

To toast food first place your food in centre position at oven rack or baking pan and set it at rack position 2 for toasting purpose. Then set the function dial at toast position and temperature dial at Toast/Broil position. Turn the toast timer dial and select the desired shade from light, med, and dark. When the toasting cycle is complete the timer will ring and the oven automatically powers off.

4. Bake Convection Bake

This setting is ideal for baking your favourite foods. Using this setting you can bake casseroles, cakes, pastry, muffins, and cookies. With the help of convection fan hot air is blows fast into the cooking chamber and it gives you baking as well as browning results. You can make roast meat and make 8*11 inch pizza into baking pan.

To start baking first set the function dial at the bake convection bake position and select the desire temperature level with the help of the temperature dial. Turn and select the appropriate cooking time as per recipe needs. After finishing the baking cycle oven power off automatically. To get the best baking results always preheat your oven for 5 minutes prior.

5. Air Fry

This function is used to air fry your favourite foods like French fries, onion rings, chicken wings, and more. This is one of the healthy methods of frying your favourite food quickly and easily. It gives a nice crispy and crunchy texture to your food.

To air fry, your food first places the air fry rack into baking try and set it into rack position 2. Then set the function dial at air fry position and select desire temperature settings. Turn the timer dial and select the desired time as per recipe needs. When the cooking cycle is complete the oven is automatically powered off.

Benefits of Using Cuisinart Air Fryer Toaster Oven

The Cuisinart Toaster oven is one of the multi-functional cooking appliances that work as an air fryer, oven, and toaster come with various benefits.

- **Cooks healthy Food**

Compare to the deep-frying method Cuisinart air fryer toaster oven requires very little oil to cook your food. You cook a wide variety of fried food like French fries, chicken wings, onion rings within a tablespoon of oil without compromising the taste and texture of food. It encourages you to change your daily eating habits towards healthy eating. Air fried food is one of the healthiest choices for daily cooking. They are lower in calories, fats, and some harmful compounds found in the traditional deep frying method.

- **Versatile Cooking Appliance**

The Cuisinart oven is performing operations of air fryer, oven, and toaster. You can use it for different operations like Air fry your French fries, broil meat or fish, toast bread or sandwich, bake your favourite cake and also keep your food warm. All these operations are made into a single appliance; you never need to buy a separate cooking appliance for each operation. It not only saves your time and energy but also saves your money.

- **Cooks your food faster**

The Cuisinart oven is loaded with a hot air circulation mechanism situated at the top side of the oven. It blows the hottest air with the help of a convection fan and cooks your food fast and evenly from all the sides. The oven consumes 1800 watt power to blow 450°F hot air which cooks your food quickly as compared to the traditional cooking method.

- **Cooks large quantity of food**

The Cuisinart oven is specially designed to hold more food. It comes with 2 rack positions and holds a large quantity of food at a time. The small frame and large interior allows you to bake a 12-inch pizza or air fry 3 pounds of chicken wings and also make a 12-inch pizza. Due to small and compact design, it also saves your kitchen countertop space.

- **Easy to clean**

The interior of the Cuisinart oven is coated with non-stick coating makes the daily cleaning process easy. The oven comes with a user manual you just need to follow the cleaning instructions as per given in the manual.

Tips

1. Air Frying Tips
   - Different types of oils are used while air frying your food. If you want mild flavour then use canola, vegetable, and grape-seed oil. If you want rich flavour then use olive oil during air fry.
   - Always flip the large food items like chicken cutlets during halfway of the cooking process. This will ensure that the food is cooked evenly from all the sides with a brown texture.
   - Do not crowd the food while air frying; this will affect the even cooking result, taste, and texture of food.
   - Cut food into even sizes, this will help to cook food more evenly and quickly.
2. Broiling Tips
   - To get a perfect broiling result always put the air fryer rack into the baking tray during the broiling process.
   - Use a sturdy metal pan during broiling. Do not use any glass while broiling even if the glass is strong.
   - To get a perfect broiling result to arrange food items in a single layer. This will ensure even cooking and browning results.
3. Baking Tips
   - A larger food item like chicken is placed into rack 1 position and while baking pizza use baking pan at rack 1 position.
   - Before start, the baking process always preheats your oven to get quick and perfect baking results.
4. Toasting Tips
   - Place your bread at the centre position of the oven to get even toasting results.
   - Always keep watch on your food from the oven window while toasting your food until how the oven cooks your food while toasting.

Chapter 2: Breakfast & Brunch

Breakfast Oatmeal Cake

Preparation Time: 10 minutes; Cooking Time: 25 minutes; Serve: 8

Ingredients:
- 2 eggs
- 1 tbsp coconut oil
- 3 tbsp yogurt
- 1/2 tsp baking powder
- 1 tsp cinnamon
- 1 tsp vanilla
- 3 tbsp honey
- 1/2 tsp baking soda
- 1 apple, peel & chopped
- 1 cup oats

Directions:
1. Fit the Cuisinart oven with the rack in position 1.
2. Line baking dish with parchment paper and set aside.
3. Add 3/4 cup oats and remaining ingredients into the blender and blend until smooth.
4. Add remaining oats and stir well.
5. Pour mixture into the prepared baking dish.
6. Set to bake at 350 F for 30 minutes. After 5 minutes place the baking dish in the preheated oven.
7. Slice and serve.

Nutritional Value (Amount per Serving):
Calories 114; Fat 3.6 g; Carbohydrates 18.2 g; Sugar 10 g; Protein 3.2 g; Cholesterol 41 mg

Banana Oat Muffins

Preparation Time: 10 minutes; Cooking Time: 25 minutes; Serve: 6

Ingredients:
- 1 egg
- 2 tbsp butter, melted
- 1/2 tsp cinnamon
- 1 tsp vanilla
- 2 tbsp yogurt
- 1 1/2 cup oats
- 1 tsp baking powder
- 2 ripe bananas, mashed

Directions:
1. Fit the Cuisinart oven with the rack in position 1.
2. Line the muffin tray with cupcake liners and set aside.
3. In a bowl, whisk the egg with banana, yogurt, vanilla, cinnamon, baking powder, and butter.
4. Add oats and mix well.
5. Pour mixture into the prepared muffin tray.
6. Set to bake at 350 F for 30 minutes. After 5 minutes place the muffin tray in the preheated oven.
7. Serve and enjoy.

Nutritional Value (Amount per Serving):
Calories 164; Fat 6.1 g; Carbohydrates 23.9 g; Sugar 5.5 g; Protein 4.4 g; Cholesterol 38 mg

Easy Cheese Egg Casserole

Preparation Time: 10 minutes; Cooking Time: 40 minutes; Serve: 10

Ingredients:
- 12 eggs
- 8 oz cheddar cheese, shredded
- 1/3 cup milk
- 1/4 tsp pepper
- 1 tsp salt

Directions:
1. Fit the Cuisinart oven with the rack in position 1.

2. Spray 9*13-inch casserole dish with cooking spray and set aside.
3. In a bowl, whisk eggs with milk, pepper, and salt.
4. Add shredded cheese and stir well.
5. Pour egg mixture into the prepared casserole dish.
6. Set to bake at 350 F for 45 minutes. After 5 minutes place the casserole dish in the preheated oven.
7. Serve and enjoy.

Nutritional Value (Amount per Serving):
Calories 171; Fat 12.9 g; Carbohydrates 1.1 g; Sugar 0.9 g; Protein 12.6 g; Cholesterol 221 mg

Quick & Easy Granola

Preparation Time: 10 minutes; Cooking Time: 8 minutes; Serve: 4
Ingredients:
- 2 cups oats
- 2 tbsp chia seeds
- 1 tsp vanilla
- 1/2 tsp cinnamon
- 1/4 cup honey
- 1/4 cup almond butter

Directions:
1. Fit the Cuisinart oven with the rack in position 1.
2. In a bowl, mix the almond butter, honey, cinnamon, and vanilla.
3. Add oats and chia seeds and mix well.
4. Transfer oats mixture onto the parchment-lined baking pan.
5. Place the baking pan in Cuisinart oven and set to bake at 350 F for 8 minutes.
6. Serve and enjoy.

Nutritional Value (Amount per Serving):
Calories 248; Fat 4.4 g; Carbohydrates 47.3 g; Sugar 18 g; Protein 6.3 g; Cholesterol 6.3 mg

Delicious Baked Eggs

Preparation Time: 10 minutes; Cooking Time: 45 minutes; Serve: 8
Ingredients:
- 12 eggs
- 1/2 cup all-purpose flour
- 16 oz cottage cheese
- 16 oz cheddar cheese, shredded
- 1 tsp salt

Directions:
1. Fit the Cuisinart oven with the rack in position 1.
2. Grease 9*13-inch baking pan with butter and set aside.
3. In a large bowl, whisk eggs with flour, cottage cheese, cheddar cheese, and salt.
4. Pour egg mixture into the prepared baking pan.
5. Set to bake at 350 F for 50 minutes. After 5 minutes place the baking pan in the preheated oven.
6. Serve and enjoy.

Nutritional Value (Amount per Serving):
Calories 402; Fat 26.5 g; Carbohydrates 9.3 g; Sugar 1 g; Protein 31 g; Cholesterol 310 mg

Apple Cinnamon Oat Muffins

Preparation Time: 10 minutes; Cooking Time: 15 minutes; Serve: 12
Ingredients:
- 1 egg
- 1 apple, peel & dice
- 1 tsp cinnamon
- 1/2 cup milk
- 2 bananas, mashed
- 2 cups rolled oats
- 1 tsp baking powder
- Pinch of salt

Directions:
1. Fit the Cuisinart oven with the rack in position 1.
2. Line the muffin tray with cupcake liners and set aside.
3. In a mixing bowl, whisk the egg with cinnamon, baking powder, milk, oats, bananas, and salt.
4. Add apple and stir well.
5. Pour mixture into the prepared muffin tray.
6. Set to bake at 375 F for 20 minutes. After 5 minutes place the muffin tray in the preheated oven.
7. Serve and enjoy.

Nutritional Value (Amount per Serving):
Calories 90; Fat 1.6 g; Carbohydrates 17.2 g; Sugar 5 g; Protein 2.9 g; Cholesterol 14 mg

Healthy Baked Oatmeal

Preparation Time: 10 minutes; Cooking Time: 20 minutes; Serve: 6

Ingredients:
- 1 egg
- 1/3 cup dried cranberries
- 1 tsp vanilla
- 1 1/2 tsp cinnamon
- 2 tbsp butter, melted
- 1/2 cup applesauce
- 1 1/2 cups milk
- 1 tsp baking powder
- 1/3 cup light brown sugar
- 2 cups old fashioned oats
- 1/4 tsp salt

Directions:
1. Fit the Cuisinart oven with the rack in position 1.
2. Grease 8*8-inch baking dish and set aside.
3. In a bowl, mix egg, vanilla, butter, applesauce, baking powder, cinnamon, brown sugar, oats, and salt.
4. Add milk and stir well.
5. Add cranberries and fold well.
6. Pour mixture into the prepared baking dish.
7. Set to bake at 350 F for 25 minutes. After 5 minutes place the baking dish in the preheated oven.
8. Serve and enjoy.

Nutritional Value (Amount per Serving):
Calories 330; Fat 9.3 g; Carbohydrates 50.6 g; Sugar 14.4 g; Protein 9.7 g; Cholesterol 42 mg

Easy Apple Pie Baked Oatmeal

Preparation Time: 10 minutes; Cooking Time: 30 minutes; Serve: 4

Ingredients:
- 1 cup rolled oats
- 1/4 tsp nutmeg
- 2 tsp cinnamon
- 2 tbsp maple syrup
- 1/4 cup milk
- 1/2 cup raisins
- 1 banana, sliced
- 2 apples, diced
- 1 cup boiling water

Directions:
1. Fit the Cuisinart oven with the rack in position 1.
2. Add oats and boiling water in a mixing bowl and let sit for 10 minutes.
3. After 10 minutes add remaining ingredients to the bowl and mix well.
4. Pour mixture into the greased baking dish.

5. Set to bake at 350 F for 35 minutes. After 5 minutes place the baking dish in the preheated oven.
   6. Serve and enjoy.

Nutritional Value (Amount per Serving):
Calories 253; Fat 2.1 g; Carbohydrates 58.8 g; Sugar 32.8 g; Protein 4.4 g; Cholesterol 1 mg

Mushroom Spinach Egg Muffins

Preparation Time: 10 minutes; Cooking Time: 20 minutes; Serve: 12

Ingredients:
- 12 eggs
- 1/2 cup fresh basil
- 1 cup mushrooms, diced
- 1 cup spinach, chopped
- 3/4 cup feta cheese, crumbled
- Pepper
- Salt

Directions:
1. Fit the Cuisinart oven with the rack in position 1.
2. Spray a muffin tray with cooking spray and set aside.
3. In a bowl, whisk eggs with pepper and salt.
4. Add basil, mushrooms, spinach, and cheese and stir well.
5. Pour egg mixture into the prepared muffin tray.
6. Set to bake at 400 F for 25 minutes. After 5 minutes place the muffin tray in the preheated oven.
7. Serve and enjoy.

Nutritional Value (Amount per Serving):
Calories 90; Fat 6.4 g; Carbohydrates 1 g; Sugar 0.8 g; Protein 7.2 g; Cholesterol 172 mg

Crunchy Vanilla Granola

Preparation Time: 10 minutes; Cooking Time: 30 minutes; Serve: 10

Ingredients:
- 4 cups old fashioned oats
- 1 1/2 tsp vanilla
- 1/4 cup coconut oil
- 1/2 cup honey
- 1/2 tsp cinnamon

Directions:
1. Fit the Cuisinart oven with the rack in position 1.
2. In a mixing bowl, mix oats and cinnamon and set aside.
3. In a small saucepan, add honey and coconut oil and heat over medium-low heat until oil is melted.
4. Remove saucepan from heat. Add vanilla and stir well.
5. Pour honey mixture over oats and stir well.
6. Pour oats mixture onto the parchment-lined baking pan and spread evenly.
7. Set to bake at 300 F for 35 minutes. After 5 minutes place the baking pan in the preheated oven.
8. Serve and enjoy.

Nutritional Value (Amount per Serving):
Calories 350; Fat 9.6 g; Carbohydrates 57.1 g; Sugar 15.7 g; Protein 8.1 g; Cholesterol 0 mg

Nutritious Egg Breakfast Muffins

Preparation Time: 10 minutes; Cooking Time: 20 minutes; Serve: 12

Ingredients:
- 12 eggs
- 1/2 cup baby spinach, shredded
- 1 cup cheddar cheese, shredded
- 1/4 cup mushrooms, diced & sautéed

- 1/4 red bell pepper, diced
- 1/4 tsp garlic powder
- 1 cup ham, cooked and diced
- 3 tbsp onion, diced
- 1/2 tsp seasoned salt

Directions:
1. Fit the Cuisinart oven with the rack in position 1.
2. Spray a 12-cup muffin tray with cooking spray and set aside.
3. In a large bowl, whisk eggs with garlic powder and salt.
4. Add remaining ingredients and stir well.
5. Pour egg mixture into the prepared muffin tray.
6. Set to bake at 350 F for 25 minutes. After 5 minutes place the muffin tray in the preheated oven.
7. Serve and enjoy.

Nutritional Value (Amount per Serving):
Calories 122; Fat 8.5 g; Carbohydrates 1.5 g; Sugar 0.7 g; Protein 9.9 g; Cholesterol 180 mg

Soft Banana Oat Muffins

Preparation Time: 10 minutes; Cooking Time: 20 minutes; Serve: 12
Ingredients:
- 1 egg
- 1 cup banana, mashed
- 1 tsp vanilla
- 1/3 cup applesauce
- 3/4 cup milk
- 1/4 tsp nutmeg
- 1/2 tsp cinnamon
- 1 tsp baking soda
- 2 tsp baking powder
- 1/4 cup brown sugar
- 1/4 cup white sugar
- 1 cup old fashioned oats
- 1 1/2 cups whole wheat flour
- 1/2 tsp salt

Directions:
1. Fit the Cuisinart oven with the rack in position 1.
2. Line a 12-cup muffin tray with cupcake liners and set aside.
3. In a mixing bowl, mix flour, nutmeg, cinnamon, baking soda, baking powder, sugar, oats, flour, and salt.
4. In a separate bowl, whisk eggs with milk, vanilla, and applesauce. Add mashed banana and stir to combine.
5. Add flour mixture into the egg mixture and mix until just combined.
6. Pour mixture into the prepared muffin tray.
7. Set to bake at 400 F for 25 minutes. After 5 minutes place the muffin tray in the preheated oven.
8. Serve and enjoy.

Nutritional Value (Amount per Serving):
Calories 165; Fat 1.7 g; Carbohydrates 33 g; Sugar 10.5 g; Protein 4.4 g; Cholesterol 15 mg

Healthy Breakfast Cookies

Preparation Time: 10 minutes; Cooking Time: 15 minutes; Serve: 12
Ingredients:
- 2 cups quick oats
- 1/4 cup chocolate chips
- 1 1/2 tbsp chia seeds
- 1/4 cup shredded coconut
- 1/2 cup mashed banana
- 1/4 cup applesauce
- 1/4 cup honey
- 1/2 tsp cinnamon
- 3/4 cup almond butter

Directions:
1. Fit the Cuisinart oven with the rack in position 1.

2. Line baking pan with parchment paper and set aside.
3. Add all ingredients into the mixing bowl and mix until well combined.
4. Using a cookie scoop drop 12 scoops of oat mixture onto a prepared baking pan and lightly flatten the cookie.
5. Set to bake at 325 F for 20 minutes. After 5 minutes place the baking pan in the preheated oven.
6. Serve and enjoy.

Nutritional Value (Amount per Serving):
Calories 117; Fat 3.4 g; Carbohydrates 20.1 g; Sugar 9.2 g; Protein 2.6 g; Cholesterol 1 mg

Banana Coconut Muffins

Preparation Time: 10 minutes; Cooking Time: 15 minutes; Serve: 12
Ingredients:
- 1 egg
- 3 ripe bananas, mashed
- 1/2 cup shredded coconut
- 2 cups all-purpose flour
- 2 tsp baking powder
- 1/2 tsp baking soda
- 1 cup of sugar
- 1 tsp vanilla
- 1/2 cup milk
- 1/2 cup applesauce
- 1/2 tsp salt

Directions:
1. Fit the Cuisinart oven with the rack in position 1.
2. Line a 12-cup muffin tray with cupcake liners and set aside.
3. In a mixing bowl, whisk the egg with vanilla, milk, applesauce, and salt until well combined.
4. Add baking powder, baking soda, and sugar and mix well.
5. Add flour and mix until just combined.
6. Add shredded coconut and stir well.
7. Pour mixture into the prepared muffin tray.
8. Set to bake at 350 F for 20 minutes. After 5 minutes place the muffin tray in the preheated oven.
9. Serve and enjoy.

Nutritional Value (Amount per Serving):
Calories 193; Fat 2 g; Carbohydrates 41.9 g; Sugar 22.1 g; Protein 3.4 g; Cholesterol 14 mg

Delicious Broccoli Quiche

Preparation Time: 10 minutes; Cooking Time: 45 minutes; Serve: 8
Ingredients:
- 2 eggs
- 2 1/2 cups broccoli, cooked & chopped
- 8 oz cheddar cheese, shredded
- 1/2 cup onion, chopped
- 1 1/2 cups milk
- 1 tsp baking powder
- 1 cup flour
- 1 tsp salt

Directions:
1. Fit the Cuisinart oven with the rack in position 1.
2. In a large bowl, mix flour, baking powder, and salt and set aside.
3. In a separate bowl, whisk eggs. Add onion and stir well.
4. Pour egg mixture into the flour mixture and stir to combine.
5. Stir in broccoli and cheese.
6. Pour egg mixture into the greased 9-inch pie dish.

7. Set to bake at 350 F for 50 minutes. After 5 minutes place the pie dish in the preheated oven.
8. Serve and enjoy.

Nutritional Value (Amount per Serving):
Calories 223; Fat 11.7 g; Carbohydrates 17.5 g; Sugar 3.1 g; Protein 12.4 g; Cholesterol 74 mg

Tator Tots Casserole

Preparation Time: 10 minutes; Cooking Time: 30 minutes; Serve: 8

Ingredients:
- 8 eggs
- 28 oz tator tots
- 8 oz pepper jack cheese, shredded
- 2 green onions, sliced
- 1/4 cup milk
- 1 lb breakfast sausage, cooked
- Pepper
- Salt

Directions:
1. Fit the Cuisinart oven with the rack in position 1.
2. Spray 13*9-inch baking pan with cooking spray and set aside.
3. In a bowl, whisk eggs with milk, pepper, and salt.
4. Layer sausage in a prepared baking pan then pour the egg mixture and sprinkle with half shredded cheese and green onions.
5. Add tator tots on top.
6. Set to bake at 400 F for 35 minutes. After 5 minutes place the baking pan in the preheated oven.
7. Top with remaining cheese and serve.

Nutritional Value (Amount per Serving):
Calories 398; Fat 31.5 g; Carbohydrates 2 g; Sugar 0.8 g; Protein 22.1 g; Cholesterol 251 mg

Simple Apple Crisp

Preparation Time: 10 minutes; Cooking Time: 35 minutes; Serve: 8

Ingredients:
- 4 medium apples, peel & slice
- 1 tsp cinnamon
- 4 tbsp sugar

For topping:
- 1/3 cup butter, melted
- 1/2 cup brown sugar
- 3/4 cup all-purpose flour
- 3/4 cup rolled oats

Directions:
1. Fit the Cuisinart oven with the rack in position 1.
2. Add sliced apples, cinnamon, and sugar in a greased 9-inch baking dish and mix well.
3. In a bowl, mix oats, brown sugar, and flour. Add melted butter and mix well.
4. Sprinkle oat mixture over sliced apples.
5. Set to bake at 375 F for 40 minutes. After 5 minutes place the baking dish in the preheated oven.
6. Serve and enjoy.

Nutritional Value (Amount per Serving):
Calories 255; Fat 8.5 g; Carbohydrates 44.7 g; Sugar 26.5 g; Protein 2.6 g; Cholesterol 20 mg

Cheesy Hash Brown Casserole

Preparation Time: 10 minutes; Cooking Time: 45 minutes; Serve: 8

Ingredients:
- 32 oz hash browns
- 1 stick butter, melted
- 1/3 tsp black pepper
- 16 oz sour cream

- 2 cups cheddar cheese, grated
- 1 small onion, diced
- 10 oz can chicken soup

Directions:
1. Fit the Cuisinart oven with the rack in position 1.
2. Spray 9*13-inch casserole dish with cooking spray and set aside.
3. In a large bowl, add hash browns, 1 1/2 cups cheddar cheese, onion, sour cream, soup, butter, and black pepper and mix until well combined.
4. Transfer hash brown mixture into the prepared casserole dish and spread well.
5. Top with remaining cheese.
6. Set to bake at 350 F for 50 minutes. After 5 minutes place the casserole dish in the preheated oven.
7. Serve and enjoy.

Nutritional Value (Amount per Serving):
Calories 673; Fat 49 g; Carbohydrates 46 g; Sugar 2.5 g; Protein 13.3 g; Cholesterol 88 mg

Egg Ham Casserole

Preparation Time: 10 minutes; Cooking Time: 20 minutes; Serve: 2
Ingredients:
- 5 eggs, lightly beaten
- 1 slice bread, cut into pieces
- 1/3 cup ham, diced
- 1 tbsp pimento, diced
- 1/2 cup cheddar cheese, shredded
- 1/3 cup heavy cream
- 2 green onion, chopped
- 1/4 tsp black pepper
- 1/4 tsp salt

Directions:
1. Fit the Cuisinart oven with the rack in position 1.
2. Add bread pieces to the bottom of the greased casserole dish.
3. In a bowl, whisk eggs with heavy cream, pimento, green onion, pepper, and salt.
4. Pour egg mixture over bread.
5. Sprinkle ham and cheese over egg mixture.
6. Set to bake at 350 F for 25 minutes. After 5 minutes place the casserole dish in the preheated oven.
7. Serve and enjoy.

Nutritional Value (Amount per Serving):
Calories 413; Fat 30 g; Carbohydrates 10.7 g; Sugar 4.6 g; Protein 26.3 g; Cholesterol 479 mg

Hashbrown Breakfast Casserole

Preparation Time: 10 minutes; Cooking Time: 50 minutes; Serve: 8
Ingredients:
- 3 cups shredded cauliflower
- 1/2 cup mayonnaise
- 1 cup sour cream
- 4 tbsp butter
- 1 tbsp bouillon powder
- 1 tbsp onion, minced
- 1 cup cheddar cheese, shredded
- 1/2 tsp pepper
- 1 tsp salt

Directions:
1. Fit the Cuisinart oven with the rack in position 1.
2. Set aside 1/3 cup shredded cheese.
3. In a bowl, add remaining ingredients and mix well.
4. Spread mixture into the greased 8*8-inch baking dish and sprinkle with remaining shredded cheese.

5. Set to bake at 350 F for 55 minutes. After 5 minutes place the baking dish in the preheated oven.
6. Serve and enjoy.

Nutritional Value (Amount per Serving):
Calories 237; Fat 21.4 g; Carbohydrates 7.1 g; Sugar 2 g; Protein 5.4 g; Cholesterol 47 mg

Easy Egg Bites

Preparation Time: 10 minutes; Cooking Time: 30 minutes; Serve: 6

Ingredients:
- 5 eggs
- 3 bacon slices, cooked & chopped
- 4 tbsp cottage cheese
- 1/2 cup cheddar cheese, shredded
- 1/4 tsp pepper
- 1/4 tsp salt

Directions:
1. Fit the Cuisinart oven with the rack in position 1.
2. Spray 6-cups muffin tin with cooking spray and set aside.
3. Add all ingredients except bacon into the blender and blend for 30 seconds.
4. Pour egg mixture into the prepared muffin tin then divide cooked bacon evenly in all egg cups.
5. Set to bake at 325 F for 35 minutes. After 5 minutes place muffin tin in the preheated oven.
6. Serve and enjoy.

Nutritional Value (Amount per Serving):
Calories 151; Fat 10.9 g; Carbohydrates 0.9 g; Sugar 0.4 g; Protein 11.8 g; Cholesterol 158 mg

Flavorful Zucchini Frittata

Preparation Time: 10 minutes; Cooking Time: 25 minutes; Serve: 4

Ingredients:
- 6 eggs
- 2 cups zucchini, grated & squeeze out excess liquid
- 1 cup cheddar cheese, shredded
- 1 cup ham, chopped
- 1/4 cup heavy cream
- 2 tbsp butter
- 1/4 tsp pepper
- 1 tsp salt

Directions:
1. Fit the Cuisinart oven with the rack in position 1.
2. Melt butter in a pan over medium heat.
3. Add zucchini in the pan and sauté until tender. Remove pan from heat.
4. In a bowl, whisk eggs and cream. Stir in zucchini, cheese, ham, pepper, and salt.
5. Pour mixture into the greased baking dish.
6. Set to bake at 325 F for 30 minutes. After 5 minutes place the baking dish in the preheated oven.
7. Serve and enjoy.

Nutritional Value (Amount per Serving):
Calories 349; Fat 27.5 g; Carbohydrates 4.3 g; Sugar 1.7 g; Protein 21.8 g; Cholesterol 320 mg

Mushroom Sausage Breakfast Bake

Preparation Time: 10 minutes; Cooking Time: 30 minutes; Serve: 6

Ingredients:
- 12 eggs
- 2 cups spinach, chopped
- 1 tbsp garlic, minced
- 8 oz mushrooms, sliced
- 1 red bell pepper, diced
- 1 small onion, diced

- 2 tbsp olive oil
- 7 oz sausage links, diced
- Pepper
- Salt

Directions:
1. Fit the Cuisinart oven with the rack in position 1.
2. Spray 9*13-inch baking pan with cooking spray and set aside.
3. Heat oil in a pan over medium-high heat.
4. Add onion and bell pepper and sauté for 2-3 minutes.
5. Add garlic and mushrooms and sauté for 2 minutes.
6. Add sausage and spinach and cook until heated through.
7. Spread pan mixture into the greased baking pan.
8. In a bowl, whisk eggs with pepper and salt.
9. Pour egg mixture over sausage mixture.
10. Set to bake at 350 F for 35 minutes. After 5 minutes place the baking pan in the preheated oven.
11. Serve and enjoy.

Nutritional Value (Amount per Serving):
Calories 293; Fat 23 g; Carbohydrates 6 g; Sugar 3.2 g; Protein 16.9 g; Cholesterol 348 mg

Delicious Baked Omelet

Preparation Time: 10 minutes; Cooking Time: 25 minutes; Serve: 6

Ingredients:
- 8 eggs
- 1/2 cup green bell pepper
- 1/2 cup onion, diced
- 1 cup ham, chopped & cooked
- 1 cup cheddar cheese, shredded
- 1/2 cup half and half
- Pepper
- Salt

Directions:
1. Fit the Cuisinart oven with the rack in position 1.
2. Spray 9*9-inch baking pan with cooking spray and set aside.
3. In a bowl, whisk eggs with half and half, pepper, and salt.
4. Add green bell pepper, onion, ham, and cheddar cheese and stir well.
5. Pour egg mixture into the prepared baking pan.
6. Set to bake at 400 F for 30 minutes. After 5 minutes place the baking pan in the preheated oven.
7. Serve and enjoy.

Nutritional Value (Amount per Serving):
Calories 230; Fat 16.4 g; Carbohydrates 4.1 g; Sugar 1.5 g; Protein 16.6 g; Cholesterol 258 mg

Spicy Egg Casserole

Preparation Time: 10 minutes; Cooking Time: 45 minutes; Serve: 8

Ingredients:
- 10 eggs
- 1 cup Colby jack cheese, shredded
- 1 cup cottage cheese
- 1 tsp baking powder
- 1/3 cup flour
- 1/2 cup milk
- 4.5 oz can green chilies, chopped
- 1/2 small onion, minced
- 2 tbsp butter
- 1 tsp seasoned salt

Directions:
1. Fit the Cuisinart oven with the rack in position 1.
2. Spray 9*13-inch casserole dish with cooking spray and set aside.
3. Melt butter in a pan over medium heat.

4. Add onion and green chilies and sauté for 5 minutes. Remove pan from heat and set aside.
5. In a small bowl, whisk milk, baking powder, and flour until smooth.
6. In a mixing bowl, whisk eggs with cheese, cottage cheese, and seasoned salt.
7. Add sautéed onion and green chilies, milk, and flour mixture to the eggs and whisk until well combined.
8. Pour egg mixture into the prepared casserole dish.
9. Set to bake at 350 F for 50 minutes. After 5 minutes place the casserole dish in the preheated oven.
10. Serve and enjoy.

Nutritional Value (Amount per Serving):
Calories 219; Fat 13.8 g; Carbohydrates 8.4 g; Sugar 1.4 g; Protein 14.9 g; Cholesterol 228 mg

Moist Banana Breakfast Bread

Preparation Time: 10 minutes; Cooking Time: 45 minutes; Serve: 12

Ingredients:
- 1 egg
- 1 3/4 cups whole wheat flour
- 1 cup mashed banana
- 3/4 tsp vanilla
- 1/2 cup honey
- 1/4 cup butter, melted
- 1/2 tsp baking soda
- 2 tsp baking powder
- 1/4 tsp salt

Directions:
1. Fit the Cuisinart oven with the rack in position 1.
2. Spray a 9-inch loaf pan with cooking spray and set aside.
3. In a mixing bowl, mix egg, vanilla, honey, and melted butter. Add mashed banana and stir well.
4. Add dry ingredients into the egg mixture and mix until just combined.
5. Pour mixture into the prepared loaf pan.
6. Set to bake at 350 F for 50 minutes. After 5 minutes place the loaf pan in the preheated oven.
7. Serve and enjoy.

Nutritional Value (Amount per Serving):
Calories 161; Fat 4.4 g; Carbohydrates 28.9 g; Sugar 13.2 g; Protein 2.6 g; Cholesterol 24 mg

Hearty Sweet Potato Baked Oatmeal

Preparation Time: 10 minutes; Cooking Time: 30 minutes; Serve: 6

Ingredients:
- 1 egg, lightly beaten
- 1 tsp vanilla
- 1 1/2 cups milk
- 1 tsp baking powder
- 2 tbsp ground flax seed
- 1 cup sweet potato puree
- 1/4 tsp nutmeg
- 2 tsp cinnamon
- 1/3 cup maple syrup
- 2 cups old fashioned oats
- 1/4 tsp salt

Directions:
1. Fit the Cuisinart oven with the rack in position 1.
2. Spray an 8-inch square baking pan with cooking spray and set aside.
3. Add all ingredients except oats into the mixing bowl and mix until well combined.
4. Add oats and stir until just combined.
5. Pour mixture into the prepared baking pan.

6. Set to bake at 350 F for 35 minutes. After 5 minutes place the baking pan in the preheated oven.
7. Serve and enjoy.

Nutritional Value (Amount per Serving):
Calories 355; Fat 6.3 g; Carbohydrates 62.3 g; Sugar 17.1 g; Protein 10.9 g; Cholesterol 32 mg

Mediterranean Spinach Frittata

Preparation Time: 10 minutes; Cooking Time: 20 minutes; Serve: 6

Ingredients:
- 6 eggs
- 1/2 cup frozen spinach, drained the excess liquid
- 1/4 cup feta cheese, crumbled
- 1/4 cup olives, chopped
- 1/4 cup kalamata olives, chopped
- 1/2 cup tomatoes, diced
- 1/2 tsp garlic powder
- 1 tsp oregano
- 1/4 cup milk
- 1/2 tsp pepper
- 1/4 tsp salt

Directions:
1. Fit the Cuisinart oven with the rack in position 1.
2. Spray 9-inch pie pan with cooking spray and set aside.
3. In a bowl, whisk eggs with oregano, garlic powder, milk, pepper, and salt until well combined.
4. Add olives, feta cheese, tomatoes, and spinach and mix well.
5. Pour egg mixture into the prepared pie pan.
6. Set to bake at 400 F for 25 minutes. After 5 minutes place the pie pan in the preheated oven.
7. Serve and enjoy.

Nutritional Value (Amount per Serving):
Calories 103; Fat 7.2 g; Carbohydrates 2.9 g; Sugar 1.5 g; Protein 7.2 g; Cholesterol 170 mg

Broccoli Asparagus Frittata

Preparation Time: 10 minutes; Cooking Time: 20 minutes; Serve: 6

Ingredients:
- 6 eggs
- 1/2 cup onion, diced & sautéed
- 1 cup asparagus, chopped & sautéed
- 1 cup broccoli, chopped & sautéed
- 3 bacon slices, cooked & chopped
- 1/3 cup parmesan cheese, grated
- 1/2 cup milk
- 1/2 tsp pepper
- 1 tsp salt

Directions:
1. Fit the Cuisinart oven with the rack in position 1.
2. In a mixing bowl, whisk eggs with milk, cheese, pepper, and salt.
3. Add onion, asparagus, broccoli, and bacon and stir well.
4. Pour egg mixture into the greased baking dish.
5. Set to bake at 350 F for 25 minutes. After 5 minutes place the baking dish in the preheated oven.
6. Serve and enjoy.

Nutritional Value (Amount per Serving):
Calories 154; Fat 9.9 g; Carbohydrates 4.6 g; Sugar 2.4 g; Protein 12.4 g; Cholesterol 179 mg

Perfect Sausage-Hash Brown Casserole

Preparation Time: 10 minutes; Cooking Time: 45 minutes; Serve: 12

Ingredients:

- 6 eggs
- 16 oz frozen hash browns, defrosted
- 1/2 cup milk
- 2 cups cheddar cheese, shredded
- 1 lb breakfast sausage, browned
- 1/2 tsp pepper
- 1 tsp kosher salt

Directions:
1. Fit the Cuisinart oven with the rack in position 1.
2. Layer hash browns in a greased 9*9-inch casserole dish.
3. Spread sausage on top of hash browns. Sprinkle cheese on top.
4. In a mixing bowl, whisk eggs with milk, pepper, and salt.
5. Pour egg mixture over hash brown mixture.
6. Set to bake at 350 F for 50 minutes. After 5 minutes place the casserole dish in the preheated oven.
7. Serve and enjoy.

Nutritional Value (Amount per Serving):
Calories 323; Fat 24.4 g; Carbohydrates 11.7 g; Sugar 0.7 g; Protein 15.8 g; Cholesterol 134 mg

Perfect Chicken Casserole

Preparation Time: 10 minutes; Cooking Time: 30 minutes; Serve: 8
Ingredients:
- 8 eggs
- 1 cup mozzarella cheese, shredded
- 8 oz can crescent rolls
- 1 1/2 cups basil pesto
- 3/4 lb chicken breasts, cooked & shredded
- Pepper
- Salt

Directions:
1. Fit the Cuisinart oven with the rack in position 1.
2. Spray a 9*13-inch baking dish with cooking spray and set aside.
3. In a bowl, mix shredded chicken and pesto and set aside.
4. In a separate bowl, eggs, pepper, and salt.
5. Roll out the crescent roll into the prepared baking dish. Top with shredded chicken.
6. Pour egg mixture over chicken and top with shredded mozzarella cheese.
7. Set to bake at 350 F for 35 minutes. After 5 minutes place the baking dish in the preheated oven.
8. Serve and enjoy.

Nutritional Value (Amount per Serving):
Calories 266; Fat 14.3 g; Carbohydrates 11.7 g; Sugar 2.4 g; Protein 21 g; Cholesterol 203 mg

Potato Egg Casserole

Preparation Time: 10 minutes; Cooking Time: 35 minutes; Serve: 6
Ingredients:
- 5 eggs
- 2 medium potatoes, cut into 1/2-inch cubes
- 1 green bell pepper, diced
- 1 small onion, chopped
- 1 tbsp olive oil
- 1/2 cup cheddar cheese, shredded
- 3/4 tsp pepper
- 3/4 tsp salt

Directions:
1. Fit the Cuisinart oven with the rack in position 1.
2. Spray 9*9-inch casserole dish with cooking spray and set aside.
3. Heat oil in a pan over medium heat.
4. Add onion and sauté for 1 minute. Add potatoes, bell peppers, 1/2 tsp pepper, and 1/2 tsp salt and sauté for 4 minutes.

5. Transfer sautéed vegetables to the prepared casserole dish and spread evenly.
6. In a bowl, whisk eggs with remaining pepper and salt.
7. Pour egg mixture over sautéed vegetables in a casserole dish. Sprinkle cheese on top.
8. Set to bake at 350 F for 40 minutes. After 5 minutes place the casserole dish in the preheated oven.
9. Serve and enjoy.

Nutritional Value (Amount per Serving):
Calories 171; Fat 9.2 g; Carbohydrates 14.3 g; Sugar 2.6 g; Protein 8.5 g; Cholesterol 146 mg

Crustless Breakfast Quiche

Preparation Time: 10 minutes; Cooking Time: 10 minutes; Serve: 4

Ingredients:
- 6 eggs
- 1 cup cheddar cheese, shredded
- 1/4 cup milk
- 1 shallot, sliced & sautéed
- 3 bacon slices, sautéed & chopped
- 1/8 tsp pepper
- 1/8 tsp kosher salt

Directions:
1. Fit the Cuisinart oven with the rack in position 1.
2. Spray an 8-inch baking dish with cooking spray and set aside.
3. In a bowl, whisk eggs with milk, pepper, and salt.
4. Add cheese, shallot, and bacon and stir well.
5. Pour egg mixture into the prepared baking dish.
6. Set to bake at 375 F for 15 minutes. After 5 minutes place the baking dish in the preheated oven.
7. Serve and enjoy.

Nutritional Value (Amount per Serving):
Calories 301; Fat 22.2 g; Carbohydrates 3.7 g; Sugar 1.4 g; Protein 21.4 g; Cholesterol 292 mg

Perfect Potato Casserole

Preparation Time: 10 minutes; Cooking Time: 35 minutes; Serve: 6

Ingredients:
- 32 oz shredded potatoes
- 1/4 cup milk
- 1/4 cup butter, melted
- 1 cup cheddar cheese, shredded
- 10.5 oz cheddar cheese soup
- 2/3 cup sour cream
- 1/2 tsp onion powder
- 1/2 tsp garlic powder

Directions:
1. Fit the Cuisinart oven with the rack in position 1.
2. Spray 9*13-inch baking pan with cooking spray and set aside.
3. Add all ingredients into the greased baking pan and mix well.
4. Set to bake at 350 F for 40 minutes. After 5 minutes place the baking pan in the preheated oven.
5. Serve and enjoy.

Nutritional Value (Amount per Serving):
Calories 341; Fat 21.7 g; Carbohydrates 28 g; Sugar 2.5 g; Protein 9.6 g; Cholesterol 58 mg

Delicious Pumpkin Bread

Preparation Time: 10 minutes; Cooking Time: 55 minutes; Serve: 12

Ingredients:
- 2 eggs
- 1/4 cup olive oil
- 1/2 cup milk
- 1 cup of sugar

- 12 eggs
- 1/2 cup heavy cream
- 8 oz parmesan cheese, shredded
- Pepper
- Salt

Directions:
1. Fit the Cuisinart oven with the rack in position 1.
2. Spray 12-cups muffin tin with cooking spray and set aside.
3. Crack each egg into each cup.
4. Divide heavy cream and parmesan cheese evenly into each cup.
5. Season with pepper and salt.
6. Set to bake at 425 F for 15 minutes. After 5 minutes place muffin tin in the preheated oven.
7. Serve and enjoy.

Nutritional Value (Amount per Serving):
Calories 141; Fat 10.3 g; Carbohydrates 1.2 g; Sugar 0.4 g; Protein 11.7 g; Cholesterol 184 mg

Basil Dill Egg Muffins

Preparation Time: 10 minutes; Cooking Time: 20 minutes; Serve: 6

Ingredients:
- 6 eggs
- 1 tbsp chives, chopped
- 1 tbsp fresh basil, chopped
- 1 tbsp fresh cilantro, chopped
- 1/4 cup mozzarella cheese, grated
- 1 tbsp fresh dill, chopped
- 1 tbsp fresh parsley, chopped
- Pepper
- Salt

Directions:
1. Fit the Cuisinart oven with the rack in position 1.
2. Spray 6-cups muffin tin with cooking spray and set aside.
3. In a bowl, whisk eggs with pepper and salt.
4. Add remaining ingredients and stir well.
5. Pour egg mixture into the prepared muffin tin.
6. Set to bake at 350 F for 25 minutes. After 5 minutes place muffin tin in the preheated oven.
7. Serve and enjoy.

Nutritional Value (Amount per Serving):
Calories 68; Fat 4.6 g; Carbohydrates 0.8 g; Sugar 0.4 g; Protein 6 g; Cholesterol 164 mg

Easy Zucchini Frittata

Preparation Time: 10 minutes; Cooking Time: 30 minutes; Serve: 4

Ingredients:
- 8 eggs
- 2 zucchinis, chopped and cooked
- 1 tbsp fresh parsley, chopped
- 3 tbsp cheddar cheese, grated
- 1/2 tsp Italian seasoning
- Pepper
- Salt

Directions:
1. Fit the Cuisinart oven with the rack in position 1.
2. In a bowl, whisk eggs with Italian seasoning, pepper, and salt.
3. Add parsley, cheese, and zucchini and stir well.
4. Pour egg mixture into the greased baking dish.
5. Set to bake at 350 F for 35 minutes. After 5 minutes place the baking dish in the preheated oven.
6. Serve and enjoy.

Nutritional Value (Amount per Serving):
Calories 165; Fat 10.9 g; Carbohydrates 4.2 g; Sugar 2.5 g; Protein 13.6 g; Cholesterol 333 mg

Berry Breakfast Oatmeal

Preparation Time: 10 minutes; Cooking Time: 20 minutes; Serve: 4

Ingredients:
- 1 egg
- 2 cups old fashioned oats
- 1 cup blueberries
- 1/4 cup maple syrup
- 1 1/2 cups milk
- 1/2 cup blackberries
- 1/2 cup strawberries, sliced
- 1 1/2 tsp baking powder
- 1/2 tsp salt

Directions:
1. Fit the Cuisinart oven with the rack in position 1.
2. In a bowl, mix together oats, salt, and baking powder.
3. Add vanilla, egg, maple syrup, and milk and stir well. Add berries and fold well.
4. Pour mixture into the greased baking dish.
5. Set to bake at 375 F for 25 minutes. After 5 minutes place the baking dish in the preheated oven.
6. Serve and enjoy.

Nutritional Value (Amount per Serving):
Calories 461; Fat 8.4 g; Carbohydrates 80.7 g; Sugar 23.4 g; Protein 15 g; Cholesterol 48 mg

Bacon Bread Egg Casserole

Preparation Time: 10 minutes; Cooking Time: 20 minutes; Serve: 4

Ingredients:
- 6 eggs
- 1 cup cheddar cheese, shredded
- 1/2 tsp garlic, minced
- 3 tbsp milk
- 2 tbsp green onion, chopped
- 1/3 bell pepper, diced
- 2 bread slices, cubed
- 5 bacon slices, diced
- Pepper
- Salt

Directions:
1. Fit the Cuisinart oven with the rack in position 1.
2. Add all ingredients into the large bowl and stir until well combined.
3. Pour into the greased baking dish.
4. Set to bake at 350 F for 25 minutes. After 5 minutes place the baking dish in the preheated oven.
5. Serve and enjoy.

Nutritional Value (Amount per Serving):
Calories 231; Fat 26.3 g; Carbohydrates 5.2 g; Sugar 1.9 g; Protein 25 g; Cholesterol 302 mg

Jalapeno Corn Egg Bake

Preparation Time: 10 minutes; Cooking Time: 25 minutes; Serve: 2

Ingredients:
- 3 eggs
- 1/4 cup can corn, drained
- 1/2 cup cottage cheese
- 1 1/2 tbsp jalapeno, chopped
- 1/2 cup pepper jack cheese, shredded
- 1/8 tsp pepper
- 1/8 tsp sea salt

Directions:
1. Fit the Cuisinart oven with the rack in position 1.
2. In a bowl, whisk eggs with pepper and salt.

3. Stir in corn, jalapeno, pepper jack cheese, and cottage cheese.
4. Pour egg mixture into the greased 7*5-inch baking dish.
5. Set to bake at 350 F for 30 minutes. After 5 minutes place the baking dish in the preheated oven.
6. Serve and enjoy.

Nutritional Value (Amount per Serving):
Calories 252; Fat 15.1 g; Carbohydrates 6.7 g; Sugar 1.5 g; Protein 22.3 g; Cholesterol 274 mg

Sweet Pineapple Oatmeal

Preparation Time: 10 minutes; Cooking Time: 45 minutes; Serve: 6
Ingredients:
- 2 cups old-fashioned oats
- 1/2 cup coconut flakes
- 1 cup pineapple, crushed
- 2 eggs, lightly beaten
- 1/3 cup yogurt
- 1/3 cup butter, melted
- 1/2 tsp baking powder
- 1/3 cup brown sugar
- 1/2 tsp vanilla
- 2/3 cup milk
- 1/2 tsp salt

Directions:
1. Fit the Cuisinart oven with the rack in position 1.
2. In a mixing bowl, mix together oats, baking powder, brown sugar, and salt.
3. In a separate bowl, beat eggs with vanilla, milk, yogurt, and butter.
4. Add egg mixture into the oat mixture and stir to combine.
5. Add coconut and pineapple and stir to combine.
6. Pour oat mixture into the greased 8-inch baking dish.
7. Set to bake at 350 F for 50 minutes, after 5 minutes, place the baking dish in the oven.
8. Serve and enjoy.

Nutritional Value (Amount per Serving):
Calories 304; Fat 16.4 g; Carbohydrates 33.2 g; Sugar 13.6 g; Protein 7.5 g; Cholesterol 85 mg

Breakfast Sweet Potato Hash

Preparation Time: 10 minutes; Cooking Time: 65 minutes; Serve: 6
Ingredients:
- 6 cups sweet potatoes, peeled and diced
- 1 tsp thyme
- 1 tsp onion powder
- 1 onion, diced
- 8 garlic cloves, minced
- 1/3 cup olive oil
- 1/2 tsp paprika
- 1 tbsp garlic powder
- 1/2 tsp pepper
- 2 tsp salt

Directions:
1. Fit the Cuisinart oven with the rack in position 1.
2. Add sweet potatoes to a casserole dish and sprinkle with paprika, thyme, onion powder, garlic powder, pepper, and salt.
3. Drizzle oil over sweet potatoes and toss well.
4. Set to bake at 450 F for 60 minutes, after 5 minutes, place the casserole dish in the oven.
5. Heat 1 tbsp of olive oil in a pan over medium heat.
6. Add onion and garlic and sauté for 10 minutes.
7. Add onion and garlic mixture to the sweet potatoes and mix well.
8. Serve and enjoy.

Nutritional Value (Amount per Serving):
Calories 294; Fat 11.6 g; Carbohydrates 46.5 g; Sugar 2.1 g; Protein 3.1 g; Cholesterol 0 mg

Nutritious Cinnamon Oat Muffins

Preparation Time: 10 minutes; Cooking Time: 30 minutes; Serve: 12
Ingredients:
- 2 cups oat flour
- 1/3 cup coconut oil, melted
- 1/2 cup maple syrup
- 1 cup applesauce
- 1 tsp cinnamon
- 2 tsp baking powder
- 1 tsp vanilla
- 1/4 tsp salt

Directions:
1. Fit the Cuisinart oven with the rack in position 1.
2. Line 12-cups muffin tin with cupcake liners and set aside.
3. In a bowl, add applesauce, cinnamon, vanilla, oil, maple syrup, and salt and stir to combine.
4. Add baking powder and oat flour and stir well.
5. Pour batter into the prepared muffin tin.
6. Set to bake at 350 F for 35 minutes, after 5 minutes, place the muffin tin in the oven.
7. Serve and enjoy.

Nutritional Value (Amount per Serving):
Calories 158; Fat 7.1 g; Carbohydrates 22.2 g; Sugar 9.9 g; Protein 2 g; Cholesterol 0 mg

Baked Peanut Butter Oatmeal

Preparation Time: 10 minutes; Cooking Time: 35 minutes; Serve: 4
Ingredients:
- 2 cups old fashioned oats
- 2 tsp vanilla
- 1/4 cup maple syrup
- 1/2 cup peanut butter
- 1 3/4 cup almond milk
- 1/4 tsp salt

Directions:
1. Fit the Cuisinart oven with the rack in position 1.
2. In a mixing bowl, whisk together almond milk, vanilla, maple syrup, peanut butter, and salt.
3. Add oats and stir to mix.
4. Pour oats mixture into the greased baking dish.
5. Set to bake at 375 F for 40 minutes, after 5 minutes, place the baking dish in the oven.
6. Serve and enjoy.

Nutritional Value (Amount per Serving):
Calories 800; Fat 46.5 g; Carbohydrates 79.3 g; Sugar 20.6 g; Protein 20.5 g; Cholesterol 0 mg

Cinnamon Sweet Potatoes

Preparation Time: 10 minutes; Cooking Time: 45 minutes; Serve: 6
Ingredients:
- 2 lbs sweet potatoes, peel and cut into 1/2-inch cubes
- 1/2 tsp chili powder
- 1/2 tsp cinnamon
- 2 tbsp olive oil
- 1/2 tsp onion powder
- 1/2 tsp garlic powder
- Pepper
- Salt

Directions:
1. Fit the Cuisinart oven with the rack in position 1.
2. Line baking pan with parchment paper and set aside.
3. Spread sweet potato cubes in a prepared baking pan.
4. Drizzle with oil and sprinkle with spices. Toss to coat.
5. Set to bake at 400 F for 50 minutes, after 5 minutes, place the baking pan in the oven.

6. Serve and enjoy.

Nutritional Value (Amount per Serving):
Calories 221; Fat 5 g; Carbohydrates 42.8 g; Sugar 0.9 g; Protein 2.4 g; Cholesterol 0 mg

Breakfast Potatoes

Preparation Time: 10 minutes; Cooking Time: 35 minutes; Serve: 4

Ingredients:
- 2 lbs potatoes, scrubbed and cut into 1/2-inch cubes
- 1 tsp garlic powder
- 1 tbsp olive oil
- 1/2 tsp sweet paprika
- Pepper
- Salt

Directions:
1. Fit the Cuisinart oven with the rack in position 1.
2. Place potato cubes on the parchment-lined baking pan.
3. Drizzle with oil and season with paprika, garlic powder, pepper, and salt. Toss potatoes well.
4. Set to bake at 425 F for 40 minutes, after 5 minutes, place the baking pan in the oven.
5. Serve and enjoy.

Nutritional Value (Amount per Serving):
Calories 190; Fat 3.8 g; Carbohydrates 36.3 g; Sugar 2.8 g; Protein 4 g; Cholesterol 0 mg

Sweet Potato Chickpeas Hash

Preparation Time: 10 minutes; Cooking Time: 30 minutes; Serve: 4

Ingredients:
- 14.5 oz can chickpeas, drained
- 1 tsp paprika
- 1 tsp garlic powder
- 1 sweet potato, peeled and cubed
- 1 tbsp olive oil
- 1 bell pepper, chopped
- 1 onion, diced
- 1/2 tsp ground black pepper
- 1 tsp salt

Directions:
1. Fit the Cuisinart oven with the rack in position 1.
2. Spread sweet potato, chickpeas, bell pepper, and onion in a baking pan.
3. Drizzle with oil and season with paprika, garlic powder, pepper, and salt. Stir well.
4. Set to bake at 390 F for 35 minutes, after 5 minutes, place the baking pan in the oven.

Nutritional Value (Amount per Serving):
Calories 203; Fat 4.9 g; Carbohydrates 34.9 g; Sugar 4.7 g; Protein 6.5 g; Cholesterol 0 mg

Poppy Seed Muffins

Preparation Time: 10 minutes; Cooking Time: 20 minutes; Serve: 12

Ingredients:
- 3 tbsp poppy seeds
- 1 tsp vanilla
- 8 tbsp maple syrup
- 2 tbsp lemon zest
- 6 tbsp lemon juice
- 4/5 cup almond milk
- 1/4 cup butter, melted
- 1/4 tsp baking soda
- 2 tsp baking powder
- 1 1/4 cups flour
- 1 1/4 cups almond flour
- Pinch of salt

Directions:
1. Fit the Cuisinart oven with the rack in position 1.
2. Line 12-cups muffin tin with cupcake liners and set aside.

3. In a large bowl, mix together melted butter, milk, lemon zest, vanilla, lemon juice, poppy seeds, maple syrup, and almond flour.
4. Add flour, baking soda, and baking powder. Stir until well combined.
5. Pour batter into the prepared muffin tin.
6. Set to bake at 350 F for 25 minutes, after 5 minutes, place the muffin tin in the oven.
7. Serve and enjoy.

Nutritional Value (Amount per Serving):
Calories 239; Fat 14.4 g; Carbohydrates 23.6 g; Sugar 9.1 g; Protein 4.7 g; Cholesterol 10 mg

Healthy Oatmeal Bars

Preparation Time: 10 minutes; Cooking Time: 20 minutes; Serve: 18
Ingredients:
- 2 cups oatmeal
- 1/2 tsp allspice
- 1 tsp baking soda
- 1 tbsp maple syrup
- 1 cup butter
- 1 cup of sugar
- 1 cup flour

Directions:
1. Fit the Cuisinart oven with the rack in position 1.
2. Add butter and maple syrup into a bowl and microwave until butter is melted. Stir well.
3. In a mixing bowl, mix oatmeal, sugar, flour, allspice, and baking soda.
4. Add melted butter and maple syrup mixture and mix until well combined.
5. Pour mixture into the parchment-lined 9*12-inch baking dish. Spread well.
6. Set to bake at 350 F for 25 minutes, after 5 minutes, place the baking dish in the oven.
7. Slice and serve.

Nutritional Value (Amount per Serving):
Calories 195; Fat 10.9 g; Carbohydrates 23.4 g; Sugar 11.9 g; Protein 2 g; Cholesterol 27 mg

Whole Wheat Carrot Bread

Preparation Time: 10 minutes; Cooking Time: 50 minutes; Serve: 10
Ingredients:
- 1 egg
- 3/4 cup whole wheat flour
- 1 cup carrots, shredded
- 3/4 tsp vanilla
- 3/4 cup all-purpose flour
- 1/2 cup brown sugar
- 1 tsp baking powder
- 1/2 tsp nutmeg
- 1 1/2 tsp cinnamon
- 3/4 cup yogurt
- 3 tbsp vegetable oil
- 1 tsp baking soda

Directions:
1. Fit the Cuisinart oven with the rack in position 1.
2. In a large bowl, mix all dry ingredients and set aside.
3. In a separate bowl, whisk the egg with vanilla, sugar, yogurt, and oil.
4. Add carrots and fold well.
5. Add dry ingredient mixture and stir until just combined.
6. Pour mixture into the 9*5-inch greased loaf pan.
7. Set to bake at 350 F for 55 minutes, after 5 minutes, place the loaf pan in the oven.
8. Slice and serve.

Nutritional Value (Amount per Serving):
Calories 159; Fat 5 g; Carbohydrates 24.4 g; Sugar 9 g; Protein 3.7 g; Cholesterol 17 mg

Zucchini Breakfast Bread

Preparation Time: 10 minutes; Cooking Time: 50 minutes; Serve: 10

Ingredients:
- 2 eggs
- 1 1/2 cups zucchini, grated
- 1 tsp vanilla extract
- 1/4 cup yogurt
- 1/2 tsp baking powder
- 1 1/2 cups whole wheat flour
- 1/2 cup applesauce
- 1/4 cup coconut sugar
- 1 tsp ground cinnamon
- 1/2 tsp baking soda
- 1/2 cup apple, grated
- 1/4 tsp sea salt

Directions:
1. Fit the Cuisinart oven with the rack in position 1.
2. In a bowl, mix all dry ingredients.
3. In another bowl, whisk eggs, coconut sugar, vanilla, yogurt, and applesauce.
4. Add dry ingredients mixture into the wet mixture and stir until well combined.
5. Add apples and zucchini and stir well.
6. Pour batter into the 9*5-inch greased loaf pan.
7. Set to bake at 350 F for 55 minutes, after 5 minutes, place the loaf pan in the oven.
8. Slice and serve.

Nutritional Value (Amount per Serving):
Calories 103; Fat 1.2 g; Carbohydrates 19.1 g; Sugar 3.3 g; Protein 3.7 g; Cholesterol 33 mg

Choco Chip Banana Bread

Preparation Time: 10 minutes; Cooking Time: 50 minutes; Serve: 10

Ingredients:
- 2 eggs
- 3 ripe bananas
- 1 tsp vanilla
- 1 cup granulated sugar
- 1/2 cup sour cream
- 1/2 cup butter, melted
- 1/2 cup chocolate chips
- 1 1/2 cups all-purpose flour
- 1 tsp baking soda
- 1 tsp salt

Directions:
1. Fit the Cuisinart oven with the rack in position 1.
2. In a large bowl, add bananas and mash using a fork until smooth.
3. Stir in sour cream and melted butter.
4. Add eggs, vanilla, sugar, and salt and stir well.
5. Add flour, baking soda, and salt and stir until just combined.
6. Add chocolate chips and stir well.
7. Pour batter into the greased 9*8-inch loaf pan.
8. Set to bake at 350 F for 55 minutes, after 5 minutes, place the loaf pan in the oven.
9. Slice and serve.

Nutritional Value (Amount per Serving):
Calories 339; Fat 15.3 g; Carbohydrates 48 g; Sugar 28.9 g; Protein 4.5 g; Cholesterol 64 mg

Flavorful Pumpkin Bread

Preparation Time: 10 minutes; Cooking Time: 55 minutes; Serve: 12

Ingredients:
- 2 eggs
- 8 oz pumpkin puree
- 1 3/4 cups flour
- 1 1/2 cups sugar
- 1/3 cup water
- 1/2 cup vegetable oil
- 1/8 tsp ground ginger
- 1/4 tsp ground cloves
- 1/2 tsp ground nutmeg
- 1/2 tsp ground cinnamon
- 1 tsp baking soda
- 3/4 tsp salt

Directions:

1. Fit the Cuisinart oven with the rack in position 1.
2. In a bowl, whisk eggs, sugar, water, oil, and pumpkin puree until combined.
3. In a separate bowl, mix dry ingredients.
4. Add dry ingredient mixture into the egg mixture and mix until well combined.
5. Pour batter into the greased loaf pan.
6. Set to bake at 350 F for 60 minutes, after 5 minutes, place the loaf pan in the oven.
7. Slice and serve.

Nutritional Value (Amount per Serving):
Calories 258; Fat 10.1 g; Carbohydrates 40.7 g; Sugar 25.8 g; Protein 3 g; Cholesterol 27 mg

Lemon Blueberry Bread

Preparation Time: 10 minutes; Cooking Time: 55 minutes; Serve: 12

Ingredients:
- 2 eggs
- 1/4 cup yogurt
- 1/2 cup maple syrup
- 1 tsp baking powder
- 1 3/4 cups all-purpose flour
- 3 tbsp lemon zest, grated
- 3/4 cup blueberries
- 1/4 cup fresh lemon juice
- 1/4 cup coconut oil, melted
- 1/2 tsp salt

Directions:
1. Fit the Cuisinart oven with the rack in position 1.
2. In a bowl, mix all-purpose flour, salt, and baking powder.
3. In a separate bowl, beat eggs with lemon juice, coconut oil, maple syrup, and yogurt.
4. Add flour mixture into the egg mixture and mix until well combined.
5. Add blueberries and lemon zest and stir well.
6. Pour batter into the greased 8*4-inch loaf pan.
7. Set to bake at 350 F for 60 minutes, after 5 minutes, place the loaf pan in the oven.
8. Slice and serve.

Nutritional Value (Amount per Serving):
Calories 162; Fat 5.6 g; Carbohydrates 25.1 g; Sugar 9.4 g; Protein 3.2 g; Cholesterol 28 mg

Moist Orange Bread Loaf

Preparation Time: 10 minutes; Cooking Time: 50 minutes; Serve: 10

Ingredients:
- 4 eggs
- 4 oz butter, softened
- 1 cup of orange juice
- 1 orange zest, grated
- 1 cup of sugar
- 2 tsp baking powder
- 2 cups all-purpose flour
- 1 tsp vanilla

Directions:
1. Fit the Cuisinart oven with the rack in position 1.
2. In a large bowl, whisk eggs and sugar until creamy.
3. Whisk in vanilla, butter, orange juice, and orange zest.
4. Add flour and baking powder and mix until combined.
5. Pour batter into the greased 9*5-inch loaf pan.
6. Set to bake at 350 F for 55 minutes, after 5 minutes, place the loaf pan in the oven.
7. Slice and serve.

Nutritional Value (Amount per Serving):
Calories 286; Fat 11.3 g; Carbohydrates 42.5 g; Sugar 22.4 g; Protein 5.1 g; Cholesterol 90 mg

Kale Egg Muffins

Preparation Time: 10 minutes; Cooking Time: 35 minutes; Serve: 12

Ingredients:
- 10 eggs
- 1/4 cup kale, chopped
- 1/4 cup sausage, sliced
- 1/4 cup sun-dried tomatoes, chopped
- 1 cup almond milk
- Pepper
- Salt

Directions:
1. Fit the Cuisinart oven with the rack in position 1.
2. Spray 12-cups muffin tin with cooking spray and set aside.
3. In a large bowl, add all ingredients and whisk until well combined.
4. Pour egg mixture into the greased muffin tin.
5. Set to bake at 350 F for 40 minutes, after 5 minutes, place the muffin tin in the oven.
6. Serve and enjoy.

Nutritional Value (Amount per Serving):
Calories 102; Fat 8.6 g; Carbohydrates 1.7 g; Sugar 1.1 g; Protein 5.3 g; Cholesterol 137 mg

Chicken Breakfast Muffins

Preparation Time: 10 minutes; Cooking Time: 15 minutes; Serve: 12

Ingredients:
- 10 eggs
- 1/3 cup green onions, chopped
- 1 cup chicken, cooked and chopped
- 1/4 tsp pepper
- 1 tsp sea salt

Directions:
1. Fit the Cuisinart oven with the rack in position 1.
2. Spray 12-cups muffin tin with cooking spray and set aside.
3. In a large bowl, whisk eggs with pepper and salt.
4. Add remaining ingredients and stir well.
5. Pour egg mixture into the greased muffin tin.
6. Set to bake at 400 F for 20 minutes, after 5 minutes, place the muffin tin in the oven.
7. Serve and enjoy.

Nutritional Value (Amount per Serving):
Calories 71; Fat 4 g; Carbohydrates 0.5 g; Sugar 0.3 g; Protein 8 g; Cholesterol 145 mg

Spinach Zucchini Egg Muffins

Preparation Time: 10 minutes; Cooking Time: 20 minutes; Serve: 12

Ingredients:
- 8 eggs
- 1 cup baby spinach, chopped
- 1 red bell pepper, diced
- 1/4 cup green onion, chopped
- 12 bacon slices, cooked and crumbled
- 2 small zucchini, sliced
- 1/4 cup almond milk
- 2 tbsp parsley, chopped
- 1 tbsp olive oil
- Pepper
- Salt

Directions:
1. Fit the Cuisinart oven with the rack in position 1.
2. Spray 12-cups muffin tin with cooking spray and set aside.
3. Heat olive oil in a pan over medium heat.
4. Add parsley, spinach, green onion, red bell pepper to the pan and sauté until spinach is wilted.
5. In a bowl, whisk eggs with almond milk, pepper, and salt.
6. Add sautéed vegetables, bacon, and zucchini to the egg mixture and stir well.
7. Pour egg mixture into the greased muffin tin.

8. Set to bake at 350 F for 25 minutes, after 5 minutes, place muffin tin in the oven.
   9. Serve and enjoy.

Nutritional Value (Amount per Serving):
Calories 174; Fat 13.3 g; Carbohydrates 2.5 g; Sugar 1.3 g; Protein 11.3 g; Cholesterol 130 mg

Spinach Egg Bites

Preparation Time: 10 minutes; Cooking Time: 20 minutes; Serve: 12

Ingredients:
- 8 eggs
- 1/4 cup almond milk
- 1/4 cup green onion, chopped
- 1 cup spinach, chopped
- 1 cup roasted red peppers, chopped
- 1/2 tsp salt

Directions:
1. Fit the Cuisinart oven with the rack in position 1.
2. Spray 12-cups muffin tin with cooking spray and set aside.
3. In a bowl, whisk eggs with milk and salt.
4. Add spinach, green onion, and red peppers to the egg mixture and stir to combine.
5. Pour egg mixture into the greased muffin tin.
6. Set to bake at 350 F for 25 minutes, after 5 minutes, place muffin tin in the oven.
7. Serve and enjoy.

Nutritional Value (Amount per Serving):
Calories 59; Fat 4.2 g; Carbohydrates 1.7 g; Sugar 1.1 g; Protein 4.1 g; Cholesterol 109 mg

Omelet Egg Muffins

Preparation Time: 10 minutes; Cooking Time: 20 minutes; Serve: 12

Ingredients:
- 12 eggs, lightly beaten
- 1 cup tomatoes, chopped
- 4 tbsp water
- 1 tsp Italian seasoning
- 1 cup fresh spinach, chopped
- 1/2 tsp pepper
- 1/4 tsp salt

Directions:
1. Fit the Cuisinart oven with the rack in position 1.
2. Spray 12-cups muffin tin with cooking spray and set aside.
3. Whisk eggs in a bowl with water, Italian seasoning, pepper, and salt.
4. Add spinach and tomatoes to the egg mixture and whisk well.
5. Pour egg mixture into the greased muffin tin.
6. Set to bake at 350 F for 25 minutes, after 5 minutes, place muffin tin in the oven.
7. Serve and enjoy.

Nutritional Value (Amount per Serving):
Calories 68; Fat 4.5 g; Carbohydrates 1.1 g; Sugar 0.8 g; Protein 5.8 g; Cholesterol 164 mg

Easy Breakfast Bake

Preparation Time: 10 minutes; Cooking Time: 45 minutes; Serve: 6

Ingredients:
- 10 eggs
- 10 bacon sliced, cooked, and crumbled
- 2 tomatoes, sliced
- 1 tbsp butter
- 3 cups baby spinach, chopped
- 1/2 tsp salt

Directions:
1. Fit the Cuisinart oven with the rack in position 1.
2. Melt butter in a pan.

3. Add spinach and cook until spinach wilted.
4. Whisk eggs and salt in a bowl. Add spinach and whisk well.
5. Pour egg mixture into the greased 9-inch baking dish. Top with bacon and tomatoes
6. Set to bake at 350 F for 50 minutes, after 5 minutes, place the baking dish in the oven.
7. Serve and enjoy.

Nutritional Value (Amount per Serving):
Calories 266; Fat 21 g; Carbohydrates 2.7 g; Sugar 1.7 g; Protein 18.4 g; Cholesterol 303 mg

Zucchini Breakfast Casserole

Preparation Time: 10 minutes; Cooking Time: 50 minutes; Serve: 8
Ingredients:
- 12 eggs
- 2 small zucchinis, shredded
- 1 lb ground sausage
- 3 tomatoes, sliced
- 3 tbsp coconut flour
- 1/4 cup coconut milk
- 1/4 tsp pepper
- 1/2 tsp salt

Directions:
1. Fit the Cuisinart oven with the rack in position 1.
2. Cook sausage in a pan until lightly brown.
3. Transfer sausage to a large mixing bowl.
4. Add coconut flour, milk, eggs, zucchini, pepper, and salt. Stir well.
5. Add eggs and whisk until well combined.
6. Pour bowl mixture into the greased casserole dish and top with tomato slices.
7. Set to bake at 350 F for 55 minutes, after 5 minutes, place the casserole dish in the oven.
8. Serve and enjoy.

Nutritional Value (Amount per Serving):
Calories 330; Fat 25 g; Carbohydrates 5.7 g; Sugar 2.7 g; Protein 20.8 g; Cholesterol 293 mg

Easy Egg Quiche

Preparation Time: 10 minutes; Cooking Time: 45 minutes; Serve: 6
Ingredients:
- 8 eggs
- 4 tbsp butter, melted
- 6 oz cream cheese
- 6 oz cheddar cheese, shredded

Directions:
1. Fit the Cuisinart oven with the rack in position 1.
2. Add eggs, cheese, butter, and cream cheese into the bowl and whisk until well combined.
3. Pour egg mixture into the greased pie dish.
4. Set to bake at 325 F for 50 minutes, after 5 minutes, place the pie dish in the oven.
5. Serve and enjoy.

Nutritional Value (Amount per Serving):
Calories 365; Fat 32.8 g; Carbohydrates 1.6 g; Sugar 0.7 g; Protein 16.7 g; Cholesterol 300 mg

Baked Breakfast Quiche

Preparation Time: 10 minutes; Cooking Time: 45 minutes; Serve: 6
Ingredients:
- 6 eggs
- 1 cup milk
- 1 cup cheddar cheese, grated
- 1 cup tomatoes, chopped
- Pepper
- Salt

Directions:
1. Fit the Cuisinart oven with the rack in position 1.
2. In a bowl, whisk eggs with cheese, milk, pepper, and salt. Stir in tomatoes.

3. Pour egg mixture into the greased pie dish.
4. Set to bake at 350 F for 50 minutes, after 5 minutes, place the pie dish in the oven.
5. Serve and enjoy.

Nutritional Value (Amount per Serving):
Calories 165; Fat 11.5 g; Carbohydrates 3.8 g; Sugar 3.1 g; Protein 11.8 g; Cholesterol 187 mg

Ham Egg Muffins

Preparation Time: 10 minutes; Cooking Time: 20 minutes; Serve: 12

Ingredients:
- 12 eggs
- 2 cups ham, diced
- 1 3/4 cup cheddar cheese, shredded
- 1/2 pepper
- 1/2 tsp salt

Directions:
1. Fit the Cuisinart oven with the rack in position 1.
2. Spray 12-cups muffin tin with cooking spray and set aside.
3. In a bowl, whisk eggs with pepper and salt.
4. Stir in cheddar cheese and ham.
5. Pour egg mixture into prepared muffin tin.
6. Set to bake at 375 F for 25 minutes, after 5 minutes, place the muffin tin in the oven.
7. Serve and enjoy.

Nutritional Value (Amount per Serving):
Calories 166; Fat 11.8 g; Carbohydrates 1.5 g; Sugar 0.4 g; Protein 13.4 g; Cholesterol 194 mg

Chapter 3: Poultry

Juicy Baked Chicken Breast

Preparation Time: 10 minutes; Cooking Time: 25 minutes; Serve: 4

Ingredients:
- 4 chicken breasts
- 1 tbsp fresh parsley, chopped
- 1/4 tsp red pepper flakes
- 1/2 tsp black pepper
- 1 tsp Italian seasoning
- 2 tbsp olive oil
- 1/4 cup balsamic vinegar
- 1 tsp kosher salt

Directions:
1. Fit the Cuisinart oven with the rack in position 1.
2. Place chicken breasts into the mixing bowl.
3. Mix together remaining ingredients and pour over chicken breasts and coat well and let marinate for 30 minutes.
4. Arrange marinated chicken breasts into a greased baking dish.
5. Set to bake at 425 F for 30 minutes. After 5 minutes place the baking dish in the preheated oven.
6. Slice and serve.

Nutritional Value (Amount per Serving):
Calories 345; Fat 18.2 g; Carbohydrates 0.6 g; Sugar 0.2 g; Protein 42.3 g; Cholesterol 131 mg

Baked Spinach Cheese Chicken

Preparation Time: 10 minutes; Cooking Time: 20 minutes; Serve: 2

Ingredients:
- 2 chicken breasts, boneless & skinless
- 1/2 tsp garlic powder
- 1/4 cup sun-dried tomatoes, chopped
- 1/4 cup cheddar cheese, shredded
- 3 oz cream cheese
- 2 cups fresh spinach, chopped
- 3/4 tsp pepper
- 3/4 tsp salt

Directions:
1. Fit the Cuisinart oven with the rack in position 1.
2. Slice the chicken breasts into the half and place them into the baking dish. Season with pepper and salt.
3. Cook spinach in the pan until wilted.
4. In a bowl, mix spinach, garlic powder, tomatoes, cheddar cheese, and cream cheese.
5. Spread spinach mixture on top of chicken breasts.
6. Set to bake at 425 F for 25 minutes. After 5 minutes place the baking dish in the preheated oven.
7. Serve and enjoy.

Nutritional Value (Amount per Serving):
Calories 498; Fat 30.5 g; Carbohydrates 4.3 g; Sugar 1.1 g; Protein 50.2 g; Cholesterol 192 mg

Green Chili Chicken Noodle Casserole

Preparation Time: 10 minutes; Cooking Time: 30 minutes; Serve: 6

Ingredients:
- 3 cups cooked chicken, shredded
- 4 oz can green chilies
- 1/3 cup parmesan cheese, shredded
- 3 cups cheddar cheese, shredded
- 1 1/3 cups milk
- 10.5 oz cream of chicken soup
- 1 tsp chili powder
- 1 onion, diced
- 1/3 cup bell pepper, diced
- 3 tbsp butter
- 3 cups shell noodles, uncooked
- 1/2 tsp salt

Directions:
1. Fit the Cuisinart oven with the rack in position 1.
2. Cook noodles according to the packet instructions and drain well.
3. Melt butter in a pan over medium heat.
4. Add bell pepper and onion and sauté for 5 minutes. Stir in chili powder and salt.
5. In a large bowl, mix chicken soup, parmesan cheese, 2 cups cheddar cheese, milk, and sautéed onion bell pepper. Stir in green chilies, noodles, and chicken.
6. Pour mixture into the greased 9*13-inch baking dish and top with remaining cheese.
7. Set to bake at 375 F for 35 minutes. After 5 minutes place the baking dish in the preheated oven.
8. Serve and enjoy.

Nutritional Value (Amount per Serving):
Calories 560; Fat 32.6 g; Carbohydrates 23.9 g; Sugar 5 g; Protein 42.2 g; Cholesterol 156 mg

Baked Chicken Noodle Casserole

Preparation Time: 10 minutes; Cooking Time: 55 minutes; Serve: 4
Ingredients:
- 2 cups cooked chicken, diced
- 3/4 cup frozen peas
- 10.5 oz cream of chicken soup
- 2 cups dry egg noodles
- 1/2 cup milk
- 1/2 cup cheddar cheese, shredded
- 2 tbsp breadcrumbs
- 1 tbsp butter, melted

Directions:
1. Fit the Cuisinart oven with the rack in position 1.
2. Cook noodles according to the packet instructions. Drain well.
3. Add cooked noodles, milk, soup, chicken, and peas into the greased casserole dish. Sprinkle with shredded cheese.
4. Mix melted butter and breadcrumbs and sprinkle over chicken noodle mixture.
5. Set to bake at 425 F for 60 minutes. After 5 minutes place the casserole dish in the preheated oven.
6. Serve and enjoy.

Nutritional Value (Amount per Serving):
Calories 417; Fat 16.5 g; Carbohydrates 33.9 g; Sugar 3.8 g; Protein 32.2 g; Cholesterol 108 mg

Simple & Healthy Baked Chicken Breasts

Preparation Time: 10 minutes; Cooking Time: 20 minutes; Serve: 6
Ingredients:
- 6 chicken breasts, skinless & boneless
- 1/4 tsp paprika
- 1 tsp Italian seasoning
- 2 tbsp olive oil
- 1/4 tsp pepper
- 1/2 tsp seasoning salt

Directions:
1. Fit the Cuisinart oven with the rack in position 1.
2. Brush chicken with oil and season with paprika, Italian seasoning, pepper, and salt.
3. Place chicken breasts into the baking dish.
4. Set to bake at 400 F for 25 minutes. After 5 minutes place the baking dish in the preheated oven.
5. Serve and enjoy.

Nutritional Value (Amount per Serving):
Calories 320; Fat 15.7 g; Carbohydrates 0.2 g; Sugar 0.1 g; Protein 42.3 g; Cholesterol 130 mg

Flavorful Lemon Pepper Chicken

Preparation Time: 10 minutes; Cooking Time: 25 minutes; Serve: 4
Ingredients:
- 4 chicken breasts, boneless & skinless
- 3 tbsp fresh lemon juice
- 2 tsp ground black pepper
- 5 tbsp olive oil
- 1/2 tsp sea salt

Directions:
1. Fit the Cuisinart oven with the rack in position 1.
2. Heat 2 tablespoons of oil in a pan over medium-high heat. Brown chicken in a pan.
3. In a small bowl, mix lemon juice, remaining oil, pepper, and salt.
4. Place browned chicken into the baking dish. Pour lemon juice mixture over chicken.
5. Set to bake at 425 F for 30 minutes. After 5 minutes place the baking dish in the preheated oven.
6. Serve and enjoy.

Nutritional Value (Amount per Serving):
Calories 433; Fat 28.4 g; Carbohydrates 0.9 g; Sugar 0.3 g; Protein 42.4 g; Cholesterol 130 mg

Delicious Tender Chicken Breasts

Preparation Time: 10 minutes; Cooking Time: 25 minutes; Serve: 6
Ingredients:
- 3 lbs chicken breasts, boneless
- 1 1/2 cups parmesan cheese, grated
- 1/2 tsp pepper
- 2 tsp garlic powder
- 1 cup sour cream
- 1 tsp salt

Directions:
1. Fit the Cuisinart oven with the rack in position 1.
2. Place chicken into the baking dish.
3. In a bowl, mix 1 cup parmesan cheese, pepper, garlic powder, sour cream, and salt.
4. Pour cheese mixture over chicken and sprinkle remaining parmesan cheese on top of chicken.
5. Set to bake at 375 F for 30 minutes. After 5 minutes place the baking dish in the preheated oven.
6. Serve and enjoy.

Nutritional Value (Amount per Serving):
Calories 589; Fat 29.7 g; Carbohydrates 3.3 g; Sugar 0.3 g; Protein 74.2 g; Cholesterol 235 mg

Potato Garlic Chicken

Preparation Time: 10 minutes; Cooking Time: 25 minutes; Serve: 4
Ingredients:
- 4 chicken breasts, skinless & boneless
- 1/2 cup cheddar cheese, shredded
- 1 cup mozzarella cheese, shredded
- 2 tsp dried parsley
- 1/2 tsp crushed red pepper
- 1 tbsp garlic, minced
- 1/2 cup butter
- 1 lb baby potatoes, cut into half
- 1/4 tsp pepper
- 1/4 tsp salt

Directions:
1. Fit the Cuisinart oven with the rack in position 1.
2. Season chicken with pepper and salt and place in a casserole dish. Top with potatoes.
3. Melt butter in a pan over medium heat. Add garlic and sauté for a minute.
4. Remove pan from heat and let it cool for 5 minutes.
5. Pour melted butter over chicken and potatoes. Sprinkle with pepper and parsley.

6. Set to bake at 400 F for 25 minutes. After 5 minutes place the casserole dish in the preheated oven.
7. Remove the casserole dish from the oven. Sprinkle mozzarella cheese and cheddar cheese on top of chicken and potatoes and bake for 5 minutes more.
8. Serve and enjoy.

Nutritional Value (Amount per Serving):
Calories 635; Fat 40 g; Carbohydrates 16.8 g; Sugar 0.3 g; Protein 51.6 g; Cholesterol 210 mg

Italian Veggie Chicken

Preparation Time: 10 minutes; Cooking Time: 30 minutes; Serve: 4

Ingredients:
- 4 chicken breasts
- 1 cup mozzarella cheese, shredded
- 6 bacon slices, cooked & chopped
- 8 oz can artichoke hearts, sliced
- 1 cup cherry tomatoes, cut in half
- 1 zucchini, sliced
- 1 tbsp dried basil
- 1/4 tsp salt

Directions:
1. Fit the Cuisinart oven with the rack in position 1.
2. Place chicken breasts into the casserole dish and sprinkle with basil and salt.
3. Spread artichoke hearts, cherry tomatoes, and zucchini on top of chicken.
4. Sprinkle shredded cheese and bacon on top of vegetables.
5. Set to bake at 375 F for 35 minutes. After 5 minutes place the casserole dish in the preheated oven.
6. Serve and enjoy.

Nutritional Value (Amount per Serving):
Calories 484; Fat 24.2 g; Carbohydrates 6.9 g; Sugar 2.5 g; Protein 56.8 g; Cholesterol 165 mg

Easy Smothered Chicken

Preparation Time: 10 minutes; Cooking Time: 55 minutes; Serve: 4

Ingredients:
- 4 chicken breasts
- 1/2 tsp garlic powder
- 1 tsp dried basil
- 1 tsp dried oregano
- 1 tbsp cornstarch
- 3/4 cup parmesan cheese, grated
- 1 cup sour cream
- 4 mozzarella cheese slices
- 1/4 tsp pepper
- 1/2 tsp salt

Directions:
1. Fit the Cuisinart oven with the rack in position 1.
2. Place chicken breasts into the baking dish and top with mozzarella cheese slices.
3. In a bowl, mix sour cream, parmesan cheese, cornstarch, oregano, basil, garlic powder, pepper, and salt.
4. Pour sour cream mixture over chicken.
5. Set to bake at 375 F for 60 minutes. After 5 minutes place the baking dish in the preheated oven.
6. Serve and enjoy.

Nutritional Value (Amount per Serving):
Calories 545; Fat 31.5 g; Carbohydrates 6.5 g; Sugar 0.2 g; Protein 57.2 g; Cholesterol 182 mg

Baked Fajita Chicken

Preparation Time: 10 minutes; Cooking Time: 35 minutes; Serve: 4

Ingredients:
- 4 chicken breasts, sliced
- 2 cups cheddar cheese, shredded

- 2 bell peppers, sliced
- 1 oz fajita seasoning
- 1/3 cup salsa
- 8 oz cream cheese, softened

Directions:
1. Fit the Cuisinart oven with the rack in position 1.
2. Place chicken into the greased 9*13-inch baking dish.
3. Mix together salsa, cream cheese, and fajita seasoning and pour over chicken.
4. Spread sliced bell peppers on top of chicken. Sprinkle shredded cheese on top.
5. Set to bake at 375 F for 40 minutes. After 5 minutes place the baking dish in the preheated oven.
6. Serve and enjoy.

Nutritional Value (Amount per Serving):
Calories 754; Fat 49.5 g; Carbohydrates 252 g; Sugar 4.1 g; Protein 61.5 g; Cholesterol 252 mg

Juicy & Tender Chicken Breast

Preparation Time: 10 minutes; Cooking Time: 20 minutes; Serve: 4
Ingredients:
- 4 chicken breasts, skinless & boneless
- 1/4 tsp pepper
- 1/4 tsp onion powder
- 1/4 tsp garlic powder
- 1 tsp paprika
- 1 tsp Italian seasoning
- 1 tbsp brown sugar
- 3 tbsp butter, melted
- 1 tsp salt

Directions:
1. Fit the Cuisinart oven with the rack in position 1.
2. In a small bowl, mix paprika, brown sugar, Italian seasoning, garlic powder, onion powder, pepper, and salt.
3. Brush chicken with melted butter and rub with spice mixture.
4. Place chicken into the baking dish.
5. Set to bake at 425 F for 25 minutes. After 5 minutes place the baking dish in the preheated oven.
6. Serve and enjoy.

Nutritional Value (Amount per Serving):
Calories 369; Fat 19.9 g; Carbohydrates 3 g; Sugar 2.4 g; Protein 42.5 g; Cholesterol 154 mg

Juicy Balsamic Chicken

Preparation Time: 10 minutes; Cooking Time: 25 minutes; Serve: 4
Ingredients:
- 4 chicken breasts, boneless & skinless
- 2 tsp dried oregano
- 2 garlic clove, minced
- 1/2 cup balsamic vinegar
- 2 tbsp soy sauce
- 1/4 cup olive oil
- 1/4 tsp pepper
- 1/4 tsp salt

Directions:
1. Fit the Cuisinart oven with the rack in position 1.
2. Place chicken into the baking dish. Mix together remaining ingredients and pour over chicken and let sit for 10 minutes.
3. Set to bake at 400 F for 30 minutes. After 5 minutes place the baking dish in the preheated oven.
4. Serve and enjoy.

Nutritional Value (Amount per Serving):
Calories 401; Fat 23.5 g; Carbohydrates 2 g; Sugar 0.3 g; Protein 42.9 g; Cholesterol 130 mg

Pesto Chicken

Preparation Time: 10 minutes; Cooking Time: 30 minutes; Serve: 4
Ingredients:
- 4 chicken breasts, boneless & skinless
- 2 tbsp fresh basil
- 8 oz mozzarella cheese, sliced
- 2 tomatoes, sliced
- 1/2 cup pesto
- 1 tbsp garlic, minced

Directions:
1. Fit the Cuisinart oven with the rack in position 1.
2. Place chicken into the baking dish and sprinkle with basil and garlic.
3. Pour pesto over chicken. Arrange sliced tomatoes and cheese on top of chicken.
4. Set to bake at 400 F for 35 minutes. After 5 minutes place the baking dish in the preheated oven.
5. Serve and enjoy.

Nutritional Value (Amount per Serving):
Calories 587; Fat 34 g; Carbohydrates 7.1 g; Sugar 3.6 g; Protein 62 g; Cholesterol 167 mg

Cheesy Bacon Chicken

Preparation Time: 10 minutes; Cooking Time: 30 minutes; Serve: 4
Ingredients:
- 4 chicken breasts, sliced in half
- 1 cup cheddar cheese, shredded
- 8 bacon slices, cooked & chopped
- 6 oz cream cheese
- Pepper
- Salt

Directions:
1. Fit the Cuisinart oven with the rack in position 1.
2. Place season chicken with pepper and salt and place it into the greased baking dish.
3. Add cream cheese and bacon on top of chicken.
4. Sprinkle shredded cheddar cheese on top of chicken.
5. Set to bake at 400 F for 35 minutes. After 5 minutes place the baking dish in the preheated oven.
6. Serve and enjoy.

Nutritional Value (Amount per Serving):
Calories 745; Fat 50.9 g; Carbohydrates 2.1 g; Sugar 0.2 g; Protein 66.6 g; Cholesterol 248 mg

Juicy Baked Chicken Wings

Preparation Time: 10 minutes; Cooking Time: 40 minutes; Serve: 4
Ingredients:
- 2 lbs chicken wings
- 1 tbsp garlic, minced
- 2 tbsp mayonnaise
- 2 tbsp ketchup
- Pepper
- Salt

Directions:
1. Fit the Cuisinart oven with the rack in position 1.
2. Add chicken wings and remaining ingredients into the bowl and mix well. Let marinate chicken wings for 3 hours.
3. Place marinated chicken wings into the baking dish.
4. Set to bake at 400 F for 45 minutes. After 5 minutes place the baking dish in the preheated oven.
5. Serve and enjoy.

Nutritional Value (Amount per Serving):
Calories 470; Fat 19.3 g; Carbohydrates 4.4 g; Sugar 2.2 g; Protein 65.9 g; Cholesterol 204 mg

Bacon Broccoli Chicken

Preparation Time: 10 minutes; Cooking Time: 30 minutes; Serve: 4
Ingredients:
- 4 chicken breasts, sliced in half
- 1/3 cup mozzarella cheese, shredded
- 1 cup cheddar cheese, shredded
- 1/2 cup ranch dressing
- 6 bacon slices, cooked & chopped
- 2 cups broccoli florets, chopped

Directions:
1. Fit the Cuisinart oven with the rack in position 1.
2. Place chicken into the greased casserole dish.
3. Add ranch dressing, bacon, and broccoli on top of chicken.
4. Sprinkle cheddar cheese and mozzarella cheese on top of chicken.
5. Set to bake at 375 F for 35 minutes. After 5 minutes place the casserole dish in the preheated oven.
6. Serve and enjoy.

Nutritional Value (Amount per Serving):
Calories 577; Fat 32.8 g; Carbohydrates 5.5 g; Sugar 1.7 g; Protein 62.2 g; Cholesterol 192 mg

Easy Creamy Chicken

Preparation Time: 10 minutes; Cooking Time: 55 minutes; Serve: 4
Ingredients:
- 4 chicken breasts
- 1 tsp garlic powder
- 1 tsp dried basil
- 1 tsp dried oregano
- 3/4 cup parmesan cheese, grated
- 1 cup sour cream
- 1 cup mozzarella cheese, shredded
- 1/2 tsp pepper
- 1/2 tsp salt

Directions:
1. Fit the Cuisinart oven with the rack in position 1.
2. Season chicken with pepper and salt and place into the greased baking dish.
3. Mix together sour cream, mozzarella cheese, parmesan cheese, oregano, basil, garlic powder, and salt and pour over chicken.
4. Set to bake at 375 F for 60 minutes. After 5 minutes place the baking dish in the preheated oven.
5. Serve and enjoy.

Nutritional Value (Amount per Serving):
Calories 479; Fat 27.8 g; Carbohydrates 4.2 g; Sugar 0.3 g; Protein 51.7 g; Cholesterol 171 mg

Easy Baked Chicken Drumsticks

Preparation Time: 10 minutes; Cooking Time: 45 minutes; Serve: 6
Ingredients:
- 6 chicken legs
- 1/4 cup Worcestershire sauce
- 2 tbsp olive oil
- 1/2 tsp paprika
- 1/2 tsp oregano
- 1 1/2 tsp onion powder
- 1 1/2 tsp garlic powder
- 1/2 tsp pepper
- 1/2 tsp salt

Directions:
1. Fit the Cuisinart oven with the rack in position 1.
2. Add chicken legs and remaining ingredients into the zip-lock bag, seal bag shake well and place in the fridge for 2 hours.
3. Place marinated chicken legs in a baking pan.

4. Set to bake at 375 F for 50 minutes. After 5 minutes place the baking pan in the preheated oven.
   5. Serve and enjoy.

Nutritional Value (Amount per Serving):
Calories 182; Fat 9.7 g; Carbohydrates 3.3 g; Sugar 2.4 g; Protein 19.5 g; Cholesterol 59 mg

Crispy Cajun Chicken Breast

Preparation Time: 10 minutes; Cooking Time: 25 minutes; Serve: 2

Ingredients:
- 2 chicken breasts
- 3/4 cup breadcrumbs
- 1 tsp garlic powder
- 1 tsp paprika
- 1 tsp Cajun seasoning
- 2 tbsp mayonnaise
- 1/2 tsp pepper
- 1/2 tsp salt

Directions:
1. Fit the Cuisinart oven with the rack in position 1.
2. In a shallow dish, mix breadcrumbs, Cajun seasoning, paprika, garlic powder, pepper, and salt.
3. Brush chicken with mayonnaise and coat with breadcrumbs.
4. Place coated chicken breasts into the baking pan.
5. Set to bake at 425 F for 30 minutes. After 5 minutes place the baking pan in the preheated oven.
6. Serve and enjoy.

Nutritional Value (Amount per Serving):
Calories 504; Fat 18.1 g; Carbohydrates 34.6 g; Sugar 3.9 g; Protein 48.3 g; Cholesterol 134 mg

Honey Garlic Chicken Wings

Preparation Time: 10 minutes; Cooking Time: 50 minutes; Serve: 6

Ingredients:
- 3 lbs chicken wings
- 1 tbsp garlic, minced
- 1 cup honey
- 2 tbsp BBQ sauce
- 1/2 cup soy sauce
- 2 tbsp olive oil
- Pepper
- Salt

Directions:
1. Fit the Cuisinart oven with the rack in position 1.
2. Add chicken wings and remaining ingredients into the mixing bowl and mix until well coated.
3. Arrange chicken wings onto the baking pan.
4. Set to bake at 350 F for 55 minutes. After 5 minutes place the baking pan in the preheated oven.
5. Serve and enjoy.

Nutritional Value (Amount per Serving):
Calories 664; Fat 21.5 g; Carbohydrates 50.5 g; Sugar 48.1 g; Protein 67.2 g; Cholesterol 202 mg

Tasty Turkey Meatballs

Preparation Time: 10 minutes; Cooking Time: 25 minutes; Serve: 6

Ingredients:
- 2 eggs
- 2 lbs ground turkey
- 1/2 cup breadcrumbs
- 1 tsp cumin
- 1 tsp oregano
- 1/2 tsp pepper
- 1 tsp fresh mint, chopped
- 1/2 cup parsley, chopped

- 1/2 cup onion, minced
- 1 tbsp garlic, minced
- 1/2 tsp pepper
- 1 tsp salt

Directions:
1. Fit the Cuisinart oven with the rack in position 1.
2. Add all ingredients into the mixing bowl and mix until well combined.
3. Make small balls from meat mixture and place onto the parchment-lined baking pan.
4. Set to bake at 375 F for 30 minutes. After 5 minutes place the baking pan in the preheated oven.
5. Serve and enjoy.

Nutritional Value (Amount per Serving):
Calories 362; Fat 18.7 g; Carbohydrates 8.8 g; Sugar 1.2 g; Protein 44.9 g; Cholesterol 209 mg

Delicious Turkey Cutlets

Preparation Time: 10 minutes; Cooking Time: 25 minutes; Serve: 4

Ingredients:
- 1 egg
- 1 1/2 lbs turkey cutlets
- 1/2 tsp garlic powder
- 1/2 tsp onion powder
- 1/2 tsp dried parsley
- 1/4 cup parmesan cheese, grated
- 1/2 cup almond flour
- 1/4 tsp pepper
- 1/2 tsp salt

Directions:
1. Fit the Cuisinart oven with the rack in position 1.
2. Add egg in a small bowl and whisk well.
3. In a shallow dish, mix almond flour, parmesan cheese, parsley, onion powder, garlic powder, pepper, and salt.
4. Dip turkey cutlet into the egg and coat with almond flour mixture.
5. Place coated turkey cutlets into the baking pan.
6. Set to bake at 350 F for 30 minutes. After 5 minutes place the baking pan in the preheated oven.
7. Serve and enjoy.

Nutritional Value (Amount per Serving):
Calories 346; Fat 12.6 g; Carbohydrates 1.6 g; Sugar 0.4 g; Protein 53.9 g; Cholesterol 174 mg

Herb Turkey Tenderloin

Preparation Time: 10 minutes; Cooking Time: 40 minutes; Serve: 4

Ingredients:
- 24 oz turkey tenderloin
- 1 tbsp dried rosemary
- 1 tbsp dried sage
- Pepper
- Salt

Directions:
1. Fit the Cuisinart oven with the rack in position 1.
2. Rub turkey tenderloin with rosemary, sage, pepper, and salt.
3. Place turkey tenderloin into the baking pan.
4. Set to bake at 350 F for 45 minutes. After 5 minutes place the baking pan in the preheated oven.
5. Slice and serve.

Nutritional Value (Amount per Serving):
Calories 185; Fat 2.4 g; Carbohydrates 0.9 g; Sugar 0 g; Protein 42.3 g; Cholesterol 68 mg

Juicy Chicken Patties

Preparation Time: 10 minutes; Cooking Time: 25 minutes; Serve: 4
Ingredients:
- 1 egg
- 1 lb ground chicken
- 1 tsp garlic, minced
- 1/2 cup onion, minced
- 3/4 cup breadcrumbs
- 1/2 cup mozzarella cheese, grated cheese
- 1 cup carrot, grated
- 1 cup cauliflower, grated
- 1/8 tsp pepper
- 3/4 tsp salt

Directions:
1. Fit the Cuisinart oven with the rack in position 1.
2. Add all ingredients into the mixing bowl and mix until well combined.
3. Make 4 equal shapes of patties from meat mixture and place onto the parchment-lined baking pan.
4. Set to bake at 400 F for 30 minutes. After 5 minutes place the baking pan in the preheated oven.
5. Serve and enjoy.

Nutritional Value (Amount per Serving):
Calories 346; Fat 11.2 g; Carbohydrates 20.4 g; Sugar 3.9 g; Protein 38.8 g; Cholesterol 144 mg

Parmesan Baked Chicken Pasta

Preparation Time: 10 minutes; Cooking Time: 30 minutes; Serve: 4
Ingredients:
- 12 oz pasta, uncooked
- 1 cup basil, chopped
- 2 garlic cloves, minced
- 25 oz tomato sauce
- 2 cups mozzarella cheese, shredded
- 1 cup parmesan cheese, shredded
- 2 cups chicken, cooked & shredded
- 1/4 tsp pepper
- Pinch of salt

Directions:
1. Fit the Cuisinart oven with the rack in position 1.
2. Cook pasta according to the packet instructions. Drain well.
3. In a bowl, mix pasta, basil, garlic, tomato sauce, chicken, pepper, and salt.
4. Pour pasta mixture into the greased 9*13-inch casserole dish. Sprinkle mozzarella and parmesan cheese on top.
5. Set to bake at 375 F for 35 minutes. After 5 minutes place the casserole dish in the preheated oven.
6. Serve and enjoy.

Nutritional Value (Amount per Serving):
Calories 509; Fat 11.8 g; Carbohydrates 58.1 g; Sugar 7.6 g; Protein 43.8 g; Cholesterol 140 mg

Ranch Chicken Thighs

Preparation Time: 10 minutes; Cooking Time: 30 minutes; Serve: 4
Ingredients:
- 2 lbs chicken thighs
- 1 oz ranch seasoning
- 1 cup cheddar cheese, shredded
- 1/2 cup mayonnaise
- 2 tsp garlic, minced

Directions:
1. Fit the Cuisinart oven with the rack in position 1.
2. Place chicken thighs into the baking dish.

3. Mix together mayonnaise, garlic, cheddar cheese, and ranch seasoning and pour over chicken thighs.
4. Set to bake at 400 F for 35 minutes. After 5 minutes place the baking dish in the preheated oven.
5. Serve and enjoy.

Nutritional Value (Amount per Serving):
Calories 684; Fat 36 g; Carbohydrates 7.8 g; Sugar 2 g; Protein 73 g; Cholesterol 239 mg

Bacon Ranch Chicken

Preparation Time: 10 minutes; Cooking Time: 45 minutes; Serve: 6
Ingredients:
- 2 lbs chicken breasts
- 1 packet dry ranch dressing mix
- 2 cups cheddar cheese, shredded
- 1 tsp garlic powder
- 4 oz cream cheese
- 1 cup sour cream
- 12 oz broccoli, steam
- 1 lb bacon, cooked & chopped

Directions:
1. Fit the Cuisinart oven with the rack in position 1.
2. Place chicken breasts and broccoli into the greased baking pan.
3. Mix together sour cream, cream cheese, garlic powder, bacon, and ranch dressing mix and pour over chicken and broccoli.
4. Sprinkle cheddar cheese on top of chicken and broccoli mixture.
5. Set to bake at 350 F for 50 minutes. After 5 minutes place the baking pan in the preheated oven.
6. Serve and enjoy.

Nutritional Value (Amount per Serving):
Calories 844; Fat 60.8 g; Carbohydrates 11.8 g; Sugar 1.5 g; Protein 65.6 g; Cholesterol 212 mg

Flavors Cheesy Chicken Breasts

Preparation Time: 10 minutes; Cooking Time: 45 minutes; Serve: 6
Ingredients:
- 3 lbs chicken breasts, sliced in half
- 1 tsp garlic powder
- 1/2 cup parmesan cheese, shredded
- 1 cup Greek yogurt
- 1/2 tsp pepper
- 1/2 tsp salt

Directions:
1. Fit the Cuisinart oven with the rack in position 1.
2. Place chicken breasts into the greased baking dish.
3. Mix parmesan cheese, yogurt, garlic powder, pepper, and salt and pour over chicken.
4. Set to bake at 375 F for 50 minutes. After 5 minutes place the baking dish in the preheated oven.
5. Serve and enjoy.

Nutritional Value (Amount per Serving):
Calories 482; Fat 19.1 g; Carbohydrates 2.1 g; Sugar 1.5 g; Protein 71.5 g; Cholesterol 209 mg

Mexican Salsa Chicken

Preparation Time: 10 minutes; Cooking Time: 30 minutes; Serve: 6
Ingredients:
- 4 chicken breasts, skinless & boneless
- 1/4 tsp cumin
- 1/4 tsp garlic powder
- 1 3/4 cups Mexican shredded cheese
- 12 oz salsa
- 1/4 tsp pepper
- 1/4 tsp salt

Directions:
1. Fit the Cuisinart oven with the rack in position 1.
2. Place chicken breasts into the baking dish and season with cumin, garlic powder, pepper, and salt.
3. Pour salsa over chicken breasts.
4. Sprinkle shredded cheese on top of chicken.
5. Set to bake at 375 F for 35 minutes. After 5 minutes place the baking dish in the preheated oven.
6. Serve and enjoy.

Nutritional Value (Amount per Serving):
Calories 330; Fat 17.8 g; Carbohydrates 6.1 g; Sugar 1.8 g; Protein 36.1 g; Cholesterol 116 mg

Baked Lemon Pepper Chicken

Preparation Time: 10 minutes; Cooking Time: 35 minutes; Serve: 4
Ingredients:
- 4 chicken thighs
- 1 tsp garlic powder
- 1/2 tsp onion powder
- 1 tbsp lemon pepper seasoning
- 2 tbsp fresh lemon juice
- 1/2 tsp paprika
- 2 tbsp olive oil
- 1 tsp salt

Directions:
1. Fit the Cuisinart oven with the rack in position 1.
2. Add chicken in the mixing bowl.
3. Pour lemon juice and olive oil over chicken and coat well.
4. Mix lemon pepper seasoning, paprika, Italian seasoning, onion powder, garlic powder, and salt and rub all over the chicken thighs.
5. Place chicken in baking pan.
6. Set to bake at 400 F for 40 minutes. After 5 minutes place the baking pan in the preheated oven.
7. Serve and enjoy.

Nutritional Value (Amount per Serving):
Calories 184; Fat 11.6 g; Carbohydrates 2.1 g; Sugar 0.5 g; Protein 17.8 g; Cholesterol 53 mg

Easy Pesto Chicken

Preparation Time: 10 minutes; Cooking Time: 35 minutes; Serve: 4
Ingredients:
- 4 chicken breasts, sliced into 8 pieces
- 8 oz mozzarella cheese, shredded
- 1/4 cup pesto
- 1/4 tsp pepper
- 1/2 tsp salt

Directions:
1. Fit the Cuisinart oven with the rack in position 1.
2. Season chicken with pepper and salt and place in a greased baking dish.
3. Spread pesto and cheese on top of chicken.
4. Set to bake at 350 F for 40 minutes. After 5 minutes place the baking dish in the preheated oven.
5. Serve and enjoy.

Nutritional Value (Amount per Serving):
Calories 505; Fat 27.3 g; Carbohydrates 3.1 g; Sugar 1 g; Protein 59.8 g; Cholesterol 164 mg

Cheesy Chicken Casserole

Preparation Time: 10 minutes; Cooking Time: 20 minutes; Serve: 4

Ingredients:
- 1 lb cooked chicken, shredded
- 1/2 cup salsa
- 4 oz cream cheese, softened
- 4 cups cauliflower florets
- 1/4 cup Greek yogurt
- 1 cup cheddar cheese, shredded
- 1/8 tsp pepper
- 1/2 tsp kosher salt

Directions:
1. Fit the Cuisinart oven with the rack in position 1.
2. Add cauliflower into the boiling water and cook until tender. Drain well.
3. In a mixing bowl, mix cauliflower, salsa, cream cheese, chicken, yogurt, pepper, and salt.
4. Pour cauliflower mixture into the greased casserole dish and top with shredded cheddar cheese.
5. Set to bake at 375 F for 25 minutes. After 5 minutes place the casserole dish in the preheated oven.
6. Serve and enjoy.

Nutritional Value (Amount per Serving):
Calories 427; Fat 23.1 g; Carbohydrates 9 g; Sugar 4.1 g; Protein 45.8 g; Cholesterol 149 mg

Chicken Pasta Broccoli Casserole

Preparation Time: 10 minutes; Cooking Time: 35 minutes; Serve: 8

Ingredients:
- 2 lbs chicken breasts, cut into large chunks
- 16 oz pasta, cooked and drained
- 12 oz frozen broccoli, thawed
- 1/2 cup cheddar cheese, shredded
- 1 can cream of chicken condensed soup
- 1 tbsp olive oil
- Pepper
- Salt

Directions:
1. Fit the Cuisinart oven with the rack in position 1.
2. Heat oil in a pan over medium heat.
3. Season chicken with pepper and salt and place into the pan. Cook chicken until lightly browned, about 3-4 minutes on each side.
4. Remove pan from heat and set aside.
5. Add chicken and remaining ingredients into the mixing bowl and mix well.
6. Pour chicken mixture into the 9*13-inch greased casserole dish.
7. Set to bake at 400 F for 40 minutes. After 5 minutes place the casserole dish in the preheated oven.
8. Serve and enjoy.

Nutritional Value (Amount per Serving):
Calories 446; Fat 14.2 g; Carbohydrates 35.2 g; Sugar 0.9 g; Protein 42.4 g; Cholesterol 151 mg

Mustard Chicken Breasts

Preparation Time: 10 minutes; Cooking Time: 30 minutes; Serve: 4

Ingredients:
- 4 frozen chicken breasts, boneless and skinless
- 1 tbsp olive oil
- 1/3 cup breadcrumbs
- 4 tsp mustard
- 1/4 tsp garlic powder
- Pepper
- Salt

Directions:
1. Fit the Cuisinart oven with the rack in position 1.
2. In a small bowl, mix breadcrumbs, garlic powder, oil, pepper, and salt. Set aside.
3. Place chicken breasts in a baking dish.

4. Spread 1 tsp of mustard on each chicken breast.
5. Sprinkle breadcrumb mixture over chicken.
6. Set to bake at 425 F for 35 minutes. After 5 minutes place the baking dish in the preheated oven.
7. Serve and enjoy.

Nutritional Value (Amount per Serving):
Calories 202; Fat 6.4 g; Carbohydrates 7.8 g; Sugar 0.8 g; Protein 28.1 g; Cholesterol 65 mg

Tasty Chicken Tenders

Preparation Time: 10 minutes; Cooking Time: 30 minutes; Serve: 4
Ingredients:
- 2 lbs frozen chicken tenders
- 1 tbsp dried oregano
- 1 cup parmesan cheese, grated
- 1/2 cup butter, melted
- 1 tsp garlic powder
- 1 tbsp paprika
- Pepper
- Salt

Directions:
1. Fit the Cuisinart oven with the rack in position 1.
2. In a shallow dish, mix parmesan cheese, oregano, paprika, garlic powder, pepper, and salt.
3. Place melted butter in a separate shallow dish.
4. Dip each chicken tender in melted butter then coat with parmesan cheese mixture.
5. Place coated chicken tenders in a baking pan.
6. Set to bake at 350 F for 35 minutes. After 5 minutes place the baking pan in the preheated oven.
7. Serve and enjoy.

Nutritional Value (Amount per Serving):
Calories 833; Fat 50.7 g; Carbohydrates 54.5 g; Sugar 0.4 g; Protein 43.3 g; Cholesterol 157 mg

Baked Chicken Fritters

Preparation Time: 10 minutes; Cooking Time: 25 minutes; Serve: 4
Ingredients:
- 1 lb ground chicken
- 1 cup breadcrumbs
- 1 egg, lightly beaten
- 1 garlic clove, minced
- 1 1/2 cup mozzarella cheese, shredded
- 1/2 cup shallots, chopped
- 2 cups broccoli, chopped
- Pepper
- Salt

Directions:
1. Fit the Cuisinart oven with the rack in position 1.
2. Add all ingredients into the bowl and mix until well combined.
3. Make small patties and place them in a parchment-lined baking pan.
4. Set to bake at 390 F for 30 minutes. After 5 minutes place the baking pan in the preheated oven.
5. Serve and enjoy.

Nutritional Value (Amount per Serving):
Calories 399; Fat 13 g; Carbohydrates 26.5 g; Sugar 2.5 g; Protein 42.6 g; Cholesterol 147 mg

Chicken Burger Patties

Preparation Time: 10 minutes; Cooking Time: 25 minutes; Serve: 4
Ingredients:
- 1 lb ground chicken
- 1 egg, lightly beaten
- 1 cup cheddar cheese, shredded
- 1 cup carrot, grated

- 1 cup cauliflower, grated
- 1/8 tsp red pepper flakes
- 2 garlic cloves, minced
- 1/2 cup onion, minced
- 3/4 cup breadcrumbs
- Pepper
- Salt

Directions:
1. Fit the Cuisinart oven with the rack in position 1.
2. Add all ingredients into the bowl and mix until well combined.
3. Make small patties and place them in a parchment-lined baking pan.
4. Set to bake at 400 F for 30 minutes. After 5 minutes place the baking pan in the preheated oven.
5. Serve and enjoy.

Nutritional Value (Amount per Serving):
Calories 451; Fat 20 g; Carbohydrates 20.9 g; Sugar 4.1 g; Protein 44.9 g; Cholesterol 172 mg

Meatballs

Preparation Time: 10 minutes; Cooking Time: 20 minutes; Serve: 6
Ingredients:
- 2 lbs ground chicken
- 1/2 cup parmesan cheese, grated
- 1 cup breadcrumbs
- 1 egg, lightly beaten
- 1 tbsp fresh parsley, chopped
- 1 tsp Italian seasoning
- 1 tsp garlic, minced
- 2 tbsp olive oil
- Pepper
- Salt

Directions:
1. Fit the Cuisinart oven with the rack in position 1.
2. Add all ingredients into the bowl and mix until well combined.
3. Make small balls from meat mixture and place in baking pan.
4. Set to bake at 400 F for 25 minutes. After 5 minutes place the baking pan in the preheated oven.
5. Serve and enjoy.

Nutritional Value (Amount per Serving):
Calories 436; Fat 19.4 g; Carbohydrates 13.6 g; Sugar 1.3 g; Protein 49.5 g; Cholesterol 168 mg

Turkey Meatballs

Preparation Time: 10 minutes; Cooking Time: 25 minutes; Serve: 4
Ingredients:
- 1 lb ground chicken
- 2 garlic cloves, minced
- 1/2 cup parmesan cheese, grated
- 1/2 cup breadcrumbs
- 1 egg, lightly beaten
- 2 tbsp cilantro, chopped
- 1 tbsp olive oil
- 1/2 tsp red pepper flakes
- 1/4 cup shallots, chopped
- Pepper
- Salt

Directions:
1. Fit the Cuisinart oven with the rack in position 1.
2. Add all ingredients into the large bowl and mix until well combined.
3. Make small balls from the meat mixture and place them into the baking pan.
4. Set to bake at 400 F for 30 minutes. After 5 minutes place the baking pan in the preheated oven.
5. Serve and enjoy.

Nutritional Value (Amount per Serving):
Calories 361; Fat 16.2 g; Carbohydrates 12.6 g; Sugar 1 g; Protein 40 g; Cholesterol 150 mg

Zucchini Chicken Meatballs

Preparation Time: 10 minutes; Cooking Time: 18 minutes; Serve: 6

Ingredients:
- 1 lb ground chicken
- 1 tbsp basil, chopped
- 1/3 cup coconut flour
- 2 cups zucchini, grated
- 1 tsp dried oregano
- 1 tbsp garlic, minced
- 1 tbsp nutritional yeast
- 1 tsp cumin
- 1 tbsp dried onion flakes
- 2 eggs, lightly beaten
- Pepper
- Salt

Directions:
1. Fit the Cuisinart oven with the rack in position 1.
2. Add all ingredients into the mixing bowl and mix until well combined.
3. Make small balls from the meat mixture and place them into the baking pan.
4. Set to bake at 400 F for 23 minutes. After 5 minutes place the baking pan in the preheated oven.
5. Serve and enjoy.

Nutritional Value (Amount per Serving):
Calories 215; Fat 8.5 g; Carbohydrates 7.6 g; Sugar 1.5 g; Protein 26.5 g; Cholesterol 122 mg

Garlic Chicken

Preparation Time: 10 minutes; Cooking Time: 40 minutes; Serve: 6

Ingredients:
- 2 lbs chicken thighs, skinless and boneless
- 10 garlic cloves, sliced
- 2 tbsp olive oil
- 2 tbsp fresh parsley, chopped
- 1 fresh lemon juice
- Pepper
- Salt

Directions:
1. Fit the Cuisinart oven with the rack in position 1.
2. Place chicken in baking pan and season with pepper and salt.
3. Sprinkle parsley and garlic over the chicken. Drizzle with oil and lemon juice.
4. Set to bake at 450 F for 45 minutes. After 5 minutes place the baking pan in the preheated oven.
5. Serve and enjoy.

Nutritional Value (Amount per Serving):
Calories 337; Fat 16 g; Carbohydrates 1.9 g; Sugar 0.2 g; Protein 44.2 g; Cholesterol 135 mg

Greek Chicken Paillard

Preparation Time: 10 minutes; Cooking Time: 25 minutes; Serve: 8

Ingredients:
- 4 chicken breasts, skinless and boneless
- 1/2 cup olives, diced
- 1 small onion, sliced
- 1 fennel bulb, sliced
- 28 oz can tomatoes, diced
- 1/4 cup fresh basil, chopped
- 1/4 cup fresh parsley, chopped
- 1/4 cup pine nuts
- 2 tbsp olive oil
- Pepper
- Salt

Directions:
1. Fit the Cuisinart oven with the rack in position 1.
2. Season chicken with pepper and salt and place in baking dish. Drizzle with oil.
3. In a bowl, mix together olives, tomatoes, pine nuts, onion, fennel, pepper, and salt.
4. Pour olive mixture over chicken.

5. Set to bake at 450 F for 30 minutes. After 5 minutes place the baking dish in the preheated oven.
6. Garnish with basil and parsley and serve.

Nutritional Value (Amount per Serving):
Calories 242; Fat 12.8 g; Carbohydrates 9.3 g; Sugar 3.9 g; Protein 23.2 g; Cholesterol 65 mg

Olive Caper Chicken

Preparation Time: 10 minutes; Cooking Time: 18 minutes; Serve: 4
Ingredients:
- 4 chicken breast, boneless and halves
- 12 olives, pitted and halved
- 2 cups cherry tomatoes
- 3 tbsp olive oil
- 3 tbsp capers, rinsed and drained
- Pepper
- Salt

Directions:
1. Fit the Cuisinart oven with the rack in position 1.
2. In a bowl, toss tomatoes, capers, olives with 2 tablespoons of oil. Set aside.
3. Season chicken with pepper and salt.
4. Heat remaining oil in a pan over high heat.
5. Place chicken in the pan and cook for 4 minutes.
6. Transfer chicken in baking dish. Top with tomato mixture.
7. Set to bake at 450 F for 23 minutes. After 5 minutes place the baking dish in the preheated oven.
8. Serve and enjoy.

Nutritional Value (Amount per Serving):
Calories 251; Fat 15 g; Carbohydrates 4.7 g; Sugar 2.4 g; Protein 24.8 g; Cholesterol 72 mg

Tasty Lemon Chicken

Preparation Time: 10 minutes; Cooking Time: 15 minutes; Serve: 1
Ingredients:
- 1 chicken breast, boneless and skinless
- 1 fresh lemon juice
- 1 fresh lemon, sliced
- 1/2 tbsp Italian seasoning
- Pepper
- Salt

Directions:
1. Fit the Cuisinart oven with the rack in position 1.
2. Season chicken with Italian season, pepper, and salt.
3. Place chicken breast in baking dish.
4. Pour lemon juice over chicken and arrange lemon slices on top of chicken.
5. Set to bake at 350 F for 20 minutes. After 5 minutes place the baking dish in the preheated oven.
6. Serve and enjoy.

Nutritional Value (Amount per Serving):
Calories 178; Fat 5.4 g; Carbohydrates 7.2 g; Sugar 3.1 g; Protein 24.8 g; Cholesterol 77 mg

Baked Italian Lemon Chicken

Preparation Time: 10 minutes; Cooking Time: 25 minutes; Serve: 4
Ingredients:
- 1 1/4 lbs chicken breasts, skinless and boneless
- 3 tbsp butter, melted
- 1 tsp Italian seasoning
- 1 tbsp olive oil
- 1 tbsp fresh parsley, chopped
- 2 tbsp fresh lemon juice
- 1/4 cup water

- Pepper
- Salt

Directions:
1. Fit the Cuisinart oven with the rack in position 1.
2. Season chicken with Italian seasoning, pepper, and salt.
3. Heat oil in a pan over medium-high heat.
4. Add chicken to the pan and cook for 3-5 minutes on each side.
5. Transfer chicken to a baking dish.
6. In a small bowl, mix together butter, lemon juice, and water.
7. Pour butter mixture over chicken.
8. Set to bake at 400 F for 30 minutes. After 5 minutes place the baking dish in the preheated oven.
9. Garnish with parsley and serve.

Nutritional Value (Amount per Serving):
Calories 382; Fat 23.1 g; Carbohydrates 0.4 g; Sugar 0.3 g; Protein 41.2 g; Cholesterol 150 mg

Meatballs

Preparation Time: 10 minutes; Cooking Time: 18 minutes; Serve: 6

Ingredients:
- 1 egg, lightly beaten
- 1 lb ground chicken
- 1 1/2 cups zucchini, grated & squeeze out all liquid
- 1 1/2 tsp Italian seasoning
- 2 tbsp chives, chopped
- 1/4 cup almond flour
- 1/2 tsp salt

Directions:
1. Fit the Cuisinart oven with the rack in position 1.
2. Add chicken, zucchini, seasoning, chives, egg, almond flour, and salt and mix until well combined.
3. Make small balls from the meat mixture and place it into the parchment-lined baking pan.
4. Set to bake at 350 F for 23 minutes. After 5 minutes place the baking pan in the preheated oven.
5. Serve and enjoy.

Nutritional Value (Amount per Serving):
Calories 169; Fat 7.3 g; Carbohydrates 1.4 g; Sugar 0.7 g; Protein 23.4 g; Cholesterol 95 mg

Meatballs

Preparation Time: 10 minutes; Cooking Time: 25 minutes; Serve: 6

Ingredients:
- 1 lb ground turkey
- 1 egg, lightly beaten
- 2 tbsp basil, chopped
- 2 tbsp coconut flour
- 1 tsp olive oil
- 1/2 tsp ground ginger
- 1/2 tsp salt

Directions:
1. Fit the Cuisinart oven with the rack in position 1.
2. In a bowl, mix turkey, basil, coconut flour, olive oil, ginger, egg, and salt until well combined.
3. Make small balls from the meat mixture and place it into the parchment-lined baking pan.
4. Set to bake at 375 F for 30 minutes. After 5 minutes place the baking pan in the preheated oven.
5. Serve and enjoy.

Nutritional Value (Amount per Serving):
Calories 185; Fat 10.5 g; Carbohydrates 2.9 g; Sugar 0.4 g; Protein 22.3 g; Cholesterol 104 mg

Spinach Turkey Meatballs

Preparation Time: 10 minutes; Cooking Time: 20 minutes; Serve: 6
Ingredients:
- 2 lbs ground turkey
- 1/2 cup breadcrumbs
- 1 egg, lightly beaten
- 1/4 cup fresh parsley, chopped
- 1 cup spinach, chopped
- 1 tbsp fresh mint, chopped
- 1/4 tsp cumin
- 1/2 tsp oregano
- 4 oz feta cheese
- 1/2 tsp pepper
- 1/2 tsp onion powder
- Salt

Directions:
1. Fit the Cuisinart oven with the rack in position 1.
2. Add all ingredients into the large bowl and mix until well combined.
3. Make small balls from the meat mixture and place it into the parchment-lined baking pan.
4. Set to bake at 375 F for 25 minutes. After 5 minutes place the baking pan in the preheated oven.
5. Serve and enjoy.

Nutritional Value (Amount per Serving):
Calories 395; Fat 21.9 g; Carbohydrates 8.1 g; Sugar 1.5 g; Protein 46.5 g; Cholesterol 198 mg

Lemon Mustard Chicken

Preparation Time: 10 minutes; Cooking Time: 20 minutes; Serve: 4
Ingredients:
- 1 lbs chicken tenders
- 1 garlic clove, minced
- 1/2 oz fresh lemon juice
- 1/2 tsp pepper
- 2 tbsp fresh tarragon, chopped
- 1/2 cup whole grain mustard
- 1/2 tsp paprika
- 1/4 tsp kosher salt

Directions:
1. Fit the Cuisinart oven with the rack in position 1.
2. Add all ingredients except chicken to the large bowl and mix well.
3. Add chicken to the bowl and stir until well coated.
4. Place chicken in a baking dish.
5. Set to bake at 425 F for 25 minutes. After 5 minutes place the baking dish in the preheated oven.
6. Serve and enjoy.

Nutritional Value (Amount per Serving):
Calories 242; Fat 9.5 g; Carbohydrates 3.1 g; Sugar 0.1 g; Protein 33.2 g; Cholesterol 101 mg

Baked Zucchini Chicken Tenders

Preparation Time: 10 minutes; Cooking Time: 30 minutes; Serve: 4
Ingredients:
- 2 lbs chicken tenders
- 1 large zucchini
- 2 tbsp feta cheese, crumbled
- 1 tbsp fresh lemon juice
- 1 tbsp fresh dill, chopped
- 1 cup grape tomatoes
- 2 tbsp olive oil

Directions:
1. Fit the Cuisinart oven with the rack in position 1.
2. Coat chicken with oil and place in baking pan along with zucchini, dill, and tomatoes. Season with salt.
3. Set to bake at 400 F for 35 minutes. After 5 minutes place the baking dish in the preheated oven.

4. Drizzle with lemon juice and top with feta cheese.
5. Serve and enjoy.

Nutritional Value (Amount per Serving):
Calories 527; Fat 25.1 g; Carbohydrates 5.2 g; Sugar 2.9 g; Protein 67.9 g; Cholesterol 206 mg

Roasted Pepper Chicken Thighs

Preparation Time: 10 minutes; **Cooking Time:** 55 minutes; **Serve:** 4

Ingredients:
- 8 chicken thighs
- 1 1/2 lbs potatoes, cut into small chunks
- 6 garlic cloves, crushed
- 1/4 cup capers, drained
- 10 oz jar roasted red peppers, drained and sliced
- 2 cups grape tomatoes
- 4 tbsp olive oil
- 1 tsp dried oregano
- Pepper
- Salt

Directions:
1. Fit the Cuisinart oven with the rack in position 1.
2. Season chicken with pepper and salt.
3. Heat 2 tablespoons of olive oil in a pan over medium heat.
4. Add chicken to the pan and sear until brown from all the sides.
5. Transfer chicken in baking pan.
6. Add tomato, potatoes, capers, oregano, garlic, and red peppers around the chicken. Drizzle with remaining olive oil.
7. Set to bake at 400 F for 60 minutes. After 5 minutes place the baking pan in the preheated oven.
8. Serve and enjoy.

Nutritional Value (Amount per Serving):
Calories 542; Fat 21.9 g; Carbohydrates 45.1 g; Sugar 4.4 g; Protein 35.6 g; Cholesterol 89 mg

Chicken with Vegetables

Preparation Time: 10 minutes; **Cooking Time:** 35 minutes; **Serve:** 4

Ingredients:
- 1 lb chicken breasts, skinless, boneless and cut into pieces
- 3 cups potatoes cut into pieces
- 4 cups Brussels sprouts, trimmed and quartered
- 1 lemon juice
- 1/3 cup vinaigrette dressing
- 1 onion, diced
- 1/4 cup olives, quartered
- 1 tsp oregano
- 1 1/2 tsp Dijon mustard
- 1/4 tsp pepper
- 1/4 tsp salt

Directions:
1. Fit the Cuisinart oven with the rack in position 1.
2. Place chicken in the center of the baking pan.
3. Place potatoes, sprouts, and onions around the chicken.
4. In a small bowl, mix vinaigrette, oregano, mustard, lemon juice, and salt and pour over chicken and vegetables.
5. Sprinkle olives and season with pepper.
6. Set to bake at 400 F for 40 minutes. After 5 minutes place the baking pan in the preheated oven.
7. Serve and enjoy.

Nutritional Value (Amount per Serving):

Calories 397; Fat 13 g; Carbohydrates 31.4 g; Sugar 6.7 g; Protein 38.3 g; Cholesterol 101 mg

Mustard Chicken Thighs

Preparation Time: 10 minutes; Cooking Time: 50 minutes; Serve: 4
Ingredients:
- 1 1/2 lbs chicken thighs, skinless and boneless
- 2 tbsp Dijon mustard
- 1/4 cup French mustard
- 1/4 cup maple syrup
- 1 tbsp olive oil

Directions:
1. Fit the Cuisinart oven with the rack in position 1.
2. In a bowl, mix maple syrup, olive oil, Dijon mustard, and French mustard.
3. Add chicken to the bowl and coat well.
4. Arrange chicken in a baking dish.
5. Set to bake at 375 F for 55 minutes. After 5 minutes place the baking dish in the preheated oven.
6. Serve and enjoy.

Nutritional Value (Amount per Serving):
Calories 410; Fat 16.5 g; Carbohydrates 13.6 g; Sugar 11.8 g; Protein 49.6 g; Cholesterol 151 mg

Coconut Chicken Tenders

Preparation Time: 10 minutes; Cooking Time: 20 minutes; Serve: 4
Ingredients:
- 1 lb chicken breast, skinless, boneless & cut into strips
- 1 egg, lightly beaten
- 1/4 cup shredded coconut
- 1/2 cup almond meal
- 1/2 tsp garlic powder
- 1/2 tsp cayenne pepper
- 1 tsp paprika
- 1/4 tsp black pepper
- 1/2 tsp sea salt

Directions:
1. Fit the Cuisinart oven with the rack in position 1.
2. In a shallow dish, mix almond meal, shredded coconut, paprika, cayenne pepper, garlic powder, pepper, and salt.
3. In a separate bowl, whisk the egg.
4. Dip each chicken strip in egg then coat with almond meal mixture,
5. Place coat chicken strips in a parchment-lined baking pan.
6. Set to bake at 400 F for 25 minutes. After 5 minutes place the baking pan in the preheated oven.
7. Serve and enjoy.

Nutritional Value (Amount per Serving):
Calories 235; Fat 11.7 g; Carbohydrates 4.2 g; Sugar 1.1 g; Protein 28.3 g; Cholesterol 114 mg

Crispy Crusted Chicken

Preparation Time: 10 minutes; Cooking Time: 30 minutes; Serve: 4
Ingredients:
- 4 chicken breasts, skinless and boneless
- 2 tbsp butter, melted
- 3 cups corn flakes, crushed
- 1 tsp poultry seasoning
- 1 tsp water
- 1 egg, lightly beaten
- Pepper
- Salt

Directions:
1. Fit the Cuisinart oven with the rack in position 1.

2. Season chicken with poultry seasoning, pepper, and salt.
3. In a shallow dish, whisk together egg and water.
4. In a separate shallow dish, mix crushed cornflakes and melted butter.
5. Dip chicken into the egg mixture then coats with crushed cornflakes.
6. Place the coated chicken into the parchment-lined baking pan.
7. Set to bake at 400 F for 35 minutes. After 5 minutes place the baking pan in the preheated oven.
8. Serve and enjoy.

Nutritional Value (Amount per Serving):
Calories 421; Fat 17.7 g; Carbohydrates 18.6 g; Sugar 1.5 g; Protein 45.1 g; Cholesterol 186 mg

Cracker Apple Chicken

Preparation Time: 10 minutes; Cooking Time: 45 minutes; Serve: 2
Ingredients:
- 2 chicken breasts, skinless and boneless
- 1 apple, sliced
- 12 Ritz cracker, crushed
- 10 oz can condensed cheddar cheese soup
- Pepper
- Salt

Directions:
1. Fit the Cuisinart oven with the rack in position 1.
2. Season chicken with pepper and salt and place into the baking dish.
3. Arrange sliced apple on top of chicken.
4. Sprinkle crushed crackers on top.
5. Set to bake at 350 F for 50 minutes. After 5 minutes place the baking dish in the preheated oven.
6. Pour cheddar cheese soup on top and serve.

Nutritional Value (Amount per Serving):
Calories 924; Fat 38.2 g; Carbohydrates 87 g; Sugar 21.4 g; Protein 51.8 g; Cholesterol 136 mg

Air Fry Chicken Drumsticks

Preparation Time: 10 minutes; Cooking Time: 25 minutes; Serve: 6
Ingredients:
- 6 chicken drumsticks
- 1/2 tsp garlic powder
- 2 tbsp olive oil
- 1/2 tsp ground cumin
- 3/4 tsp paprika
- Pepper
- Salt

Directions:
1. Fit the Cuisinart oven with the rack in position 2.
2. Add chicken drumsticks and olive oil in a large bowl and toss well.
3. Sprinkle garlic powder, paprika, cumin, pepper, and salt over chicken drumsticks and toss until well coated.
4. Place chicken drumsticks in the air fryer basket then place an air fryer basket in the baking pan.
5. Place a baking pan on the oven rack. Set to air fry at 400 F for 25 minutes.
6. Serve and enjoy.

Nutritional Value (Amount per Serving):
Calories 120; Fat 7.4 g; Carbohydrates 0.4 g; Sugar 0.1 g; Protein 12.8 g; Cholesterol 40 mg

Honey Chicken Wings

Preparation Time: 10 minutes; Cooking Time: 15 minutes; Serve: 2

Ingredients:
- 2 chicken drumsticks
- 2 tsp honey
- 2 tsp olive oil
- 2 garlic cloves, minced

Directions:
1. Fit the Cuisinart oven with the rack in position 2.
2. In a bowl, mix honey, garlic, and olive oil.
3. Add chicken drumsticks and coat well and let it sit for 20 minutes.
4. Arrange chicken drumsticks in the air fryer basket then place an air fryer basket in the baking pan.
5. Place a baking pan on the oven rack. Set to air fry at 400 F for 15 minutes.
6. Serve and enjoy.

Nutritional Value (Amount per Serving):
Calories 143; Fat 7.3 g; Carbohydrates 6.8 g; Sugar 5.8 g; Protein 12.9 g; Cholesterol 40 mg

Crispy Chicken Nuggets

Preparation Time: 10 minutes; Cooking Time: 25 minutes; Serve: 4

Ingredients:
- 1 1/2 lbs chicken breast, boneless & cut into chunks
- 1/4 cup parmesan cheese, shredded
- 1/4 cup mayonnaise
- 1/2 tsp garlic powder
- 1/4 tsp salt

Directions:
1. Fit the Cuisinart oven with the rack in position 2.
2. In a bowl, mix mayonnaise, cheese, garlic powder, and salt.
3. Add chicken and mix until well coated.
4. Arrange coated chicken in the air fryer basket then place an air fryer basket in the baking pan.
5. Place a baking pan on the oven rack. Set to air fry at 400 F for 25 minutes.
6. Serve and enjoy.

Nutritional Value (Amount per Serving):
Calories 270; Fat 10.4 g; Carbohydrates 4 g; Sugar 1 g; Protein 38.1 g; Cholesterol 117 mg

Ranch Chicken Wings

Preparation Time: 10 minutes; Cooking Time: 20 minutes; Serve: 2

Ingredients:
- 1 lb chicken wings
- 2 tbsp butter, melted
- 1 1/2 tbsp ranch seasoning
- 3 garlic cloves, minced

Directions:
1. Fit the Cuisinart oven with the rack in position 2.
2. In a bowl, mix butter, garlic, ranch seasoning.
3. Add chicken wings and toss well.
4. Cover and place in the refrigerator for 1 hour.
5. Arrange marinated chicken wings in an air fryer basket then place an air fryer basket in a baking pan.
6. Place a baking pan on the oven rack. Set to air fry at 360 F for 20 minutes.
7. Serve and enjoy.

Nutritional Value (Amount per Serving):
Calories 562; Fat 28.4 g; Carbohydrates 1.5 g; Sugar 0.1 g; Protein 66 g; Cholesterol 232 mg

Sweet & Spicy Chicken Wings

Preparation Time: 10 minutes; Cooking Time: 30 minutes; Serve: 4

Ingredients:
- 12 chicken wings
- 1/2 cup hot sauce
- 1/2 cup honey
- Pepper
- Salt

Directions:
1. Fit the Cuisinart oven with the rack in position 2.
2. Season chicken wings with pepper and salt.
3. Arrange chicken wings in the air fryer basket then place an air fryer basket in the baking pan.
4. Place a baking pan on the oven rack. Set to air fry at 400 F for 25 minutes.
5. Meanwhile, add honey and hot sauce in a saucepan and heat over medium heat for 5 minutes.
6. Add chicken wings in a bowl. Pour
7. sauce over chicken wings and toss well.
8. Serve and enjoy.

Nutritional Value (Amount per Serving):
Calories 698; Fat 22.2 g; Carbohydrates 35.4 g; Sugar 35.2 g; Protein 89.4 g; Cholesterol 256 mg

Garlic Butter Wings

Preparation Time: 10 minutes; Cooking Time: 25 minutes; Serve: 4

Ingredients:
- 1 lb chicken wings
- 1 tsp garlic powder
- 1/4 tsp pepper
- 1/2 tsp Italian seasoning
- 1/2 tsp salt

For sauce:
- 1 tbsp butter, melted
- 1/8 tsp garlic powder

Directions:
1. Fit the Cuisinart oven with the rack in position 2.
2. In a large bowl, toss chicken wings with Italian seasoning, garlic powder, pepper, and salt.
3. Arrange chicken wings in the air fryer basket then place an air fryer basket in the baking pan.
4. Place a baking pan on the oven rack. Set to air fry at 390 F for 25 minutes.
5. In a bowl, mix melted butter and garlic powder.
6. Add chicken wings and toss until well coated.
7. Serve and enjoy.

Nutritional Value (Amount per Serving):
Calories 246; Fat 11.5 g; Carbohydrates 0.7 g; Sugar 0.2 g; Protein 33 g; Cholesterol 109 mg

Garlic Chicken Wings

Preparation Time: 10 minutes; Cooking Time: 25 minutes; Serve: 2

Ingredients:
- 1 lb chicken wings
- 2 tbsp butter, melted
- 1 tbsp garlic, minced

Directions:
1. Fit the Cuisinart oven with the rack in position 2.
2. In a large bowl, mix butter and garlic. Add chicken wings and toss to coat.
3. Add marinated chicken wings to the air fryer basket then place an air fryer basket in the baking pan.
4. Place a baking pan on the oven rack. Set to air fry at 360 F for 25 minutes.
5. Serve and enjoy.

Nutritional Value (Amount per Serving):
Calories 539; Fat 28.4 g; Carbohydrates 1.4 g; Sugar 0.1 g; Protein 66 g; Cholesterol 232 mg

Simple Jerk Chicken Wings

Preparation Time: 10 minutes; Cooking Time: 20 minutes; Serve: 2
Ingredients:
- 1 lb chicken wings
- 1 tbsp jerk seasoning
- 1 tsp olive oil
- 1 tbsp cornstarch
- Pepper
- Salt

Directions:
1. Fit the Cuisinart oven with the rack in position 2.
2. In a large bowl, add chicken wings.
3. Add remaining ingredients on top of chicken wings and toss to coat.
4. Add chicken wings to the air fryer basket then place an air fryer basket in the baking pan.
5. Place a baking pan on the oven rack. Set to air fry at 380 F for 20 minutes.
6. Serve and enjoy.

Nutritional Value (Amount per Serving):
Calories 466; Fat 19.1 g; Carbohydrates 3.7 g; Sugar 0 g; Protein 65.6 g; Cholesterol 202 mg

Sriracha Chicken Wings

Preparation Time: 10 minutes; Cooking Time: 30 minutes; Serve: 4
Ingredients:
- 1 lb chicken wings
- 2 tbsp sriracha sauce
- 1/4 cup honey
- 1 tbsp butter
- 1 1/2 tbsp soy sauce
- Pepper
- Salt

Directions:
1. Fit the Cuisinart oven with the rack in position 2.
2. Season chicken wings with pepper and salt.
3. Add chicken wings to the air fryer basket then place an air fryer basket in the baking pan.
4. Place a baking pan on the oven rack. Set to air fry at 360 F for 30 minutes.
5. Meanwhile, add butter, soy sauce, sriracha sauce, and honey in a saucepan and cook for 3 minutes.
6. Add chicken wings into the bowl.
7. Pour sauce over chicken wings and toss until well coated.
8. Serve and enjoy.

Nutritional Value (Amount per Serving):
Calories 359; Fat 16.3 g; Carbohydrates 18.4 g; Sugar 18 g; Protein 33.3 g; Cholesterol 114 mg

Easy BBQ Chicken Drumsticks

Preparation Time: 10 minutes; Cooking Time: 25 minutes; Serve: 4
Ingredients:
- 4 chicken drumsticks
- 1/4 tsp paprika
- 1/2 tsp garlic powder
- 2 tbsp olive oil
- 1/2 cup BBQ sauce
- 1/2 tsp onion powder
- Pepper
- Salt

Directions:
1. Fit the Cuisinart oven with the rack in position 2.
2. In a mixing bowl, add chicken drumsticks, onion powder, garlic powder, olive oil, paprika, pepper, and salt and toss well.

3. Add chicken drumsticks to the air fryer basket then place an air fryer basket in baking pan.
4. Place a baking pan on the oven rack. Set to air fry at 400 F for 20 minutes.
5. Brush chicken drumsticks with BBQ sauce and air fry for 5 minutes.
6. Serve and enjoy.

Nutritional Value (Amount per Serving):
Calories 187; Fat 9.7 g; Carbohydrates 11.9 g; Sugar 8.4 g; Protein 12.8 g; Cholesterol 40 mg

Air Fryer Chicken Tenders

Preparation Time: 10 minutes; Cooking Time: 16 minutes; Serve: 4

Ingredients:
- 1 lb chicken tenders
- For rub:
- 1/2 tbsp dried thyme
- 1 tbsp garlic powder
- 1 tbsp paprika
- 1/2 tbsp onion powder
- 1/2 tsp cayenne pepper
- Pepper
- Salt

Directions:
1. Fit the Cuisinart oven with the rack in position 2.
2. In a bowl, add all rub ingredients and mix well.
3. Add chicken tenders into the bowl and coat well.
4. Place chicken tenders in the air fryer basket then place an air fryer basket in the baking pan.
5. Place a baking pan on the oven rack. Set to air fry at 370 F for 16 minutes.
6. Serve and enjoy.

Nutritional Value (Amount per Serving):
Calories 232; Fat 8.7 g; Carbohydrates 3.6 g; Sugar 1 g; Protein 33.6 g; Cholesterol 101 mg

Greek Chicken Breast

Preparation Time: 10 minutes; Cooking Time: 25 minutes; Serve: 4

Ingredients:
- 4 chicken breasts, skinless & boneless
- 1 tbsp olive oil

For rub:
- 1 tsp oregano
- 1 tsp thyme
- 1 tsp parsley
- 1 tsp onion powder
- 1 tsp basil
- Pepper
- Salt

Directions:
1. Fit the Cuisinart oven with the rack in position 2.
2. Brush chicken with olive oil.
3. In a small bowl, mix together all rub ingredients and rub all over the chicken breasts.
4. Place chicken into the air fryer basket then places the air fryer basket in the baking pan.
5. Place a baking pan on the oven rack. Set to air fry at 390 F for 25 minutes.
6. Serve and enjoy.

Nutritional Value (Amount per Serving):
Calories 312; Fat 14.4 g; Carbohydrates 0.9 g; Sugar 0.2 g; Protein 42.4 g; Cholesterol 130 mg

Meatballs

Preparation Time: 10 minutes; Cooking Time: 20 minutes; Serve: 4

Ingredients:
- 1 lb ground turkey
- 1/4 cup basil, chopped

- 3 tbsp scallions, chopped
- 1 egg, lightly beaten
- 1/2 cup almond flour
- 1/2 tsp red pepper, crushed
- 1 tbsp lemongrass, chopped
- 1 1/2 tbsp fish sauce
- 2 garlic cloves, minced

Directions:
1. Fit the Cuisinart oven with the rack in position 2.
2. Line the air fryer basket with parchment paper.
3. Add all ingredients into a large bowl and mix until well combined.
4. Make small balls from meat mixture and place in the air fryer basket then place the air fryer basket in the baking pan.
5. Place a baking pan on the oven rack. Set to air fry at 380 F for 20 minutes.
6. Serve and enjoy.

Nutritional Value (Amount per Serving):
Calories 269; Fat 15.4 g; Carbohydrates 3.4 g; Sugar 1.3 g; Protein 33.9 g; Cholesterol 157 mg

Chapter 4: Beef, Pork & Lamb

Perfect Beef Hash brown Bake

Preparation Time: 10 minutes; Cooking Time: 40 minutes; Serve: 4
Ingredients:
- 1 lb ground beef
- 2 cups cheddar cheese, shredded
- 1 cup milk
- 10 oz can cream of mushroom soup
- 30 oz frozen shredded hash browns
- 1 tsp garlic powder
- 1 tbsp onion, minced
- Pepper
- Salt

Directions:
1. Fit the Cuisinart oven with the rack in position 1.
2. In a pan, brown ground beef with garlic powder, onion, pepper, and salt. Drain.
3. In a bowl, mix meat, shredded cheese, milk, soup, and hash browns.
4. Pour meat mixture into the greased 9*13-inch baking dish.
5. Set to bake at 350 F for 45 minutes. After 5 minutes place the baking dish in the preheated oven.
6. Serve and enjoy.

Nutritional Value (Amount per Serving):
Calories 514; Fat 28.3 g; Carbohydrates 11.4 g; Sugar 4.8 g; Protein 51.6 g; Cholesterol 168 mg

Spicy Meatballs

Preparation Time: 10 minutes; Cooking Time: 30 minutes; Serve: 4
Ingredients:
- 1 lb ground beef
- 4 oz cream cheese
- 1 tsp dried basil
- 2 tbsp Worcestershire sauce
- 1/3 cup milk
- 1/2 cup cheddar cheese, shredded
- 3/4 cup breadcrumbs
- 2 jalapenos, minced
- 1/2 onion, minced
- 1 tsp salt

Directions:
1. Fit the Cuisinart oven with the rack in position 1.
2. Add all ingredients into the mixing bowl and mix until well combined.
3. Make small balls from the meat mixture and place it into the parchment-lined baking pan.
4. Set to bake at 400 F for 35 minutes. After 5 minutes place the baking pan in the preheated oven.
5. Serve and enjoy.

Nutritional Value (Amount per Serving):
Calories 472; Fat 23.2 g; Carbohydrates 19.7 g; Sugar 4.6 g; Protein 43.7 g; Cholesterol 149 mg

Juicy & Tender Pork Chops

Preparation Time: 10 minutes; Cooking Time: 15 minutes; Serve: 4
Ingredients:
- 4 pork chops, boneless
- 1 tsp onion powder
- 1 tsp smoked paprika
- 1/4 cup olive oil
- 1 tsp pepper
- 2 tsp salt

Directions:
1. Fit the Cuisinart oven with the rack in position 1.
2. Brush pork chops with oil and season with onion powder, paprika, pepper, and salt.
3. Place pork chops in a baking pan.

4. Set to bake at 400 F for 20 minutes. After 5 minutes place the baking pan in the preheated oven.
   5. Serve and enjoy.

Nutritional Value (Amount per Serving):
Calories 369; Fat 32.6 g; Carbohydrates 1.1 g; Sugar 0.3 g; Protein 18.2 g; Cholesterol 69 mg

Ranch Pork Chops

Preparation Time: 10 minutes; Cooking Time: 35 minutes; Serve: 6
Ingredients:
- 6 pork chops, boneless
- 1 tsp dried parsley
- 2 tbsp dry ranch mix
- 1/4 cup olive oil

Directions:
1. Fit the Cuisinart oven with the rack in position 1.
2. Place pork chops in baking dish.
3. Mix together remaining ingredients and pour over pork chops.
4. Set to bake at 425 F for 40 minutes. After 5 minutes place the baking dish in the preheated oven.
5. Serve and enjoy.

Nutritional Value (Amount per Serving):
Calories 330; Fat 28.3 g; Carbohydrates 0.4 g; Sugar 0 g; Protein 18 g; Cholesterol 69 mg

Pesto Pork Chops

Preparation Time: 10 minutes; Cooking Time: 25 minutes; Serve: 6
Ingredients:
- 6 pork chops
- 1/2 cup pesto
- 2 lbs cherry tomatoes
- 2 tbsp olive oil
- Pepper
- Salt

Directions:
1. Fit the Cuisinart oven with the rack in position 1.
2. Brush pork chops with oil and season with pepper and salt.
3. Place pork chops into the baking dish. Add cherry tomatoes around the pork chops.
4. Pour pesto over pork chops.
5. Set to bake at 425 F for 30 minutes. After 5 minutes place the baking dish in the preheated oven.
6. Serve and enjoy.

Nutritional Value (Amount per Serving):
Calories 413; Fat 33.5 g; Carbohydrates 7.2 g; Sugar 5.3 g; Protein 21.3 g; Cholesterol 74 mg

Pork Chops with Potatoes

Preparation Time: 10 minutes; Cooking Time: 25 minutes; Serve: 6
Ingredients:
- 6 pork chops
- 1 oz dried Italian dressing
- 1/4 cup olive oil
- 1 onion, chopped
- 1 lb baby potatoes, quartered
- Pepper
- Salt

Directions:
1. Fit the Cuisinart oven with the rack in position 1.
2. Brush pork chops with oil and season with pepper and salt.
3. Place pork chops into the baking dish.

4. Toss potatoes, onion, and Italian dressing in a bowl and place potatoes and onion around the pork chops in baking dish.
5. Set to bake at 425 F for 30 minutes. After 5 minutes place the baking dish in the preheated oven.
6. Serve and enjoy.

Nutritional Value (Amount per Serving):
Calories 393; Fat 29.7 g; Carbohydrates 11.6 g; Sugar 1.2 g; Protein 20.1 g; Cholesterol 72 mg

Meatballs

Preparation Time: 10 minutes; Cooking Time: 25 minutes; Serve: 4

Ingredients:
- 1 lb ground beef
- 1 tsp fresh rosemary, chopped
- 1 tbsp garlic, chopped
- 1/2 tsp pepper
- 1 tsp garlic powder
- 1 tsp onion powder
- 1/4 cup breadcrumbs
- 2 eggs
- 1 lb ground pork
- 1/2 tsp pepper
- 1 tsp sea salt

Directions:
1. Fit the Cuisinart oven with the rack in position 1.
2. Add all ingredients into the mixing bowl and mix until well combined.
3. Make small balls from the meat mixture and place it into the parchment-lined baking pan.
4. Set to bake at 400 F for 30 minutes. After 5 minutes place the baking pan in the preheated oven.
5. Serve and enjoy.

Nutritional Value (Amount per Serving):
Calories 441; Fat 13.7 g; Carbohydrates 7.2 g; Sugar 1 g; Protein 68.1 g; Cholesterol 266 mg

Crunchy Parmesan Pork Chops

Preparation Time: 10 minutes; Cooking Time: 10 minutes; Serve: 4

Ingredients:
- 4 pork chops, boneless
- 2 tbsp olive oil
- 1/4 tsp pepper
- 1/2 tsp garlic powder
- 1 tsp dried parsley
- 1/4 tsp smoked paprika
- 2 tbsp breadcrumbs
- 1/4 cup parmesan cheese, grated

Directions:
1. Fit the Cuisinart oven with the rack in position 1.
2. In a shallow dish, mix breadcrumbs, paprika, parmesan cheese, garlic powder, parsley, and pepper.
3. Brush pork chops with oil and coat with breadcrumb mixture.
4. Place coated pork chops into the baking pan.
5. Set to bake at 450 F for 15 minutes. After 5 minutes place the baking pan in the preheated oven.
6. Serve and enjoy.

Nutritional Value (Amount per Serving):
Calories 350; Fat 28.3 g; Carbohydrates 3.1 g; Sugar 0.3 g; Protein 20.4 g; Cholesterol 73 mg

Delicious Pork Belly

Preparation Time: 10 minutes; Cooking Time: 55 minutes; Serve: 6

Ingredients:
- 3 lbs pork belly, cut into 2-inch cubes
- 3 green onions stalk, chopped

- 1/4 tsp pepper
- 1 tbsp sesame oil
- 2 tbsp brown sugar
- 1/4 cup rice vinegar
- 1/4 cup soy sauce
- 1 tsp red chili flakes
- 1 tsp garlic, minced
- 1/4 tsp salt

Directions:
1. Fit the Cuisinart oven with the rack in position 1.
2. Add all ingredients into the zip-lock bag, seal bag shake well and place in the refrigerator for 1 hour.
3. Place marinated pork belly cubes into the parchment-lined baking pan.
4. Set to bake at 400 F for 60 minutes. After 5 minutes place the baking pan in the preheated oven.
5. Turn pork belly cubes after 30 minutes.
6. Serve and enjoy.

Nutritional Value (Amount per Serving):
Calories 362; Fat 32.3 g; Carbohydrates 5.5 g; Sugar 3.3 g; Protein 10.4 g; Cholesterol 51 mg

Cheesy Pork Chops

Preparation Time: 10 minutes; Cooking Time: 40 minutes; Serve: 4

Ingredients:
- 4 pork chops
- 1/2 tsp garlic powder
- 1/2 tsp pepper
- 1/2 tsp dried parsley
- 1/4 tsp paprika
- 1/4 cup Italian seasoned breadcrumbs
- 1/2 cup parmesan cheese, grated
- 1 tbsp olive oil
- Salt

Directions:
1. Fit the Cuisinart oven with the rack in position 1.
2. In a shallow dish, mix cheese, paprika, breadcrumbs, parsley, pepper, garlic powder, and salt.
3. Brush pork chops with oil and coat with parmesan cheese.
4. Place coated pork chops into the baking dish.
5. Set to bake at 350 F for 45 minutes. After 5 minutes place the baking dish in the preheated oven.
6. Serve and enjoy.

Nutritional Value (Amount per Serving):
Calories 353; Fat 26.2 g; Carbohydrates 6 g; Sugar 0.5 g; Protein 22.8 g; Cholesterol 77 mg

Baked Pork Ribs

Preparation Time: 10 minutes; Cooking Time: 30 minutes; Serve: 8

Ingredients:
- 2 lbs pork ribs, boneless
- 1 tbsp onion powder
- 1 1/2 tbsp garlic powder
- Pepper
- Salt

Directions:
1. Fit the Cuisinart oven with the rack in position 1.
2. Place pork ribs in baking pan and season with onion powder, garlic powder, pepper, and salt.
3. Set to bake at 350 F for 35 minutes. After 5 minutes place the baking pan in the preheated oven.
4. Serve and enjoy.

Nutritional Value (Amount per Serving):

Calories 318; Fat 20.1 g; Carbohydrates 1.9 g; Sugar 0.7 g; Protein 30.4 g; Cholesterol 117 mg

Herb Beef Tips

Preparation Time: 10 minutes; Cooking Time: 20 minutes; Serve: 6

Ingredients:
- 2 lbs sirloin steak, cut into 1-inch cubes
- 1/4 tsp red chili flakes
- 1/2 tsp pepper
- 1/2 tsp dried thyme
- 1 tsp onion powder
- 1 tsp dried oregano
- 2 tbsp lemon juice
- 2 tbsp water
- 1/4 cup olive oil
- 1 cup parsley, chopped
- 1 tsp garlic, minced
- 1/2 tsp salt

Directions:
1. Fit the Cuisinart oven with the rack in position 1.
2. Add all ingredients into the zip-lock bag, seal bag shake well and place in the refrigerator for 1 hour.
3. Place marinated steak cubes into the parchment-lined baking pan.
4. Set to bake at 400 F for 25 minutes. After 5 minutes place the baking pan in the preheated oven.
5. Serve and enjoy.

Nutritional Value (Amount per Serving):
Calories 361; Fat 18 g; Carbohydrates 1.6 g; Sugar 0.4 g; Protein 46.3 g; Cholesterol 135 mg

Meatballs

Preparation Time: 10 minutes; Cooking Time: 20 minutes; Serve: 4

Ingredients:
- 1 lb ground beef
- 2 tbsp parmesan cheese, grated
- 2 tsp Italian seasoning
- 1/4 cup rolled oats
- 1 egg, lightly beaten
- 1/2 cup spinach, chopped
- 1 tsp garlic, minced
- 1/2 onion, minced
- 4 oz mushrooms, chopped
- 3/4 cup cooked quinoa

Directions:
1. Fit the Cuisinart oven with the rack in position 1.
2. Add all ingredients into the mixing bowl and mix until well combined.
3. Make small balls from the meat mixture and place it into the parchment-lined baking pan.
4. Set to bake at 400 F for 25 minutes. After 5 minutes place the baking pan in the preheated oven.
5. Serve and enjoy.

Nutritional Value (Amount per Serving):
Calories 395; Fat 12 g; Carbohydrates 27 g; Sugar 1.4 g; Protein 43.3 g; Cholesterol 146 mg

Meatballs

Preparation Time: 10 minutes; Cooking Time: 12 minutes; Serve: 6

Ingredients:
- 1 egg
- 20 oz ground beef
- 1/2 cup parmesan cheese, grated
- 8 tbsp almond milk
- 6 garlic cloves, minced
- 3/4 cups almond meal
- 2 tbsp basil, chopped
- 2 tbsp parsley, chopped
- 1 tsp black pepper
- 1 tsp salt

Directions:

1. Fit the Cuisinart oven with the rack in position 1.
2. Add all ingredients into the mixing bowl and mix until well combined.
3. Make small balls from the meat mixture and place it into the parchment-lined baking pan.
4. Set to bake at 350 F for 17 minutes. After 5 minutes place the baking pan in the preheated oven.
5. Serve and enjoy.

Nutritional Value (Amount per Serving):
Calories 331; Fat 19 g; Carbohydrates 5.3 g; Sugar 1.3 g; Protein 35.3 g; Cholesterol 117 mg

Meatloaf

Preparation Time: 10 minutes; Cooking Time: 60 minutes; Serve: 8

Ingredients:
- 3 eggs
- 45 Ritz crackers, crushed
- 1 1/2 lbs lean ground beef
- 1/2 cup milk
- 4 oz sharp cheddar cheese, shredded
- 1/4 cup green pepper, diced
- 1/2 cup onion, chopped
- 1/4 tsp black pepper
- 1 tsp salt

For topping:
- 1 tsp yellow mustard
- 1/2 cup brown sugar
- 1/2 cup ketchup

Directions:
1. Fit the Cuisinart oven with the rack in position 1.
2. In a small bowl, mix together all topping ingredients and set aside.
3. In a mixing bowl, beat the eggs then add cheese, green pepper, onion, cracker crumbs, milk pepper, and salt. Stir well to combine.
4. Add ground meat and mix well.
5. Make a loaf of meat mixture and place it into the parchment-lined baking pan.
6. Set to bake at 350 F for 35 minutes. After 5 minutes place the baking pan in the preheated oven.
7. Spread topping mixture on top of the meatloaf and bake for 30 minutes more.
8. Slice and serve.

Nutritional Value (Amount per Serving):
Calories 316; Fat 12.7 g; Carbohydrates 17 g; Sugar 13.7 g; Protein 32.7 g; Cholesterol 154 mg

Delicious Lamb Patties

Preparation Time: 10 minutes; Cooking Time: 15 minutes; Serve: 4

Ingredients:
- 1 lb ground lamb
- 1 tsp ground coriander
- 1 tsp ground cumin
- 1/4 cup fresh parsley, chopped
- 1/4 cup onion, minced
- 1 tbsp garlic, minced
- 1/4 tsp cayenne pepper
- 1/2 tsp ground allspice
- 1 tsp ground cinnamon
- 1/4 tsp pepper
- 1 tsp kosher salt

Directions:
1. Fit the Cuisinart oven with the rack in position 1.
2. Add all ingredients into the mixing bowl and mix until well combined.
3. Make small patties from meat mixture and place onto the parchment-lined baking pan.
4. Set to bake at 450 F for 20 minutes. After 5 minutes place the baking pan in the preheated oven.
5. Serve and enjoy.

Nutritional Value (Amount per Serving):
Calories 223; Fat 8.5 g; Carbohydrates 2.6 g; Sugar 0.4 g; Protein 32.3 g; Cholesterol 102 mg

Meatballs

Preparation Time: 10 minutes; Cooking Time: 20 minutes; Serve: 4
Ingredients:
- 1 egg, lightly beaten
- 1 lb ground lamb
- 2 tbsp fresh parsley, chopped
- 1 tbsp garlic, minced
- 1/4 tsp red pepper flakes
- 1 tsp ground cumin
- 2 tsp fresh oregano, chopped
- 1/4 tsp pepper
- 1 tsp kosher salt

Directions:
1. Fit the Cuisinart oven with the rack in position 1.
2. Add all ingredients into the mixing bowl and mix until well combined.
3. Make small balls from meat mixture and place onto the parchment-lined baking pan.
4. Set to bake at 425 F for 25 minutes. After 5 minutes place the baking pan in the preheated oven.
5. Serve and enjoy.

Nutritional Value (Amount per Serving):
Calories 235; Fat 9.7 g; Carbohydrates 1.7 g; Sugar 0.2 g; Protein 33.6 g; Cholesterol 143 mg

Tender Pork Tenderloin

Preparation Time: 10 minutes; Cooking Time: 20 minutes; Serve: 4
Ingredients:
- 1 1/2 lbs pork tenderloin
- 1 tsp garlic powder
- 1 tsp Italian seasoning
- 2 tbsp olive oil
- 1 tsp ground coriander
- 1/4 tsp pepper
- 1 tsp sea salt

Directions:
1. Fit the Cuisinart oven with the rack in position 1.
2. Brush pork tenderloin with 1 tablespoon of olive oil.
3. Mix coriander, garlic powder, Italian seasoning, pepper, and salt and rub over pork tenderloin.
4. Heat remaining oil in a pan over medium-high heat.
5. Add pork tenderloin in a pan and sear until brown.
6. Place pork tenderloin in baking pan.
7. Set to bake at 400 F for 25 minutes. After 5 minutes place the baking pan in the preheated oven.
8. Slice and serve.

Nutritional Value (Amount per Serving):
Calories 310; Fat 13.3 g; Carbohydrates 0.7 g; Sugar 0.3 g; Protein 44.7 g; Cholesterol 125 mg

Easy Pork Chops

Preparation Time: 10 minutes; Cooking Time: 25 minutes; Serve: 2
Ingredients:
- 2 pork chops
- 2 tsp brown sugar
- 1 tsp smoked paprika
- Pepper
- Salt

Directions:
1. Fit the Cuisinart oven with the rack in position 1.

2. Mix smoked paprika, brown sugar, pepper, and salt and rub all over pork chops.
3. Place pork chops in a baking pan.
4. Set to bake at 325 F for 30 minutes. After 5 minutes place the baking pan in the preheated oven.
5. Serve and enjoy.

Nutritional Value (Amount per Serving):
Calories 271; Fat 20 g; Carbohydrates 3.6 g; Sugar 3 g; Protein 18.1 g; Cholesterol 69 mg

Baked Sweet & Tangy Pork Chops

Preparation Time: 10 minutes; Cooking Time: 35 minutes; Serve: 2
Ingredients:
- 2 pork chops
- 2 tbsp brown sugar
- 2 tbsp ketchup
- 2 onion sliced
- Pepper
- Salt

Directions:
1. Fit the Cuisinart oven with the rack in position 1.
2. Season pork chops with pepper and salt.
3. Place pork chops in a baking dish.
4. Mix ketchup and brown sugar and pour over pork chops.
5. Top with onion slices.
6. Set to bake at 375 F for 40 minutes. After 5 minutes place the baking dish in the preheated oven.
7. Serve and enjoy.

Nutritional Value (Amount per Serving):
Calories 308; Fat 19.9 g; Carbohydrates 13.5 g; Sugar 12.5 g; Protein 18.4 g; Cholesterol 69 mg

Curried Beef Patties

Preparation Time: 10 minutes; Cooking Time: 25 minutes; Serve: 6
Ingredients:
- 1 lb ground beef
- 2 eggs, lightly beaten
- 1/2 onion, chopped
- 2 medium zucchini, grated and squeeze out all liquid
- 1/2 tsp chili powder
- 1 tsp curry powder
- 1 cup breadcrumbs
- Pepper
- Salt

Directions:
1. Fit the Cuisinart oven with the rack in position 1.
2. Add all ingredients into the large bowl and mix until well combined.
3. Make small patties from the meat mixture and place it into the baking pan.
4. Set to bake at 400 F for 30 minutes. After 5 minutes place the baking pan in the preheated oven.
5. Serve and enjoy.

Nutritional Value (Amount per Serving):
Calories 248; Fat 7.3 g; Carbohydrates 16.4 g; Sugar 2.8 g; Protein 28.1 g; Cholesterol 122 mg

Tender Baked Pork Chops

Preparation Time: 10 minutes; Cooking Time: 15 minutes; Serve: 4
Ingredients:
- 4 pork chops, boneless
- 1/4 tsp onion powder
- 1/2 tsp garlic powder
- 2 tbsp olive oil
- 2 tbsp brown sugar
- 1/2 tsp chili powder

- Pepper
- Salt

Directions:
1. Fit the Cuisinart oven with the rack in position 1.
2. Brush pork chops with oil.
3. In a small bowl, mix brown sugar, chili powder, onion powder, garlic powder, pepper, and salt and rub all over pork chops.
4. Place pork chops in a baking pan.
5. Set to bake at 400 F for 20 minutes. After 5 minutes place the baking pan in the preheated oven.
6. Serve and enjoy.

Nutritional Value (Amount per Serving):
Calories 336; Fat 26.9 g; Carbohydrates 5 g; Sugar 4.5 g; Protein 18.1 g; Cholesterol 69 mg

Cripsy Crusted Pork Chops

Preparation Time: 10 minutes; Cooking Time: 40 minutes; Serve: 4

Ingredients:
- 4 pork chops, boneless
- 1 cup parmesan cheese
- 1 tbsp olive oil
- 1 tsp garlic powder
- 1 cup breadcrumbs
- 1/2 tsp Italian seasoning
- Pepper
- Salt

Directions:
1. Fit the Cuisinart oven with the rack in position 1.
2. In a shallow dish, mix breadcrumbs, parmesan cheese, Italian seasoning, garlic powder, pepper, and salt.
3. Brush pork chops with oil and coat with breadcrumb mixture.
4. Place coated pork chops in a baking pan.
5. Set to bake at 350 F for 45 minutes. After 5 minutes place the baking pan in the preheated oven.
6. Serve and enjoy.

Nutritional Value (Amount per Serving):
Calories 469; Fat 29.8 g; Carbohydrates 20.8 g; Sugar 1.9 g; Protein 28.9 g; Cholesterol 85 mg

Easy Ranch Pork Chops

Preparation Time: 10 minutes; Cooking Time: 35 minutes; Serve: 6

Ingredients:
- 6 pork chops, boneless
- 2 tbsp olive oil
- 1 oz ranch seasoning

Directions:
1. Fit the Cuisinart oven with the rack in position 1.
2. Brush pork chops with oil and rub with ranch seasoning.
3. Place pork chops in a baking pan.
4. Set to bake at 400 F for 40 minutes. After 5 minutes place the baking pan in the preheated oven.
5. Serve and enjoy.

Nutritional Value (Amount per Serving):
Calories 311; Fat 24.6 g; Carbohydrates 0 g; Sugar 0 g; Protein 18 g; Cholesterol 69 mg

Meatballs

Preparation Time: 10 minutes; Cooking Time: 15 minutes; Serve: 4

Ingredients:

- 1 lb ground pork
- 1 tsp paprika
- 1 tsp garlic powder
- 1 tsp onion powder
- 1/2 tsp ground cumin
- 1/2 tsp coriander
- 1/2 tsp dried thyme
- Pepper
- Salt

Directions:
1. Fit the Cuisinart oven with the rack in position 1.
2. Add all ingredients into the mixing bowl and mix until well combined.
3. Make small balls from the meat mixture and place them into the baking pan.
4. Set to bake at 400 F for 20 minutes. After 5 minutes place the baking pan in the preheated oven.
5. Serve and enjoy.

Nutritional Value (Amount per Serving):
Calories 170; Fat 4.1 g; Carbohydrates 1.5 g; Sugar 0.4 g; Protein 30 g; Cholesterol 83 mg

Pork Burger Patties

Preparation Time: 10 minutes; Cooking Time: 35 minutes; Serve: 6

Ingredients:
- 2 lbs ground pork
- 1 egg, lightly beaten
- 1 onion, minced
- 1 carrot, minced
- 1/2 cup breadcrumbs
- 1 tsp garlic powder
- 1 tsp paprika
- Pepper
- Salt

Directions:
1. Fit the Cuisinart oven with the rack in position 1.
2. Add all ingredients into the mixing bowl and mix until well combined.
3. Make small patties from the meat mixture and place it into the baking pan.
4. Set to bake at 375 F for 40 minutes. After 5 minutes place the baking pan in the preheated oven.
5. Serve and enjoy.

Nutritional Value (Amount per Serving):
Calories 276; Fat 6.6 g; Carbohydrates 9.8 g; Sugar 2.1 g; Protein 42.1 g; Cholesterol 138 mg

Parmesan Herb Meatballs

Preparation Time: 10 minutes; Cooking Time: 20 minutes; Serve: 6

Ingredients:
- 1 lb ground beef
- 1/2 small onion, minced
- 2 garlic cloves, minced
- 1 egg, lightly beaten
- 1 1/2 tbsp fresh basil, chopped
- 1 tbsp fresh parsley, chopped
- 1/2 tbsp fresh rosemary, chopped
- 1/4 cup parmesan cheese, grated
- 1/2 cup breadcrumbs
- Pepper
- Salt

Directions:
1. Fit the Cuisinart oven with the rack in position 1.
2. Add all ingredients into the mixing bowl and mix until well combined.
3. Make small balls from the meat mixture and place them into the baking pan.
4. Set to bake at 375 F for 25 minutes. After 5 minutes place the baking pan in the preheated oven.
5. Serve and enjoy.

Nutritional Value (Amount per Serving):

Calories 204; Fat 6.8 g; Carbohydrates 7.8 g; Sugar 0.9 g; Protein 26.5 g; Cholesterol 98 mg

Meatballs

Preparation Time: 10 minutes; Cooking Time: 20 minutes; Serve: 6

Ingredients:
- 8 oz ground beef
- 1/2 onion, diced
- 1 egg, lightly beaten
- 1/4 cup parmesan cheese, grated
- 1/2 cup breadcrumbs
- 1/4 cup parsley, chopped
- 1 tsp garlic, minced
- 8 oz ground pork
- Pepper
- Salt

Directions:
1. Fit the Cuisinart oven with the rack in position 1.
2. Add all ingredients into the mixing bowl and mix until well combined.
3. Make small balls from the meat mixture and place them into the baking pan.
4. Set to bake at 400 F for 25 minutes. After 5 minutes place the baking pan in the preheated oven.
5. Serve and enjoy.

Nutritional Value (Amount per Serving):
Calories 188; Fat 5.7 g; Carbohydrates 7.9 g; Sugar 1 g; Protein 24.9 g; Cholesterol 91 mg

Crispy Cracker Crusted Pork Chops

Preparation Time: 10 minutes; Cooking Time: 30 minutes; Serve: 3

Ingredients:
- 3 pork chops, boneless
- 2 tbsp milk
- 1 egg, lightly beaten
- 1/2 cup crackers, crushed
- 4 tbsp parmesan cheese, grated
- Pepper
- Salt

Directions:
1. Fit the Cuisinart oven with the rack in position 1.
2. In a shallow bowl, whisk egg and milk.
3. In a separate shallow dish, mix cheese, crackers, pepper, and salt.
4. Dip pork chops in egg then coat with cheese mixture.
5. Place coated pork chops in a baking pan.
6. Set to bake at 350 F for 35 minutes. After 5 minutes place the baking pan in the preheated oven.
7. Serve and enjoy.

Nutritional Value (Amount per Serving):
Calories 360; Fat 25.9 g; Carbohydrates 7.2 g; Sugar 0.8 g; Protein 23.5 g; Cholesterol 130 mg

Meatballs

Preparation Time: 10 minutes; Cooking Time: 15 minutes; Serve: 4

Ingredients:
- 1 lb ground lamb
- 1 tsp onion powder
- 1 tbsp garlic, minced
- 1 tsp ground coriander
- 1 tsp ground cumin
- Pepper
- Salt

Directions:
1. Fit the Cuisinart oven with the rack in position 1.
2. Add all ingredients into the mixing bowl and mix until well combined.
3. Make small balls from the meat mixture and place them into the baking pan.

4. Set to bake at 400 F for 20 minutes. After 5 minutes place the baking pan in the preheated oven.
5. Serve and enjoy.

Nutritional Value (Amount per Serving):
Calories 218; Fat 8.5 g; Carbohydrates 1.4 g; Sugar 0.2 g; Protein 32.1 g; Cholesterol 102 mg

Cheesy Baked Burger Patties

Preparation Time: 10 minutes; Cooking Time: 15 minutes; Serve: 6

Ingredients:
- 2 lbs ground beef
- 1 tsp onion powder
- 1 tsp garlic powder
- 1/2 cup mozzarella cheese, shredded
- 1/2 cup cheddar cheese, shredded
- Pepper
- Salt

Directions:
1. Fit the Cuisinart oven with the rack in position 1.
2. Add all ingredients into the large bowl and mix until well combined.
3. Make patties from the meat mixture and place it into the baking pan.
4. Set to bake at 400 F for 20 minutes. After 5 minutes place the baking pan in the preheated oven.
5. Serve and enjoy.

Nutritional Value (Amount per Serving):
Calories 329; Fat 13 g; Carbohydrates 0.9 g; Sugar 0.3 g; Protein 49 g; Cholesterol 146 mg

Meatballs

Preparation Time: 10 minutes; Cooking Time: 20 minutes; Serve: 4

Ingredients:
- 1 lb ground beef
- 1/2 small onion, chopped
- 1 egg, lightly beaten
- 2 garlic cloves, minced
- 1 tbsp basil, chopped
- 1/4 cup parmesan cheese, grated
- 1/2 cup breadcrumbs
- 1 tbsp Italian parsley, chopped
- 1 tbsp rosemary, chopped
- 2 tbsp milk
- Pepper
- Salt

Directions:
1. Fit the Cuisinart oven with the rack in position 1.
2. Add all ingredients into the mixing bowl and mix until well combined.
3. Make small balls from the meat mixture and place them into the baking pan.
4. Set to bake at 375 F for 25 minutes. After 5 minutes place the baking pan in the preheated oven.
5. Serve and enjoy.

Nutritional Value (Amount per Serving):
Calories 311; Fat 10.4 g; Carbohydrates 12.3 g; Sugar 1.7 g; Protein 39.9 g; Cholesterol 147 mg

Baked Beef & Broccoli

Preparation Time: 10 minutes; Cooking Time: 25 minutes; Serve: 2

Ingredients:
- 1/2 lb beef meat, cut into pieces
- 1 tbsp vinegar
- 1 garlic clove, minced
- 1 tbsp olive oil
- 1/2 tsp Italian seasoning
- 1/2 cup broccoli florets
- 1 onion, sliced
- Pepper
- Salt

Directions:
1. Fit the Cuisinart oven with the rack in position 1.
2. Add meat and remaining ingredients into the large bowl and toss well and spread in baking pan.
3. Set to bake at 390 F for 30 minutes. After 5 minutes place the baking pan in the preheated oven.
4. Serve and enjoy.

Nutritional Value (Amount per Serving):
Calories 316; Fat 16.1 g; Carbohydrates 7.4 g; Sugar 2.9 g; Protein 34.4 g; Cholesterol 102 mg

Meatballs

Preparation Time: 10 minutes; Cooking Time: 12 minutes; Serve: 4
Ingredients:
- 4 oz ground lamb meat
- 1/2 tbsp lemon zest
- 1 egg, lightly beaten
- 1 tbsp oregano, chopped
- 1/4 tsp dried thyme
- Pepper
- Salt

Directions:
1. Fit the Cuisinart oven with the rack in position 1.
2. Add all ingredients into the mixing bowl and mix until well combined.
3. Make small balls from the meat mixture and place them into the baking pan.
4. Set to bake at 400 F for 17 minutes. After 5 minutes place the baking pan in the preheated oven.
5. Serve and enjoy.

Nutritional Value (Amount per Serving):
Calories 100; Fat 6.8 g; Carbohydrates 1 g; Sugar 0.2 g; Protein 8.6 g; Cholesterol 68 mg

Meatloaf

Preparation Time: 10 minutes; Cooking Time: 20 minutes; Serve: 4
Ingredients:
- 1 lb ground pork
- 1 egg, lightly beaten
- 1 tbsp thyme, chopped
- 1/4 tsp garlic powder
- 4 tbsp breadcrumbs
- 1 onion, chopped
- 1/2 tsp Italian seasoning
- Pepper
- Salt

Directions:
1. Fit the Cuisinart oven with the rack in position 1.
2. Add all ingredients into the mixing bowl and mix until well combined.
3. Pour meat mixture into the greased loaf pan.
4. Set to bake at 375 F for 25 minutes. After 5 minutes place the loaf pan in the preheated oven.
5. Serve and enjoy.

Nutritional Value (Amount per Serving):
Calories 220; Fat 5.7 g; Carbohydrates 8.2 g; Sugar 1.8 g; Protein 32.4 g; Cholesterol 124 mg

Jalapeno Basil Lamb Patties

Preparation Time: 10 minutes; Cooking Time: 8 minutes; Serve: 4
Ingredients:
- 1 lb ground lamb
- 5 basil leaves, minced
- 8 mint leaves, minced
- 1/4 cup fresh parsley, chopped

- 1 tsp dried oregano
- 1 cup goat cheese, crumbled
- 1 tbsp garlic, minced
- 1 jalapeno pepper, minced
- 1/4 tsp pepper
- 1/2 tsp kosher salt

Directions:
1. Fit the Cuisinart oven with the rack in position 1.
2. Add all ingredients into the mixing bowl and mix until well combined.
3. Make the equal shape of patties from the meat mixture and place it into the baking pan.
4. Set to bake at 450 F for 13 minutes. After 5 minutes place the baking pan in the preheated oven.
5. Serve and enjoy.

Nutritional Value (Amount per Serving):
Calories 296; Fat 13.9 g; Carbohydrates 3.7 g; Sugar 0.5 g; Protein 37.5 g; Cholesterol 118 mg

Meatballs

Preparation Time: 10 minutes; Cooking Time: 20 minutes; Serve: 6

Ingredients:
- 2 lbs ground beef
- 1 egg, lightly beaten
- 1 tsp cinnamon
- 2 tsp cumin
- 2 tsp coriander
- 1 tsp garlic, minced
- 1 tbsp fresh basil, chopped
- 1/4 cup fresh parsley, minced
- 1 tsp smoked paprika
- 1 tsp oregano
- 1 onion, grated
- 1/4 tsp pepper
- 1/2 tsp salt

Directions:
1. Fit the Cuisinart oven with the rack in position 1.
2. Add all ingredients into the large mixing bowl and mix until well combined.
3. Make small balls from the meat mixture and place it into the parchment-lined baking pan.
4. Set to bake at 400 F for 25 minutes. After 5 minutes place the baking pan in the preheated oven.
5. Serve and enjoy.

Nutritional Value (Amount per Serving):
Calories 306; Fat 10.4 g; Carbohydrates 3.1 g; Sugar 0.9 g; Protein 47.3 g; Cholesterol 162 mg

Meatloaf

Preparation Time: 10 minutes; Cooking Time: 55 minutes; Serve: 6

Ingredients:
- 2 lbs ground beef
- 1/2 cup sunflower seed flour
- 1/2 cup salsa, low-fodmap
- 2 eggs, lightly beaten
- 1 tsp oregano
- 1 tsp paprika
- 1 tsp cumin
- 1/4 cup fresh cilantro, chopped
- 1/4 cup green onion, chopped
- 1 bell pepper, diced & sautéed
- 1/2 tsp salt

Directions:
1. Fit the Cuisinart oven with the rack in position 1.
2. Add all ingredients into the mixing bowl and mix until well combined.
3. Pour mixture into the greased loaf pan.
4. Set to bake at 375 F for 60 minutes. After 5 minutes place the loaf pan in the preheated oven.
5. Slice and serve.

Nutritional Value (Amount per Serving):

Calories 306; Fat 10.4 g; Carbohydrates 3.1 g; Sugar 0.9 g; Protein 47.3 g; Cholesterol 162 mg

Pork Chops with Potatoes

Preparation Time: 10 minutes; Cooking Time: 35 minutes; Serve: 4

Ingredients:
- 4 pork chops, boneless
- 1/4 tsp ground oregano
- 1 tsp dried parsley
- 3 tbsp olive oil
- 1 oz ranch seasoning
- 2 1lbs potatoes, cut into bite-size pieces
- 1/4 tsp pepper
- Salt

Directions:
1. Fit the Cuisinart oven with the rack in position 1.
2. Season pork chops with ranch seasoning and pepper.
3. Place pork chops into the center of the baking pan.
4. In a bowl, toss potatoes with oil, parsley, oregano, and salt.
5. Place potatoes around the pork chops.
6. Set to bake at 400 F for 40 minutes. After 5 minutes place the baking pan in the preheated oven.
7. Serve and enjoy.

Nutritional Value (Amount per Serving):
Calories 433; Fat 30.5 g; Carbohydrates 15.4 g; Sugar 0.6 g; Protein 19.8 g; Cholesterol 69 mg

Herb Pork Tenderloin

Preparation Time: 10 minutes; Cooking Time: 35 minutes; Serve: 4

Ingredients:
- 1 lb pork tenderloin
- 1/2 tbsp dried rosemary
- 1/2 tsp dried thyme
- 1 tbsp olive oil
- Pepper
- Salt

Directions:
1. Fit the Cuisinart oven with the rack in position 1.
2. Mix rosemary, thyme, oil, pepper, and salt and rub over pork tenderloin.
3. Place pork tenderloin in baking pan.
4. Set to bake at 400 F for 40 minutes. After 5 minutes place the baking pan in the preheated oven.
5. Slice and serve.

Nutritional Value (Amount per Serving):
Calories 194; Fat 7.6 g; Carbohydrates 0.4 g; Sugar 0 g; Protein 29.7 g; Cholesterol 83 mg

Paprika Pork Tenderloin

Preparation Time: 10 minutes; Cooking Time: 30 minutes; Serve: 6

Ingredients:
- 2 lbs pork tenderloin
- For rub:
- 1 tbsp smoked paprika
- 1/2 tsp chili powder
- 1 tbsp garlic powder
- 1 tbsp onion powder
- 1/2 tsp salt

Directions:
1. Fit the Cuisinart oven with the rack in position 1.
2. In a small bowl, mix all rub ingredients.
3. Coat pork tenderloin with the rub and place in baking pan.
4. Set to bake at 425 F for 35 minutes. After 5 minutes place the baking pan in the preheated oven.

5. Slice and serve.

Nutritional Value (Amount per Serving):
   Calories 229; Fat 5.5 g; Carbohydrates 2.7 g; Sugar 0.9 g; Protein 40.1 g; Cholesterol 110 mg

Garlic Pork Roast

Preparation Time: 10 minutes; Cooking Time: 55 minutes; Serve: 4
Ingredients:
- 2 lbs pork sirloin roast
- 6 garlic cloves, sliced
- 2 tbsp olive oil
- 1/2 tsp pepper
- 1 tsp salt

Directions:
1. Fit the Cuisinart oven with the rack in position 1.
2. Using a sharp knife make slits on top of the roast and stuff sliced garlic in each slit.
3. Season pork roast with pepper and salt.
4. Heat oil in a pan over medium-high heat.
5. Place roast in a pan and brown from all the sides.
6. Transfer roast in a baking pan.
7. Set to bake at 300 F for 60 minutes. After 5 minutes place the baking pan in the preheated oven.
8. Slice and serve.

Nutritional Value (Amount per Serving):
   Calories 537; Fat 28.4 g; Carbohydrates 1.7 g; Sugar 0.1 g; Protein 65 g; Cholesterol 195 mg

Baked Pork Tenderloin

Preparation Time: 10 minutes; Cooking Time: 35 minutes; Serve: 6
Ingredients:
- 2 lbs pork tenderloin
- 3 garlic cloves, chopped
- Pepper
- Salt

For the spice mix:
- 1/4 tsp chili powder
- 1/4 tsp cayenne
- 1 tsp cinnamon
- 1 tsp cumin
- 1 tsp coriander
- 1 tsp oregano
- 1/4 tsp cloves

Directions:
1. Fit the Cuisinart oven with the rack in position 1.
2. In a small bowl, mix all spice ingredients and set aside.
3. Using a sharp knife make slits on pork tenderloin and insert garlic into each slit.
4. Rub spice mixture over pork tenderloin.
5. Place pork tenderloin in baking pan.
6. Set to bake at 375 F for 40 minutes. After 5 minutes place the baking pan in the preheated oven.
7. Slice and serve.

Nutritional Value (Amount per Serving):
   Calories 222; Fat 5.5 g; Carbohydrates 1.3 g; Sugar 0.1 g; Protein 39.8 g; Cholesterol 110 mg

Rosemary Pork Chops

Preparation Time: 10 minutes; Cooking Time: 30 minutes; Serve: 4
Ingredients:
- 4 pork chops, boneless
- 1 tsp dried rosemary, crushed
- 4 garlic cloves, minced
- 1 tbsp fresh rosemary, chopped

- 1/4 tsp pepper
- 1/4 tsp salt

Directions:
1. Fit the Cuisinart oven with the rack in position 1.
2. Season pork chops with pepper and salt and set aside.
3. In a small bowl, mix together garlic and rosemary and rub over pork chops.
4. Place pork chops in a baking pan.
5. Set to bake at 425 F for 35 minutes. After 5 minutes place the baking pan in the preheated oven.
6. Serve and enjoy.

Nutritional Value (Amount per Serving):
Calories 265; Fat 20.1 g; Carbohydrates 1.8 g; Sugar 0 g; Protein 18.2 g; Cholesterol 69 mg

Stuffed Pork Chops

Preparation Time: 10 minutes; Cooking Time: 35 minutes; Serve: 4

Ingredients:
- 4 pork chops, boneless and thick-cut
- 2 tbsp olives, chopped
- 3 tbsp sun-dried tomatoes, chopped
- 1/2 cup goat cheese, crumbled
- 3 garlic cloves, minced
- 2 tbsp fresh parsley, chopped

Directions:
1. Fit the Cuisinart oven with the rack in position 1.
2. In a bowl, combine together cheese, garlic, parsley, olives, and sun-dried tomatoes.
3. Stuff cheese mixture all the pork chops.
4. Season pork chops with pepper and salt and place in baking pan.
5. Set to bake at 375 F for 40 minutes. After 5 minutes place the baking pan in the preheated oven.
6. Serve and enjoy.

Nutritional Value (Amount per Serving):
Calories 295; Fat 22.6 g; Carbohydrates 1.6 g; Sugar 0.4 g; Protein 20.2 g; Cholesterol 75 mg

Crispy Crusted Pork Chops

Preparation Time: 10 minutes; Cooking Time: 15 minutes; Serve: 2

Ingredients:
- 2 pork chops, bone-in
- 1 cup pork rinds, crushed
- 1/2 tsp parsley
- 1 tbsp olive oil
- 1/2 tsp garlic powder
- 1/2 tsp onion powder
- 1/2 tsp paprika

Directions:
1. Fit the Cuisinart oven with the rack in position 2.
2. In a large bowl, mix pork rinds, garlic powder, onion powder, parsley, and paprika.
3. Brush pork chops with oil and coat with pork rind mixture.
4. place coated pork chops in air fryer basket then place air fryer basket in baking pan.
5. Place a baking pan on the oven rack. Set to air fry at 400 F for 15 minutes.
6. Serve and enjoy.

Nutritional Value (Amount per Serving):
Calories 413; Fat 32.7 g; Carbohydrates 1.3 g; Sugar 0.4 g; Protein 28.5 g; Cholesterol 92 mg

Spiced Pork Chops

Preparation Time: 10 minutes; Cooking Time: 16 minutes; Serve: 4

Ingredients:
- 4 pork chops, boneless
- 1/2 tsp granulated onion

- 1/2 tsp granulated garlic
- 1/4 tsp sugar
- 2 tsp olive oil
- 1/2 tsp celery seed
- 1/2 tsp parsley
- 1/2 tsp salt

Directions:
1. Fit the Cuisinart oven with the rack in position 2.
2. Brush pork chops with olive oil.
3. Mix celery seed, parsley, granulated onion, garlic, sugar, and salt and sprinkle over pork chops.
4. Place pork chops in the air fryer basket then place an air fryer basket in the baking pan.
5. Place a baking pan on the oven rack. Set to air fry at 350 F for 16 minutes.
6. Serve and enjoy.

Nutritional Value (Amount per Serving):
Calories 279; Fat 22.3 g; Carbohydrates 0.6 g; Sugar 0.3 g; Protein 18.1 g; Cholesterol 69 mg

Meatballs

Preparation Time: 10 minutes; Cooking Time: 25 minutes; Serve: 8
Ingredients:
- 3 eggs
- 2 lbs ground beef
- 2 tsp cumin
- 5 garlic cloves, minced
- 1 onion, grated
- 1 cup breadcrumbs
- 1/2 cup fresh parsley, minced
- 1 tsp cinnamon
- 2 tsp dried oregano
- 1 tsp pepper
- 2 tsp salt

Directions:
1. Fit the Cuisinart oven with the rack in position 1.
2. Add all ingredients into the large mixing bowl and mix until well combined.
3. Make small meatballs from mixture and place in baking pan.
4. Set to bake at 400 F for 30 minutes. After 5 minutes place the baking pan in the preheated oven.
5. Serve and enjoy.

Nutritional Value (Amount per Serving):
Calories 302; Fat 9.7 g; Carbohydrates 12.9 g; Sugar 1.6 g; Protein 38.8 g; Cholesterol 163 mg

Meatballs

Preparation Time: 10 minutes; Cooking Time: 10 minutes; Serve: 4
Ingredients:
- 2 eggs
- 1 tsp sesame oil
- 1 tsp ginger, minced
- 1 tsp garlic, minced
- 1/2 cup breadcrumbs
- 2 lbs ground pork
- 1/3 tsp red chili pepper flakes
- 1 tbsp scallions, diced
- 1 tsp soy sauce
- Pepper
- Salt

Directions:
1. Fit the Cuisinart oven with the rack in position 2.
2. Add all ingredients into the large bowl and mix until well combined.
3. Make small balls from meat mixture and place in the air fryer basket then place the air fryer basket in the baking pan.
4. Place a baking pan on the oven rack. Set to air fry at 400 F for 10 minutes.
5. Serve and enjoy.

Nutritional Value (Amount per Serving):

Calories 423; Fat 12 g; Carbohydrates 10.7 g; Sugar 1.1 g; Protein 64.1 g; Cholesterol 247 mg

Goat Cheese Meatballs

Preparation Time: 10 minutes; Cooking Time: 12 minutes; Serve: 8

Ingredients:
- 1 lb ground beef
- 1 lb ground pork
- 2 eggs, lightly beaten
- 1/4 cup fresh parsley, chopped
- 1 tbsp garlic, minced
- 1 onion, chopped
- 1 tbsp Worcestershire sauce
- 1/2 cup goat cheese, crumbled
- 1/2 cup breadcrumbs
- Pepper
- Salt

Directions:
1. Fit the Cuisinart oven with the rack in position 2.
2. Line the air fryer basket with parchment paper.
3. Add all ingredients into a large bowl and mix until well combined.
4. Make small balls from meat mixture and place in the air fryer basket then place an air fryer basket in the baking pan.
5. Place a baking pan on the oven rack. Set to air fry at 400 F for 12 minutes.
6. Serve and enjoy.

Nutritional Value (Amount per Serving):
Calories 253; Fat 8.1 g; Carbohydrates 7.2 g; Sugar 1.6 g; Protein 35.6 g; Cholesterol 136 mg

Quick Baked Pork Patties

Preparation Time: 10 minutes; Cooking Time: 10 minutes; Serve: 4

Ingredients:
- 1 1/4 lbs ground pork
- 2 tsp honey
- 1 small onion, chopped
- 1 tsp pork seasoning
- 1 tsp garlic paste
- Pepper
- Salt

Directions:
1. Fit the Cuisinart oven with the rack in position 2.
2. Line the air fryer basket with parchment paper.
3. Add all ingredients into the mixing bowl and mix until well combined.
4. Make the equal shape of patties from meat mixture and place in the air fryer basket then place an air fryer basket in the baking pan.
5. Place a baking pan on the oven rack. Set to air fry at 360 F for 10 minutes.
6. Serve and enjoy.

Nutritional Value (Amount per Serving):
Calories 228; Fat 5 g; Carbohydrates 5.7 g; Sugar 4.5 g; Protein 37.3 g; Cholesterol 103 mg

Asian Meatballs

Preparation Time: 10 minutes; Cooking Time: 15 minutes; Serve: 4

Ingredients:
- 1 lb ground pork
- 1/2 lime juice
- 2 tsp curry paste
- 1 tbsp Worcestershire sauce
- 1 tbsp soy sauce
- 1 tsp garlic puree
- 1 tsp coriander
- 1 tsp Chinese spice
- 1 tsp mixed spice
- 1 onion, chopped
- Pepper
- Salt

Directions:

1. Fit the Cuisinart oven with the rack in position 2.
2. Line the air fryer basket with parchment paper.
3. Add all ingredients into a large bowl and mix until well combined.
4. Make small balls from meat mixture and place in the air fryer basket then place an air fryer basket in the baking pan.
5. Place a baking pan on the oven rack. Set to air fry at 350 F for 15 minutes.
6. Serve and enjoy.

Nutritional Value (Amount per Serving):
Calories 199; Fat 5.7 g; Carbohydrates 4.8 g; Sugar 2.1 g; Protein 30.4 g; Cholesterol 83 mg

Cajun Burger Patties

Preparation Time: 10 minutes; Cooking Time: 10 minutes; Serve: 2
Ingredients:
- 1 egg, lightly beaten
- 1/2 lb ground pork
- 1/2 cup breadcrumbs
- 1 tbsp Cajun seasoning
- Pepper
- Salt

Directions:
1. Fit the Cuisinart oven with the rack in position 2.
2. Line the air fryer basket with parchment paper.
3. Add all ingredients into the large bowl and mix until well combined.
4. Make two equal shapes of patties from meat mixture and place in the air fryer basket then place an air fryer basket in the baking pan.
5. Place a baking pan on the oven rack. Set to air fry at 360 F for 10 minutes.
6. Serve and enjoy.

Nutritional Value (Amount per Serving):
Calories 300; Fat 7.6 g; Carbohydrates 19.6 g; Sugar 1.8 g; Protein 36.1 g; Cholesterol 165 mg

Asian Pork Shoulder

Preparation Time: 10 minutes; Cooking Time: 15 minutes; Serve: 4
Ingredients:
- 1 lb pork shoulder, boneless
- 1 tbsp wine
- 1 tbsp sugar
- 2 tbsp soy sauce
- 4 tbsp honey
- 1 tsp Chinese five-spice
- 2 tsp ginger, minced
- 2 tsp garlic, minced

Directions:
1. Fit the Cuisinart oven with the rack in position 2.
2. Add all ingredients except pork into the large zip-lock bag and mix well.
3. Add pork and seal the bag and place it in the fridge overnight.
4. Remove pork from marinade and place in an air fryer basket then place an air fryer basket in baking pan.
5. Place a baking pan on the oven rack. Set to air fry at 390 F for 15 minutes.
6. Serve and enjoy.

Nutritional Value (Amount per Serving):
Calories 419; Fat 24.3 g; Carbohydrates 22.1 g; Sugar 20.5 g; Protein 27.1 g; Cholesterol 102 mg

Tasty Breaded Pork Chops

Preparation Time: 10 minutes; Cooking Time: 12 minutes; Serve: 3
Ingredients:
- 1 egg
- 3 pork chops
- 1/2 cup breadcrumbs
- 1/4 tsp smoked paprika

- 1/2 tsp garlic powder
- 1/2 tsp onion powder
- Pepper
- Salt

Directions:
1. Fit the Cuisinart oven with the rack in position 2.
2. Line the air fryer basket with parchment paper.
3. Season pork chops with paprika, garlic powder, onion powder, pepper, and salt.
4. Place breadcrumbs in a shallow bowl.
5. In a separate shallow bowl, add the egg.
6. Dip pork chop in egg and coat with breadcrumb.
7. Place coated pork chops in the air fryer basket then place an air fryer basket in the baking pan.
8. Place a baking pan on the oven rack. Set to air fry at 380 F for 12 minutes.
9. Serve and enjoy.

Nutritional Value (Amount per Serving):
Calories 352; Fat 22.3 g; Carbohydrates 13.9 g; Sugar 1.5 g; Protein 22.4 g; Cholesterol 123 mg

Air Fryer Herb Pork Chops

Preparation Time: 10 minutes; Cooking Time: 15 minutes; Serve: 4

Ingredients:
- 4 pork chops
- 2 tsp oregano
- 2 tsp thyme
- 2 tsp sage
- 1 tsp garlic powder
- 1 tsp paprika
- 1 tsp rosemary
- Pepper
- Salt

Directions:
1. Fit the Cuisinart oven with the rack in position 2.
2. Line the air fryer basket with parchment paper.
3. Mix garlic powder, paprika, rosemary, oregano, thyme, sage, pepper, and salt and rub over pork chops.
4. Place pork chops in the air fryer basket then place an air fryer basket in the baking pan.
5. Place a baking pan on the oven rack. Set to air fry at 360 F for 15 minutes.
6. Serve and enjoy.

Nutritional Value (Amount per Serving):
Calories 266; Fat 20.2 g; Carbohydrates 2 g; Sugar 0.3 g; Protein 18.4 g; Cholesterol 69 mg

Steak Seasoned Pork Chops

Preparation Time: 10 minutes; Cooking Time: 12 minutes; Serve: 4

Ingredients:
- 1 lb pork chops, boneless
- 1 tsp steak seasoning blend
- 1 tbsp yellow mustard
- 2 tsp honey

Directions:
1. Fit the Cuisinart oven with the rack in position 2.
2. Line the air fryer basket with parchment paper.
3. In a small bowl, mix honey, mustard, and steak seasoning.
4. Brush pork chops with honey mixture and place in air fryer basket then place air fryer basket in baking pan.
5. Place a baking pan on the oven rack. Set to air fry at 350 F for 12 minutes.
6. Serve and enjoy.

Nutritional Value (Amount per Serving):
Calories 376; Fat 28.3 g; Carbohydrates 3.1 g; Sugar 2.9 g; Protein 25.7 g; Cholesterol 98 mg

Parmesan Cajun Pork Chops

Preparation Time: 10 minutes; Cooking Time: 9 minutes; Serve: 2
Ingredients:
- 2 pork chops, boneless
- 1 tsp dried mixed herbs
- 1 tsp paprika
- 3 tbsp parmesan cheese, grated
- 1 tsp Cajun seasoning
- 1/3 cup almond flour

Directions:
1. Fit the Cuisinart oven with the rack in position 2.
2. Line the air fryer basket with parchment paper.
3. In a shallow dish, mix parmesan cheese, almond flour, paprika, mixed herbs, and Cajun seasoning.
4. Spray pork chops with cooking spray and coat with parmesan cheese.
5. Place coated pork chops in the air fryer basket then place an air fryer basket in the baking pan.
6. Place a baking pan on the oven rack. Set to air fry at 350 F for 9 minutes.
7. Serve and enjoy.

Nutritional Value (Amount per Serving):
Calories 324; Fat 24.8 g; Carbohydrates 2.2 g; Sugar 0.3 g; Protein 22.9 g; Cholesterol 77 mg

Pork Belly Strips

Preparation Time: 10 minutes; Cooking Time: 15 minutes; Serve: 4
Ingredients:
- 1 lb pork belly strips
- 1/4 tsp paprika
- 1/2 tsp garlic powder
- Pepper
- Salt

Directions:
1. Fit the Cuisinart oven with the rack in position 2.
2. Toss pork belly strips with paprika, garlic powder, pepper, and salt.
3. Place pork strips in the air fryer basket then place an air fryer basket in the baking pan.
4. Place a baking pan on the oven rack. Set to air fry at 390 F for 15 minutes.
5. Serve and enjoy.

Nutritional Value (Amount per Serving):
Calories 162; Fat 6 g; Carbohydrates 0.3 g; Sugar 0.1 g; Protein 24.2 g; Cholesterol 65 mg

Easy Pork Bites

Preparation Time: 10 minutes; Cooking Time: 15 minutes; Serve: 4
Ingredients:
- 1 lb pork belly, cut into 3/4-inch cubes
- 1/2 tsp onion powder
- 1/2 tsp garlic powder
- 1 tsp soy sauce
- Pepper
- Salt

Directions:
1. Fit the Cuisinart oven with the rack in position 2.
2. In a mixing bowl, toss pork cubes with onion powder, garlic powder, soy sauce, pepper, and salt.
3. Place pork cubes in the air fryer basket then place an air fryer basket in the baking pan.
4. Place a baking pan on the oven rack. Set to air fry at 400 F for 15 minutes.
5. Serve and enjoy.

Nutritional Value (Amount per Serving):
Calories 526; Fat 30.5 g; Carbohydrates 0.6 g; Sugar 0.2 g; Protein 52.5 g; Cholesterol 131 mg

Juicy Pork Loin

Preparation Time: 10 minutes; Cooking Time: 18 minutes; Serve: 8
Ingredients:
- 2 lbs pork loin, cut in half
- 3 tbsp brown sugar
- 1 tsp basil
- 1/2 tsp mint
- 1 tsp garlic powder
- 1 tsp salt

Directions:
1. Fit the Cuisinart oven with the rack in position 2.
2. Mix brown sugar, basil, mint, garlic powder, and salt and rub all over the pork loin and place in air fryer basket then place air fryer basket in baking pan.
3. Place a baking pan on the oven rack. Set to air fry at 400 F for 18 minutes.
4. Serve and enjoy.

Nutritional Value (Amount per Serving):
Calories 289; Fat 15.8 g; Carbohydrates 3.6 g; Sugar 3.4 g; Protein 31 g; Cholesterol 91 mg

Honey Garlic Pork Chops

Preparation Time: 10 minutes; Cooking Time: 12 minutes; Serve: 4
Ingredients:
- 4 pork chops
- 2 tbsp lemon juice
- 1/4 cup honey
- 2 garlic cloves, minced
- 1 tbsp olive oil
- 1 tbsp sweet chili sauce
- Pepper
- Salt

Directions:
1. Fit the Cuisinart oven with the rack in position 2.
2. Season pork chops with pepper and salt and place in air fryer basket then place air fryer basket in baking pan.
3. Place a baking pan on the oven rack. Set to air fry at 400 F for 12 minutes.
4. Meanwhile, heat oil in a pan over medium heat.
5. Add garlic and sauté for 30 seconds.
6. Add remaining ingredients and stir well and cook for 3 minutes.
7. Place pork chops on serving dish.
8. Pour sauce over pork chops and serve.

Nutritional Value (Amount per Serving):
Calories 362; Fat 23.5 g; Carbohydrates 19.6 g; Sugar 19.1 g; Protein 18.2 g; Cholesterol 69 mg

Air Fryer Juicy Pork Chops

Preparation Time: 10 minutes; Cooking Time: 12 minutes; Serve: 2
Ingredients:
- 2 pork chops
- 2 tbsp brown sugar
- 1 tbsp olive oil
- 1/4 tsp garlic powder
- 1/2 tsp onion powder
- 1 tsp ground mustard
- 1 tbsp paprika
- Pepper
- Salt

Directions:
1. Fit the Cuisinart oven with the rack in position 2.
2. Add all dry ingredients into the small bowl and mix well.
3. Brush pork chops with oil and rub with spice mixture.
4. Place pork chops in the air fryer basket then place an air fryer basket in the baking pan.
5. Place a baking pan on the oven rack. Set to air fry at 400 F for 12 minutes.
6. Serve and enjoy.

Nutritional Value (Amount per Serving):
Calories 371; Fat 27.8 g; Carbohydrates 12.1 g; Sugar 9.5 g; Protein 19 g; Cholesterol 69 mg

Meatballs

Preparation Time: 10 minutes; Cooking Time: 10 minutes; Serve: 4
Ingredients:
- 1 egg, lightly beaten
- 1 lb ground beef
- 1/4 cup onion, chopped
- 2 tbsp taco seasoning
- 1 tbsp garlic, minced
- 1/2 cup cheddar cheese, shredded
- 1/4 cup cilantro, chopped
- Pepper
- Salt

Directions:
1. Fit the Cuisinart oven with the rack in position 2.
2. Line the air fryer basket with parchment paper.
3. Add ground beef and remaining ingredients into the large bowl and mix until well combined.
4. Make small meatballs from meat mixture and place in the air fryer basket then place an air fryer basket in the baking pan.
5. Place a baking pan on the oven rack. Set to air fry at 400 F for 10 minutes.
6. Serve and enjoy.

Nutritional Value (Amount per Serving):
Calories 290; Fat 12.9 g; Carbohydrates 1.7 g; Sugar 0.5 g; Protein 39.5 g; Cholesterol 157 mg

Delicious Air Fryer Kebabs

Preparation Time: 10 minutes; Cooking Time: 15 minutes; Serve: 4
Ingredients:
- 1 lb ground beef
- 1/4 cup cilantro, chopped
- 1/2 cup onion, minced
- 1/4 tsp ground cinnamon
- 1/2 tsp turmeric
- 1 tbsp ginger garlic paste
- 1/4 tsp ground cardamom
- 1/2 tsp cayenne
- 1 tsp salt

Directions:
1. Fit the Cuisinart oven with the rack in position 2.
2. Add meat and remaining ingredients into the large bowl and mix until well combined.
3. Make sausage shape kebabs and place them in an air fryer basket then place an air fryer basket in the baking pan.
4. Place a baking pan on the oven rack. Set to air fry at 350 F for 15 minutes.
5. Serve and enjoy.

Nutritional Value (Amount per Serving):
Calories 219; Fat 7.2 g; Carbohydrates 1.9 g; Sugar 0.7 g; Protein 34.7 g; Cholesterol 101 mg

Tasty Steak Tips

Preparation Time: 10 minutes; Cooking Time: 5 minutes; Serve: 4
Ingredients:
- 1 lb steak, cut into cubes
- 1 tsp olive oil
- 1/4 tsp garlic powder
- 1 tsp Montreal steak seasoning
- Pepper
- Salt

Directions:
1. Fit the Cuisinart oven with the rack in position 2.
2. In a bowl, add steak cubes and remaining ingredients and toss well.

3. Add marinated steak cubes to the air fryer basket then place an air fryer basket in the baking pan.
4. Place a baking pan on the oven rack. Set to air fry at 400 F for 5 minutes.
5. Serve and enjoy.

Nutritional Value (Amount per Serving):
Calories 236; Fat 6.8 g; Carbohydrates 0.2 g; Sugar 0 g; Protein 41 g; Cholesterol 102 mg

Meatballs

Preparation Time: 10 minutes; Cooking Time: 20 minutes; Serve: 4

Ingredients:
- 1 lb ground beef
- 1/2 cup kale, chopped
- 2 garlic cloves, finely chopped
- 1/2 onion, finely chopped
- 4 oz mushrooms, finely chopped
- 3/4 cup cooked quinoa
- 2 tsp Italian seasoning
- 1/4 cup rolled oats
- 1 egg, lightly beaten
- Pepper
- Salt

Directions:
1. Fit the Cuisinart oven with the rack in position 2.
2. Line the air fryer basket with parchment paper.
3. Add all ingredients into a large bowl and mix until well combined.
4. Make small balls from meat mixture and place in the air fryer basket then place the air fryer basket in the baking pan.
5. Place a baking pan on the oven rack. Set to air fry at 380 F for 20 minutes.
6. Serve and enjoy.

Nutritional Value (Amount per Serving):
Calories 388; Fat 11.2 g; Carbohydrates 27.9 g; Sugar 1.4 g; Protein 42.4 g; Cholesterol 144 mg

Simple Burger Patties

Preparation Time: 10 minutes; Cooking Time: 8 minutes; Serve: 4

Ingredients:
- 1 lb ground beef
- 1/2 tsp garlic powder
- 1/4 tsp onion powder
- 1 tbsp soy sauce
- Pepper
- Salt

Directions:
1. Fit the Cuisinart oven with the rack in position 2.
2. Line the air fryer basket with parchment paper.
3. Add all ingredients into the mixing bowl and mix until well combined.
4. Make four equal shape patties from the meat mixture and place in the air fryer basket then place an air fryer basket in the baking pan.
5. Place a baking pan on the oven rack. Set to air fry at 375 F for 8 minutes.
6. Serve and enjoy.

Nutritional Value (Amount per Serving):
Calories 215; Fat 7.1 g; Carbohydrates 0.7 g; Sugar 0.2 g; Protein 34.7 g; Cholesterol 101 mg

Ranch Beef Patties

Preparation Time: 10 minutes; Cooking Time: 12 minutes; Serve: 4

Ingredients:
- 1 lb ground beef
- 1/2 tsp onion powder
- 1/2 tsp garlic powder
- 2 tsp dried parsley
- 1/8 tsp dried dill
- 1/2 tsp paprika

- 1/2 tsp dried dill
- Pepper
- Salt

Directions:
1. Fit the Cuisinart oven with the rack in position 2.
2. Line the air fryer basket with parchment paper.
3. Add all ingredients into the large bowl and mix until well combined.
4. Make four even shape patties from the meat mixture and place in the air fryer basket then place an air fryer basket in the baking pan.
5. Place a baking pan on the oven rack. Set to air fry at 350 F for 12 minutes.
6. Serve and enjoy.

Nutritional Value (Amount per Serving):
Calories 214; Fat 7.1 g; Carbohydrates 0.8 g; Sugar 0.2 g; Protein 34.6 g; Cholesterol 101 mg

Flavorful Sirloin Steak

Preparation Time: 10 minutes; Cooking Time: 14 minutes; Serve: 2

Ingredients:
- 1 lb sirloin steaks
- 1/2 tsp garlic powder
- 1/2 tsp onion powder
- 1/4 tsp smoked paprika
- 1 tsp olive oil
- Pepper
- Salt

Directions:
1. Fit the Cuisinart oven with the rack in position 2.
2. Line the air fryer basket with parchment paper.
3. Brush steak with olive oil and rub with garlic powder, onion powder, paprika, pepper, and salt.
4. Place the steak in the air fryer basket then places an air fryer basket in the baking pan.
5. Place a baking pan on the oven rack. Set to air fry at 400 F for 14 minutes.
6. Serve and enjoy.

Nutritional Value (Amount per Serving):
Calories 447; Fat 16.5 g; Carbohydrates 1.2 g; Sugar 0.4 g; Protein 69 g; Cholesterol 203 mg

Chapter 5: Fish & Seafood

Tender & Juicy Cajun Cod

Preparation Time: 10 minutes; Cooking Time: 15 minutes; Serve: 6
Ingredients:
- 3 cod fillets, cut in half
- 1 tbsp Cajun seasoning
- 1 tbsp garlic, minced
- 1 tbsp olive oil
- 1/4 cup butter, melted
- Pepper
- Salt

Directions:
1. Fit the Cuisinart oven with the rack in position 1.
2. Season fish fillets with pepper and salt and place in a 9*13-inch baking dish.
3. Mix together the remaining ingredients and pour over fish fillets.
4. Set to bake at 400 F for 20 minutes. After 5 minutes place the baking dish in the preheated oven.
5. Serve and enjoy.

Nutritional Value (Amount per Serving):
Calories 126; Fat 10.4 g; Carbohydrates 0.5 g; Sugar 0 g; Protein 8.2 g; Cholesterol 42 mg

Lemon Butter Shrimp

Preparation Time: 10 minutes; Cooking Time: 12 minutes; Serve: 4
Ingredients:
- 1 1/4 lbs shrimp, peeled & deveined
- 2 tbsp fresh parsley, chopped
- 2 tbsp fresh lemon juice
- 1 tbsp garlic, minced
- 1/4 cup butter
- Pepper
- Salt

Directions:
1. Fit the Cuisinart oven with the rack in position 1.
2. Add shrimp into the baking dish.
3. Melt butter in a pan over low heat. Add garlic and sauté for 30 seconds. Stir in lemon juice.
4. Pour melted butter mixture over shrimp. Season with pepper and salt.
5. Set to bake at 350 F for 17 minutes. After 5 minutes place the baking dish in the preheated oven.
6. Garnish with parsley and serve.

Nutritional Value (Amount per Serving):
Calories 276; Fat 14 g; Carbohydrates 3.2 g; Sugar 0.2 g; Protein 32.7 g; Cholesterol 329 mg

Spicy Lemon Garlic Tilapia

Preparation Time: 10 minutes; Cooking Time: 15 minutes; Serve: 2
Ingredients:
- 4 tilapia fillets
- 1 lemon, cut into slices
- 1/2 tsp pepper
- 1/2 tsp chili powder
- 1 tsp garlic, minced
- 3 tbsp butter, melted
- 1 tbsp fresh lemon juice
- Salt

Directions:
1. Fit the Cuisinart oven with the rack in position 1.
2. Place fish fillets into the baking dish.
3. Arrange lemon slices on top of fish fillets.
4. Mix together the remaining ingredients and pour over fish fillets.

5. Set to bake at 350 F for 20 minutes. After 5 minutes place the baking dish in the preheated oven.
   6. Serve and enjoy.

Nutritional Value (Amount per Serving):
Calories 354; Fat 19.6 g; Carbohydrates 4 g; Sugar 1 g; Protein 42.8 g; Cholesterol 156 mg

Cajun Red Snapper

Preparation Time: 10 minutes; Cooking Time: 12 minutes; Serve: 2
Ingredients:
- 8 oz red snapper fillets
- 2 tbsp parmesan cheese, grated
- 1/4 cup breadcrumbs
- 1/2 tsp Cajun seasoning
- 1/4 tsp Worcestershire sauce
- 1 garlic clove, minced
- 1/4 cup butter

Directions:
1. Fit the Cuisinart oven with the rack in position 1.
2. Melt butter in a pan over low heat. Add Cajun seasoning, garlic, and Worcestershire sauce into the melted butter and stir well.
3. Brush fish fillets with melted butter and place into the baking dish.
4. Mix together parmesan cheese and breadcrumbs and sprinkle over fish fillets.
5. Set to bake at 400 F for 17 minutes. After 5 minutes place the baking dish in the preheated oven.
6. Serve and enjoy.

Nutritional Value (Amount per Serving):
Calories 424; Fat 27 g; Carbohydrates 10.6 g; Sugar 1 g; Protein 33.9 g; Cholesterol 119 mg

Perfect Baked Cod

Preparation Time: 10 minutes; Cooking Time: 15 minutes; Serve: 4
Ingredients:
- 4 cod fillets
- 1 tbsp olive oil
- 1 tsp dried parsley
- 2 tsp paprika
- 3/4 cup parmesan cheese, grated
- 1/4 tsp salt

Directions:
1. Fit the Cuisinart oven with the rack in position 1.
2. In a shallow dish, mix parmesan cheese, paprika, parsley, and salt.
3. Brush fish fillets with oil and coat with parmesan cheese mixture.
4. Place coated fish fillets into the baking dish.
5. Set to bake at 400 F for 20 minutes. After 5 minutes place the baking dish in the preheated oven.
6. Serve and enjoy.

Nutritional Value (Amount per Serving):
Calories 160; Fat 8.1 g; Carbohydrates 1.2 g; Sugar 0.1 g; Protein 21.7 g; Cholesterol 56 mg

Flavorful Baked Halibut

Preparation Time: 10 minutes; Cooking Time: 12 minutes; Serve: 4
Ingredients:
- 1 lb halibut fillets
- 1/4 tsp garlic powder
- 1/4 tsp paprika
- 1/4 tsp smoked paprika
- 1/4 tsp pepper
- 1/4 cup olive oil
- 1 lemon juice
- 1/2 tsp salt

Directions:

1. Fit the Cuisinart oven with the rack in position 1.
2. Place fish fillets into the baking dish.
3. In a small bowl, mix lemon juice, oil, paprika, smoked paprika, garlic powder, and salt.
4. Brush lemon juice mixture over fish fillets.
5. Set to bake at 425 F for 17 minutes. After 5 minutes place the baking dish in the preheated oven.
6. Serve and enjoy.

Nutritional Value (Amount per Serving):
Calories 236; Fat 15.3 g; Carbohydrates 0.4 g; Sugar 0.1 g; Protein 24 g; Cholesterol 36 mg

Healthy Haddock

Preparation Time: 10 minutes; Cooking Time: 25 minutes; Serve: 2

Ingredients:
- 1 lb haddock fillets
- 1/4 cup parsley, chopped
- 1 lemon juice
- 1/4 cup brown sugar
- 1/4 cup onion, diced
- 1 tsp ginger, grated
- 3/4 cup soy sauce
- Pepper
- Salt

Directions:
1. Fit the Cuisinart oven with the rack in position 1.
2. Add fish fillets and remaining ingredients into the large bowl and coat well and place in the refrigerator for 1 hour.
3. Place marinated fish fillets into the baking dish.
4. Set to bake at 325 F for 30 minutes. After 5 minutes place the baking dish in the preheated oven.
5. Serve and enjoy.

Nutritional Value (Amount per Serving):
Calories 391; Fat 2.5 g; Carbohydrates 28 g; Sugar 20.4 g; Protein 61.7 g; Cholesterol 168 mg

Delicious Baked Basa

Preparation Time: 10 minutes; Cooking Time: 10 minutes; Serve: 4

Ingredients:
- 4 basa fish fillets
- 1/4 cup green onion, sliced
- 1/2 tsp garlic powder
- 1/4 tsp lemon pepper seasoning
- 4 tbsp fresh lemon juice
- 8 tsp butter, melted
- Salt

Directions:
1. Fit the Cuisinart oven with the rack in position 1.
2. Place fish fillets into the baking dish.
3. Pour remaining ingredients over fish fillets.
4. Set to bake at 425 F for 15 minutes. After 5 minutes place the baking dish in the preheated oven.
5. Serve and enjoy.

Nutritional Value (Amount per Serving):
Calories 214; Fat 15.3 g; Carbohydrates 3.8 g; Sugar 2.3 g; Protein 15.4 g; Cholesterol 20 mg

Baked Pesto Salmon

Preparation Time: 10 minutes; Cooking Time: 15 minutes; Serve: 4

Ingredients:
- 4 salmon fillets
- 1/3 cup parmesan cheese, grated

- 1/3 cup breadcrumbs
- 6 tbsp pesto

Directions:
1. Fit the Cuisinart oven with the rack in position 1.
2. Place fish fillets into the baking dish.
3. Pour pesto over fish fillets.
4. Mix together breadcrumbs and parmesan cheese and sprinkle over fish.
5. Set to bake at 325 F for 20 minutes. After 5 minutes place the baking dish in the preheated oven.
6. Serve and enjoy.

Nutritional Value (Amount per Serving):
Calories 396; Fat 22.8 g; Carbohydrates 8.3 g; Sugar 2.1 g; Protein 40.4 g; Cholesterol 89 mg

Paprika Basil Baked Basa

Preparation Time: 10 minutes; Cooking Time: 30 minutes; Serve: 2

Ingredients:
- 2 basa fish fillets
- 4 lemon slices
- 1/8 tsp lemon juice
- 1/2 tbsp dried basil
- 1/2 tbsp sweet paprika
- 4 tbsp butter, melted
- 1/8 tsp salt

Directions:
1. Fit the Cuisinart oven with the rack in position 1.
2. Place fish fillets into the baking dish.
3. Pour remaining ingredients over fish fillets.
4. Set to bake at 350 F for 30 minutes. After 5 minutes place the baking dish in the preheated oven.
5. Serve and enjoy.

Nutritional Value (Amount per Serving):
Calories 433; Fat 35.2 g; Carbohydrates 6.5 g; Sugar 3.4 g; Protein 24.4 g; Cholesterol 61 mg

Delicious Shrimp Casserole

Preparation Time: 10 minutes; Cooking Time: 30 minutes; Serve: 10

Ingredients:
- 1 lb shrimp, peeled & tail off
- 2 tsp onion powder
- 2 tsp old bay seasoning
- 2 cups cheddar cheese, shredded
- 10.5 oz can cream of mushroom soup
- 12 oz long-grain rice
- 1 tsp salt

Directions:
1. Fit the Cuisinart oven with the rack in position 1.
2. Cook rice according to the packet instructions.
3. Add shrimp into the boiling water and cook for 4 minutes or until cooked. Drain shrimp.
4. In a bowl, mix rice, shrimp, and remaining ingredients and pour into the greased 13*9-inch casserole dish.
5. Set to bake at 350 F for 35 minutes. After 5 minutes place the casserole dish in the preheated oven.
6. Serve and enjoy.

Nutritional Value (Amount per Serving):
Calories 286; Fat 9 g; Carbohydrates 31 g; Sugar 1 g; Protein 18.8 g; Cholesterol 120 mg

Easy Blackened Shrimp

Preparation Time: 10 minutes; Cooking Time: 10 minutes; Serve: 6

Ingredients:
- 1 lb shrimp, deveined
- 1 tbsp olive oil
- 1/4 tsp pepper
- 2 tsp blackened seasoning
- 1/4 tsp salt

Directions:
1. Fit the Cuisinart oven with the rack in position 1.
2. Toss shrimp with oil, pepper, blackened seasoning, and salt.
3. Transfer shrimp into the baking pan.
4. Set to bake at 400 F for 15 minutes. After 5 minutes place the baking pan in the preheated oven.
5. Serve and enjoy.

Nutritional Value (Amount per Serving):
Calories 167; Fat 4.3 g; Carbohydrates 10.5 g; Sugar 0 g; Protein 20.6 g; Cholesterol 159 mg

Old Bay Shrimp

Preparation Time: 10 minutes; Cooking Time: 10 minutes; Serve: 4

Ingredients:
- 1 lb shrimp, deveined
- 1 1/2 tsp old bay seasoning
- 2 garlic cloves, minced
- 1 tbsp olive oil

Directions:
1. Fit the Cuisinart oven with the rack in position 1.
2. Toss shrimp with oil, garlic, and old bay seasoning.
3. Transfer shrimp into the baking pan.
4. Set to bake at 400 F for 15 minutes. After 5 minutes place the baking pan in the preheated oven.
5. Serve and enjoy.

Nutritional Value (Amount per Serving):
Calories 167; Fat 5.4 g; Carbohydrates 2.2 g; Sugar 0 g; Protein 25.9 g; Cholesterol 239 mg

Spicy Baked Shrimp

Preparation Time: 10 minutes; Cooking Time: 8 minutes; Serve: 4

Ingredients:
- 2 lbs shrimp, peeled & deveined
- 1/4 tsp cayenne pepper
- 1 tsp garlic powder
- 2 tbsp chili powder
- 2 tbsp olive oil
- 1 tsp kosher salt

Directions:
1. Fit the Cuisinart oven with the rack in position 1.
2. Toss shrimp with remaining ingredients.
3. Transfer shrimp into the baking pan.
4. Set to bake at 400 F for 13 minutes. After 5 minutes place the baking pan in the preheated oven.
5. Serve and enjoy.

Nutritional Value (Amount per Serving):
Calories 344; Fat 11.5 g; Carbohydrates 6.1 g; Sugar 0.5 g; Protein 52.3 g; Cholesterol 478 mg

Baked Scallops

Preparation Time: 10 minutes; Cooking Time: 15 minutes; Serve: 4

Ingredients:
- 1 lb scallops, frozen & thawed
- 1 tbsp garlic, grated
- 1/2 cup butter, melted
- 1 lemon, cut into wedges

- 1 tbsp olive oil
- Pepper
- Salt

Directions:
1. Fit the Cuisinart oven with the rack in position 1.
2. Add scallops and lemon into the baking dish and spread well.
3. Mix melted butter, oil, garlic, pepper, and salt and pour over scallops.
4. Set to bake at 400 F for 20 minutes. After 5 minutes place the baking dish in the preheated oven.
5. Serve and enjoy.

Nutritional Value (Amount per Serving):
Calories 341; Fat 27.4 g; Carbohydrates 4.8 g; Sugar 0.4 g; Protein 19.6 g; Cholesterol 98 mg

Blackened Mahi Mahi

Preparation Time: 10 minutes; Cooking Time: 12 minutes; Serve: 4
Ingredients:
- 4 mahi-mahi fillets
- 1 tsp cumin
- 1 tsp paprika
- 1/2 tsp cayenne pepper
- 1 tsp oregano
- 1 tsp garlic powder
- 1 tsp onion powder
- 1/2 tsp pepper
- 3 tbsp olive oil
- 1/2 tsp salt

Directions:
1. Fit the Cuisinart oven with the rack in position 1.
2. Brush fish fillets with oil and place them into the baking dish.
3. Mix together the remaining ingredients and sprinkle over fish fillets.
4. Set to bake at 450 F for 17 minutes. After 5 minutes place the baking dish in the preheated oven.
5. Serve and enjoy.

Nutritional Value (Amount per Serving):
Calories 189; Fat 11.7 g; Carbohydrates 2.1 g; Sugar 0.5 g; Protein 19.4 g; Cholesterol 86 mg

Herb Baked Catfish Fillets

Preparation Time: 10 minutes; Cooking Time: 20 minutes; Serve: 4
Ingredients:
- 4 catfish fillets
- 1/2 tsp garlic powder
- 2 tbsp butter, melted
- 1 lemon juice
- 1/2 tsp pepper
- 1/2 tsp dried basil
- 1/2 tsp dried thyme
- 3/4 tsp paprika
- 1/2 tsp dried oregano
- 1 tsp salt

Directions:
1. Fit the Cuisinart oven with the rack in position 1.
2. Place fish fillets into the baking pan.
3. Mix together garlic powder, pepper, basil, oregano, thyme, paprika, and salt and sprinkle over fish fillets.
4. Pour lemon juice and melted butter over fish fillets.
5. Set to bake at 350 F for 25 minutes. After 5 minutes place the baking pan in the preheated oven.
6. Serve and enjoy.

Nutritional Value (Amount per Serving):
Calories 274; Fat 18.1 g; Carbohydrates 1.1 g; Sugar 0.4 g; Protein 25.2 g; Cholesterol 90 mg

Moist & Juicy Baked Cod

Preparation Time: 10 minutes; Cooking Time: 10 minutes; Serve: 2

Ingredients:
- 1 lb cod fillets
- 1 1/2 tbsp olive oil
- 3 dashes cayenne pepper
- 1 tbsp fresh lemon juice
- 1/4 tsp salt

Directions:
1. Fit the Cuisinart oven with the rack in position 1.
2. Place fish fillets in a baking pan.
3. Drizzle with oil and lemon juice and sprinkle with cayenne pepper and salt.
4. Set to bake at 400 F for 15 minutes. After 5 minutes place the baking pan in the preheated oven.
5. Serve and enjoy.

Nutritional Value (Amount per Serving):
Calories 275; Fat 12.7 g; Carbohydrates 0.4 g; Sugar 0.2 g; Protein 40.6 g; Cholesterol 111 mg

Parmesan Salmon & Asparagus

Preparation Time: 10 minutes; Cooking Time: 20 minutes; Serve: 4

Ingredients:
- 4 salmon fillets
- 1 cup parmesan cheese, shredded
- 1 tbsp garlic, minced
- 3 tbsp olive oil
- 1 lb asparagus, ends trimmed
- 1/4 tsp pepper
- 1/4 tsp salt

Directions:
1. Fit the Cuisinart oven with the rack in position 1.
2. Place fish fillets and asparagus in a parchment-lined baking pan.
3. Brush fish fillets with olive oil. Season with pepper and salt.
4. Sprinkle with garlic and shredded parmesan cheese on top.
5. Set to bake at 400 F for 25 minutes. After 5 minutes place the baking pan in the preheated oven.
6. Serve and enjoy.

Nutritional Value (Amount per Serving):
Calories 424; Fat 26.5 g; Carbohydrates 6 g; Sugar 2.2 g; Protein 44.4 g; Cholesterol 95 mg

Baked Spinach Tilapia

Preparation Time: 10 minutes; Cooking Time: 10 minutes; Serve: 4

Ingredients:
- 1 lb tilapia fillets
- 1 cup Monterey jack cheese, shredded
- 3 tbsp butter, sliced
- 8 oz spinach

Directions:
1. Fit the Cuisinart oven with the rack in position 1.
2. Add spinach into the baking dish and top with butter slices.
3. Place fish fillets on top of spinach.
4. Sprinkle shredded cheese over fish fillets.
5. Set to bake at 450 F for 15 minutes. After 5 minutes place the baking dish in the preheated oven.
6. Serve and enjoy.

Nutritional Value (Amount per Serving):
Calories 288; Fat 18.4 g; Carbohydrates 2.3 g; Sugar 0.4 g; Protein 29.7 g; Cholesterol 103 mg

Paprika Cod

Preparation Time: 10 minutes; Cooking Time: 15 minutes; Serve: 4

Ingredients:
- 4 cod fillets
- 1 tsp smoked paprika
- 1/2 cup parmesan cheese, grated
- 1/2 tbsp olive oil
- 1 tsp parsley
- Pepper
- Salt

Directions:
1. Fit the Cuisinart oven with the rack in position 1.
2. Brush fish fillets with oil and season with pepper and salt.
3. In a shallow dish, mix parmesan cheese, paprika, and parsley.
4. Coat fish fillets with cheese mixture and place into the baking dish.
5. Set to bake at 400 F for 20 minutes. After 5 minutes place the baking dish in the preheated oven.
6. Serve and enjoy.

Nutritional Value (Amount per Serving):
Calories 125; Fat 5 g; Carbohydrates 0.7 g; Sugar 0.1 g; Protein 19.8 g; Cholesterol 52 mg

Salmon Beans & Mushrooms

Preparation Time: 10 minutes; Cooking Time: 25 minutes; Serve: 6

Ingredients:
- 4 salmon fillets
- 2 tbsp fresh parsley, minced
- 1/4 cup fresh lemon juice
- 1 tsp garlic, minced
- 1 tbsp olive oil
- 1/2 lb mushrooms, sliced
- 1/2 lb green beans, trimmed
- 1/2 cup parmesan cheese, grated
- Pepper
- Salt

Directions:
1. Fit the Cuisinart oven with the rack in position 1.
2. Heat oil in a small saucepan over medium-high heat.
3. Add garlic and sauté for 30 seconds.
4. Remove from heat and stir in lemon juice, parsley, pepper, and salt.
5. Arrange fish fillets, mushrooms, and green beans in baking pan and drizzle with oil mixture.
6. Sprinkle with grated parmesan cheese.
7. Set to bake at 400 F for 30 minutes. After 5 minutes place the baking pan in the preheated oven.
8. Serve and enjoy.

Nutritional Value (Amount per Serving):
Calories 225; Fat 11.5 g; Carbohydrates 4.7 g; Sugar 1.4 g; Protein 27.5 g; Cholesterol 58 mg

Baked Tilapia

Preparation Time: 10 minutes; Cooking Time: 10 minutes; Serve: 4

Ingredients:
- 1 1/4 lbs tilapia fillets
- 2 tsp onion powder
- 2 tbsp olive oil
- 1/2 tsp garlic powder
- 1/2 tsp dried thyme
- 1/2 tsp oregano
- 1/2 tsp chili powder
- 2 tbsp sweet paprika
- 1 tsp pepper
- 1/2 tsp salt

Directions:
1. Fit the Cuisinart oven with the rack in position 1.

2. Brush fish fillets with oil and place in baking dish.
3. Mix together spices and sprinkle over the fish fillets.
4. Set to bake at 425 F for 15 minutes. After 5 minutes place the baking dish in the preheated oven.
5. Serve and enjoy.

Nutritional Value (Amount per Serving):
Calories 195; Fat 8.9 g; Carbohydrates 3.9 g; Sugar 0.9 g; Protein 27.2 g; Cholesterol 69 mg

Easy Baked Fish Fillet

Preparation Time: 10 minutes; Cooking Time: 15 minutes; Serve: 4

Ingredients:
- 1 lb white fish fillets
- 2 tbsp dried parsley
- 1/4 tsp red chili flakes
- 2 tbsp garlic, minced
- 2 tbsp olive oil
- Pepper
- Salt

Directions:
1. Fit the Cuisinart oven with the rack in position 1.
2. Place fish fillets in a baking dish and drizzle with oil.
3. Sprinkle with chili flakes, parsley, and garlic. Season with pepper and salt.
4. Set to bake at 400 F for 20 minutes. After 5 minutes place the baking dish in the preheated oven.
5. Serve and enjoy.

Nutritional Value (Amount per Serving):
Calories 262; Fat 15.6 g; Carbohydrates 1.5 g; Sugar 0.1 g; Protein 28.1 g; Cholesterol 87 mg

Italian Salmon

Preparation Time: 10 minutes; Cooking Time: 20 minutes; Serve: 4

Ingredients:
- 1 3/4 lbs salmon fillet
- 1/4 cup sun-dried tomatoes, drained
- 1 tbsp fresh dill, chopped
- 1/4 cup capers
- 1/4 cup olives, pitted and chopped
- 1/3 cup basil pesto
- 1/3 cup artichoke hearts
- 1 tsp paprika
- 1/4 tsp salt

Directions:
1. Fit the Cuisinart oven with the rack in position 1.
2. Arrange salmon fillet in a baking pan and season with paprika and salt.
3. Pour remaining ingredients on top of salmon.
4. Set to bake at 400 F for 25 minutes. After 5 minutes place the baking pan in the preheated oven.
5. Serve and enjoy.

Nutritional Value (Amount per Serving):
Calories 286; Fat 13.4 g; Carbohydrates 3.6 g; Sugar 0.5 g; Protein 39.6 g; Cholesterol 88 mg

Flavorful Herb Salmon

Preparation Time: 10 minutes; Cooking Time: 15 minutes; Serve: 4

Ingredients:
- 1 lb salmon fillets
- 1/2 tbsp dried rosemary
- 1 tbsp olive oil
- 1/4 tsp dried basil
- 1 tbsp dried chives
- 1/4 tsp dried thyme
- Pepper
- Salt

Directions:
1. Fit the Cuisinart oven with the rack in position 2.
2. Place salmon skin side down in air fryer basket then place an air fryer basket in baking pan.
3. Mix olive oil, thyme, basil, chives, and rosemary in a small bowl.
4. Brush salmon with oil mixture.
5. Place a baking pan on the oven rack. Set to air fry at 400 F for 15 minutes.
6. Serve and enjoy.

Nutritional Value (Amount per Serving):
Calories 182; Fat 10.6 g; Carbohydrates 0.4 g; Sugar 0 g; Protein 22.1 g; Cholesterol 50 mg

Spicy Halibut

Preparation Time: 10 minutes; Cooking Time: 12 minutes; Serve: 4

Ingredients:
- 1 lb halibut fillets
- 1/2 tsp chili powder
- 1/2 tsp smoked paprika
- 1/4 cup olive oil
- 1/4 tsp garlic powder
- Pepper
- Salt

Directions:
1. Fit the Cuisinart oven with the rack in position 1.
2. Place halibut fillets in a baking dish.
3. In a small bowl, mix oil, garlic powder, paprika, pepper, chili powder, and salt.
4. Brush fish fillets with oil mixture.
5. Set to bake at 425 F for 17 minutes. After 5 minutes place the baking dish in the preheated oven.
6. Serve and enjoy.

Nutritional Value (Amount per Serving):
Calories 236; Fat 15.3 g; Carbohydrates 0.5 g; Sugar 0.1 g; Protein 24 g; Cholesterol 36 mg

Air Fryer Spicy Shrimp

Preparation Time: 10 minutes; Cooking Time: 6 minutes; Serve: 4

Ingredients:
- 1 lb shrimp, peeled and deveined
- 1/4 tsp chili powder
- 1 tsp dried oregano
- 1 tsp garlic powder
- 1 tsp onion powder
- 2 tsp paprika
- 1/4 tsp cayenne
- 2 tbsp olive oil
- Pepper
- Salt

Directions:
1. Fit the Cuisinart oven with the rack in position 2.
2. In a bowl, toss shrimp with remaining ingredients.
3. Add shrimp to the air fryer basket then place an air fryer basket in the baking pan.
4. Place a baking pan on the oven rack. Set to air fry at 400 F for 6 minutes.
5. Serve and enjoy.

Nutritional Value (Amount per Serving):
Calories 204; Fat 9.2 g; Carbohydrates 3.7 g; Sugar 0.5 g; Protein 26.2 g; Cholesterol 239 mg

Thyme Rosemary Shrimp

Preparation Time: 10 minutes; Cooking Time: 10 minutes; Serve: 4

Ingredients:
- 1 lb shrimp, peeled and deveined
- 1/2 tbsp fresh rosemary, chopped

- 1 tbsp olive oil
- 2 garlic cloves, minced
- 1/2 tbsp fresh thyme, chopped
- Pepper
- Salt

Directions:
1. Fit the Cuisinart oven with the rack in position 1.
2. Add shrimp and remaining ingredients in a large bowl and toss well.
3. Pour shrimp mixture into the baking dish.
4. Set to bake at 400 F for 15 minutes. After 5 minutes place the baking dish in the preheated oven.
5. Serve and enjoy.

Nutritional Value (Amount per Serving):
Calories 169; Fat 5.5 g; Carbohydrates 2.7 g; Sugar 0 g; Protein 26 g; Cholesterol 239 mg

Easy Shrimp Fajitas

Preparation Time: 10 minutes; Cooking Time: 20 minutes; Serve: 10
Ingredients:
- 1 lb shrimp
- 1 tbsp olive oil
- 2 bell peppers, diced
- 2 tbsp taco seasoning
- 1/2 cup onion, diced

Directions:
1. Fit the Cuisinart oven with the rack in position 2.
2. Add shrimp and remaining ingredients into the bowl and toss well.
3. Add shrimp mixture to the air fryer basket then place an air fryer basket in baking pan.
4. Place a baking pan on the oven rack. Set to air fry at 390 F for 20 minutes.
5. Serve and enjoy.

Nutritional Value (Amount per Serving):
Calories 76; Fat 2.2 g; Carbohydrates 3 g; Sugar 1.4 g; Protein 10.6 g; Cholesterol 96 mg

Tasty Lemon Pepper Basa

Preparation Time: 10 minutes; Cooking Time: 12 minutes; Serve: 4
Ingredients:
- 4 basa fish fillets
- 8 tsp olive oil
- 2 tbsp fresh parsley, chopped
- 1/4 cup green onion, sliced
- 1/2 tsp garlic powder
- 1/4 tsp lemon pepper seasoning
- 4 tbsp fresh lemon juice
- Pepper
- Salt

Directions:
1. Fit the Cuisinart oven with the rack in position 1.
2. Place fish fillets in a baking dish.
3. Pour remaining ingredients over fish fillets.
4. Set to bake at 425 F for 12 minutes. After 5 minutes place the baking dish in the preheated oven.
5. Serve and enjoy.

Nutritional Value (Amount per Serving):
Calories 308; Fat 21.4 g; Carbohydrates 5.5 g; Sugar 3.4 g; Protein 24.1 g; Cholesterol 0 mg

Baked Buttery Shrimp

Preparation Time: 10 minutes; Cooking Time: 15 minutes; Serve: 4
Ingredients:
- 1 lb shrimp, peel & deveined
- 2 tsp garlic powder

- 2 tsp dry mustard
- 2 tsp cumin
- 2 tsp paprika
- 2 tsp black pepper
- 4 tsp cayenne pepper
- 1/2 cup butter, melted
- 2 tsp onion powder
- 1 tsp dried oregano
- 1 tsp dried thyme
- 3 tsp salt

Directions:
1. Fit the Cuisinart oven with the rack in position 1.
2. Add shrimp, butter, and remaining ingredients into the mixing bowl and toss well.
3. Transfer shrimp mixture into the baking pan.
4. Set to bake at 400 F for 20 minutes. After 5 minutes place the baking pan in the preheated oven.
5. Serve and enjoy.

Nutritional Value (Amount per Serving):
Calories 372; Fat 26.2 g; Carbohydrates 7.5 g; Sugar 1.3 g; Protein 27.6 g; Cholesterol 300 mg

Orange Fish Fillets

Preparation Time: 10 minutes; Cooking Time: 25 minutes; Serve: 2

Ingredients:
- 1 lb salmon fillets
- 1 orange juice
- 1 orange zest, grated
- 2 tbsp honey
- 3 tbsp soy sauce

Directions:
1. Fit the Cuisinart oven with the rack in position 1.
2. In a small bowl, whisk together honey, soy sauce, orange juice, and orange zest.
3. Place salmon fillets in a baking dish and pour honey mixture over salmon fillets.
4. Set to bake at 425 F for 30 minutes. After 5 minutes place the baking dish in the preheated oven.
5. Serve and enjoy.

Nutritional Value (Amount per Serving):
Calories 399; Fat 14.1 g; Carbohydrates 24.4 g; Sugar 21.3 g; Protein 45.9 g; Cholesterol 100 mg

Baked Garlic Paprika Halibut

Preparation Time: 10 minutes; Cooking Time: 12 minutes; Serve: 4

Ingredients:
- 1 lb halibut fillets
- 1/2 tsp smoked paprika
- 1/4 cup olive oil
- 1/4 tsp garlic powder
- Pepper
- Salt

Directions:
1. Fit the Cuisinart oven with the rack in position 1.
2. Place fish fillets in a baking dish.
3. In a small bowl, mix together oil, garlic powder, paprika, pepper, and salt.
4. Brush fish fillets with oil mixture.
5. Set to bake at 425 F for 17 minutes. After 5 minutes place the baking dish in the preheated oven.
6. Serve and enjoy.

Nutritional Value (Amount per Serving):
Calories 235; Fat 15.3 g; Carbohydrates 0.3 g; Sugar 0.1 g; Protein 23.9 g; Cholesterol 36 mg

Spicy Catfish

Preparation Time: 10 minutes; Cooking Time: 15 minutes; Serve: 4

Ingredients:
- 1 lb catfish fillets, cut 1/2-inch thick
- 1 tsp crushed red pepper
- 2 tsp onion powder
- 1 tbsp dried oregano, crushed
- 1/2 tsp ground cumin
- 1/2 tsp chili powder
- Pepper
- Salt

Directions:
1. Fit the Cuisinart oven with the rack in position 1.
2. In a small bowl, mix cumin, chili powder, crushed red pepper, onion powder, oregano, pepper, and salt.
3. Rub fish fillets with the spice mixture and place in baking dish.
4. Set to bake at 350 F for 20 minutes. After 5 minutes place the baking dish in the preheated oven.
5. Serve and enjoy.

Nutritional Value (Amount per Serving):
Calories 164; Fat 8.9 g; Carbohydrates 2.3 g; Sugar 0.6 g; Protein 18 g; Cholesterol 53 mg

Baked Lemon Swordfish

Preparation Time: 10 minutes; Cooking Time: 10 minutes; Serve: 2

Ingredients:
- 12 oz swordfish fillets
- 1/8 tsp crushed red pepper
- 1 garlic clove, minced
- 2 tsp fresh parsley, chopped
- 3 tbsp olive oil
- 1/2 tsp lemon zest, grated
- 1/2 tsp ginger, grated

Directions:
1. Fit the Cuisinart oven with the rack in position 1.
2. In a small bowl, mix 2 tbsp oil, lemon zest, red pepper, ginger, garlic, and parsley.
3. Season fish fillets with salt.
4. Heat remaining oil in a pan over medium-high heat.
5. Place fish fillets in the pan and cook until browned, about 2-3 minutes.
6. Transfer fish fillets in a baking dish.
7. Set to bake at 400 F for 15 minutes. After 5 minutes place the baking dish in the preheated oven.
8. Pour oil mixture over fish fillets and serve.

Nutritional Value (Amount per Serving):
Calories 449; Fat 29.8 g; Carbohydrates 1.1 g; Sugar 0.1 g; Protein 43.4 g; Cholesterol 85 mg

Baked Garlic Tilapia

Preparation Time: 10 minutes; Cooking Time: 15 minutes; Serve: 4

Ingredients:
- 1 lb tilapia fillets
- 2 tbsp garlic, minced
- 2 tbsp olive oil
- 2 tbsp dried parsley
- Pepper
- Salt

Directions:
1. Fit the Cuisinart oven with the rack in position 1.
2. Place fish fillets in a baking dish. Drizzle with oil and season with pepper and salt.
3. Sprinkle garlic and parsley over fish fillets.
4. Set to bake at 400 F for 20 minutes. After 5 minutes place the baking dish in the preheated oven.
5. Serve and enjoy.

Nutritional Value (Amount per Serving):

Calories 160; Fat 8.1 g; Carbohydrates 1.5 g; Sugar 0.1 g; Protein 21.4 g; Cholesterol 55 mg

Sweet & Spicy Lime Salmon

Preparation Time: 10 minutes; Cooking Time: 15 minutes; Serve: 6

Ingredients:
- 1 1/2 lbs salmon fillets
- 3 tbsp brown sugar
- 2 tbsp fresh lime juice
- 1/3 cup olive oil
- 1/2 tsp red pepper flakes
- 2 garlic cloves, minced
- Pepper
- Salt

Directions:
1. Fit the Cuisinart oven with the rack in position 1.
2. Place salmon on a prepared baking sheet and season with pepper and salt.
3. In a small bowl, whisk oil, red pepper flakes, garlic, brown sugar, and lime juice.
4. Pour oil mixture over salmon.
5. Set to bake at 350 F for 20 minutes. After 5 minutes place the baking dish in the preheated oven.
6. Serve and enjoy.

Nutritional Value (Amount per Serving):
Calories 269; Fat 18.3 g; Carbohydrates 6.1 g; Sugar 4.7 g; Protein 22.2 g; Cholesterol 50 mg

Spicy Lemon Cod

Preparation Time: 10 minutes; Cooking Time: 10 minutes; Serve: 2

Ingredients:
- 1 lb cod fillets
- 1/4 tsp chili powder
- 1 tbsp fresh parsley, chopped
- 1 1/2 tbsp olive oil
- 1 tbsp fresh lemon juice
- 1/8 tsp cayenne pepper
- 1/4 tsp salt

Directions:
1. Fit the Cuisinart oven with the rack in position 1.
2. Arrange fish fillets in a baking dish. Drizzle with oil and lemon juice.
3. Sprinkle with chili powder, salt, and cayenne pepper.
4. Set to bake at 400 F for 15 minutes. After 5 minutes place the baking dish in the preheated oven.
5. Garnish with parsley and serve.

Nutritional Value (Amount per Serving):
Calories 276; Fat 12.7 g; Carbohydrates 0.5 g; Sugar 0.2 g; Protein 40.7 g; Cholesterol 111 mg

Rosemary Garlic Shrimp

Preparation Time: 10 minutes; Cooking Time: 10 minutes; Serve: 4

Ingredients:
- 1 lb shrimp, peeled and deveined
- 2 garlic cloves, minced
- 1/2 tbsp fresh rosemary, chopped
- 1 tbsp olive oil
- Pepper
- Salt

Directions:
1. Fit the Cuisinart oven with the rack in position 1.
2. Add shrimp and remaining ingredients in a large bowl and toss well.
3. Pour shrimp mixture into the baking dish.
4. Set to bake at 400 F for 15 minutes. After 5 minutes place the baking dish in the preheated oven.
5. Serve and enjoy.

Nutritional Value (Amount per Serving):
Calories 168; Fat 5.5 g; Carbohydrates 2.5 g; Sugar 0 g; Protein 26 g; Cholesterol 239 mg

Tomato Garlic Shrimp

Preparation Time: 10 minutes; Cooking Time: 25 minutes; Serve: 4
Ingredients:
- 1 lb shrimp, peeled
- 1 tbsp garlic, sliced
- 2 cups cherry tomatoes
- 1 tbsp olive oil
- Pepper
- Salt

Directions:
1. Fit the Cuisinart oven with the rack in position 1.
2. Add shrimp, oil, garlic, tomatoes, pepper, and salt into the large bowl and toss well.
3. Transfer shrimp mixture into the baking dish.
4. Set to bake at 400 F for 30 minutes. After 5 minutes place the baking dish in the preheated oven.
5. Serve and enjoy.

Nutritional Value (Amount per Serving):
Calories 184; Fat 5.6 g; Carbohydrates 5.9 g; Sugar 2.4 g; Protein 26.8 g; Cholesterol 239 mg

Delicious Crab Cakes

Preparation Time: 10 minutes; Cooking Time: 10 minutes; Serve: 5
Ingredients:
- 18 oz can crab meat, drained
- 2 1/2 tbsp mayonnaise
- 2 eggs, lightly beaten
- 1/4 cup breadcrumbs
- 1 1/2 tsp dried parsley
- 1 tbsp dried celery
- 1 tsp Old bay seasoning
- 1 1/2 tbsp Dijon mustard
- Pepper
- Salt

Directions:
1. Fit the Cuisinart oven with the rack in position 2.
2. Add all ingredients into the mixing bowl and mix until well combined.
3. Make patties from mixture and place in the air fryer basket then place an air fryer basket in the baking pan.
4. Place a baking pan on the oven rack. Set to air fry at 320 F for 10 minutes.
5. Serve and enjoy.

Nutritional Value (Amount per Serving):
Calories 138; Fat 4.7 g; Carbohydrates 7.8 g; Sugar 2.7 g; Protein 16.8 g; Cholesterol 127 mg

Quick Tuna Patties

Preparation Time: 10 minutes; Cooking Time: 10 minutes; Serve: 10
Ingredients:
- 15 oz can tuna, drained and flaked
- 3 tbsp parmesan cheese, grated
- 1/2 cup breadcrumbs
- 1 tbsp lemon juice
- 2 eggs, lightly beaten
- 1/2 tsp dried mixed herbs
- 1/2 tsp garlic powder
- 2 tbsp onion, minced
- 1 celery stalk, chopped
- Pepper
- Salt

Directions:
1. Fit the Cuisinart oven with the rack in position 2.
2. Add all ingredients into the mixing bowl and mix until well combined.

3. Make patties from mixture and place in the air fryer basket then place the air fryer basket in the baking pan.
4. Place a baking pan on the oven rack. Set to air fry at 360 F for 10 minutes.
5. Serve and enjoy.

Nutritional Value (Amount per Serving):
Calories 90; Fat 1.8 g; Carbohydrates 4.4 g; Sugar 0.6 g; Protein 13.2 g; Cholesterol 47 mg

Simple Salmon Patties

Preparation Time: 10 minutes; Cooking Time: 7 minutes; Serve: 2
Ingredients:
- 8 oz salmon fillet, minced
- 1 egg, lightly beaten
- 1/4 tsp garlic powder
- 1/4 tsp onion powder
- 1/8 tsp paprika
- 2 tbsp breadcrumbs
- Pepper
- Salt

Directions:
1. Fit the Cuisinart oven with the rack in position 2.
2. Add all ingredients into the bowl and mix until well combined.
3. Make patties from mixture and place in the air fryer basket then place an air fryer basket in the baking pan.
4. Place a baking pan on the oven rack. Set to air fry at 390 F for 7 minutes.
5. Serve and enjoy.

Nutritional Value (Amount per Serving):
Calories 211; Fat 9.6 g; Carbohydrates 5.6 g; Sugar 0.8 g; Protein 25.8 g; Cholesterol 132 mg

Herb Fish Fillets

Preparation Time: 10 minutes; Cooking Time: 5 minutes; Serve: 2
Ingredients:
- 2 salmon fillets
- 1/4 tsp smoked paprika
- 1 tsp herb de Provence
- 1 tbsp butter, melted
- 2 tbsp olive oil
- Pepper
- Salt

Directions:
1. Fit the Cuisinart oven with the rack in position 2.
2. Brush salmon fillets with oil and sprinkle with paprika, herb de Provence, pepper, and salt.
3. Place salmon fillets in the air fryer basket then place an air fryer basket in the baking pan.
4. Place a baking pan on the oven rack. Set to air fry at 390 F for 5 minutes.
5. Drizzle melted butter over salmon and serve.

Nutritional Value (Amount per Serving):
Calories 413; Fat 31.1 g; Carbohydrates 0.2 g; Sugar 0 g; Protein 35.4 g; Cholesterol 94 mg

Marinated Salmon

Preparation Time: 10 minutes; Cooking Time: 10 minutes; Serve: 2
Ingredients:
- 2 salmon fillets, skinless and boneless
- For marinade:
- 2 tbsp scallions, minced
- 1 tbsp ginger, grated
- 2 garlic cloves, minced
- 2 tbsp mirin
- 2 tbsp soy sauce
- 1 tbsp olive oil

Directions:
1. Fit the Cuisinart oven with the rack in position 2.

2. Add all marinade ingredients into the zip-lock bag and mix well.
3. Add salmon in the bag. The sealed bag shakes well and places it in the fridge for 30 minutes.
4. Arrange marinated salmon fillets in an air fryer basket then place an air fryer basket in the baking pan.
5. Place a baking pan on the oven rack. Set to air fry at 360 F for 10 minutes.
6. Serve and enjoy.

Nutritional Value (Amount per Serving):
Calories 345; Fat 18.2 g; Carbohydrates 11.6 g; Sugar 4.5 g; Protein 36.1 g; Cholesterol 78 mg

Honey Glazed Salmon

Preparation Time: 10 minutes; Cooking Time: 8 minutes; Serve: 4
Ingredients:
- 4 salmon fillets
- 2 tsp soy sauce
- 1 tbsp honey
- Pepper
- Salt

Directions:
1. Fit the Cuisinart oven with the rack in position 2.
2. Brush salmon with soy sauce and season with pepper and salt.
3. Place salmon in the air fryer basket then place an air fryer basket in the baking pan.
4. Place a baking pan on the oven rack. Set to air fry at 375 F for 8 minutes.
5. Brush salmon with honey and serve.

Nutritional Value (Amount per Serving):
Calories 253; Fat 11 g; Carbohydrates 4.6 g; Sugar 4.4 g; Protein 34.7 g; Cholesterol 78 mg

Air Fry Prawns

Preparation Time: 10 minutes; Cooking Time: 6 minutes; Serve: 4
Ingredients:
- 24 prawns
- 6 tbsp mayonnaise
- 1 1/2 tsp chili powder
- 2 tbsp vinegar
- 2 tbsp ketchup
- 1 tsp red chili flakes
- 1/2 tsp sea salt

Directions:
1. Fit the Cuisinart oven with the rack in position 2.
2. In a bowl, toss prawns with chili flakes, chili powder, and salt.
3. Add shrimp to the air fryer basket then place an air fryer basket in the baking pan.
4. Place a baking pan on the oven rack. Set to air fry at 350 F for 6 minutes.
5. In a small bowl, mix mayonnaise, vinegar, and ketchup and serve with shrimp.

Nutritional Value (Amount per Serving):
Calories 255; Fat 9.8 g; Carbohydrates 9.8 g; Sugar 3.2 g; Protein 30.5 g; Cholesterol 284 mg

Tasty Parmesan Shrimp

Preparation Time: 10 minutes; Cooking Time: 10 minutes; Serve: 4
Ingredients:
- 1 lb shrimp, peeled and deveined
- 1/4 cup parmesan cheese, grated
- 4 garlic cloves, minced
- 1 tbsp olive oil
- 1/4 tsp oregano
- 1/2 tsp pepper
- 1/2 tsp onion powder
- 1/2 tsp basil

Directions:
1. Fit the Cuisinart oven with the rack in position 2.

2. Add all ingredients into the large bowl and toss well.
3. Add shrimp to the air fryer basket then place an air fryer basket in the baking pan.
4. Place a baking pan on the oven rack. Set to air fry at 350 F for 10 minutes.
5. Serve and enjoy.

Nutritional Value (Amount per Serving):
Calories 189; Fat 6.7 g; Carbohydrates 3.4 g; Sugar 0.1 g; Protein 27.9 g; Cholesterol 243 mg

Dill Salmon Patties

Preparation Time: 10 minutes; Cooking Time: 10 minutes; Serve: 2
Ingredients:
- 14 oz can salmon, drained and discard bones
- 1 tsp dill, chopped
- 1 egg, lightly beaten
- 1/4 tsp garlic powder
- 1/2 cup breadcrumbs
- 1/4 cup onion, diced
- Pepper
- Salt

Directions:
1. Fit the Cuisinart oven with the rack in position 2.
2. Add all ingredients into the large bowl and mix well.
3. Make equal shapes of patties from mixture and place in the air fryer basket then place the air fryer basket in the baking pan.
4. Place a baking pan on the oven rack. Set to air fry at 370 F for 10 minutes.
5. Serve and enjoy.

Nutritional Value (Amount per Serving):
Calories 422; Fat 15.7 g; Carbohydrates 21.5 g; Sugar 2.5 g; Protein 46 g; Cholesterol 191 mg

Air Fry Tuna Patties

Preparation Time: 10 minutes; Cooking Time: 6 minutes; Serve: 4
Ingredients:
- 1 egg, lightly beaten
- 8 oz can tuna, drained
- 1/4 cup breadcrumbs
- 1 tbsp mustard
- 1/4 tsp garlic powder
- Pepper
- Salt

Directions:
1. Fit the Cuisinart oven with the rack in position 2.
2. Add all ingredients into the large bowl and mix until well combined.
3. Make four equal shapes of patties from the mixture and place in the air fryer basket then place an air fryer basket in the baking pan.
4. Place a baking pan on the oven rack. Set to air fry at 400 F for 6 minutes.
5. Serve and enjoy.

Nutritional Value (Amount per Serving):
Calories 122; Fat 2.7 g; Carbohydrates 6.1 g; Sugar 0.7 g; Protein 17.5 g; Cholesterol 58 mg

Dijon Salmon Fillets

Preparation Time: 10 minutes; Cooking Time: 15 minutes; Serve: 4
Ingredients:
- 1 lb salmon fillets
- 2 tbsp Dijon mustard
- 1/4 cup brown sugar
- Pepper
- Salt

Directions:
1. Fit the Cuisinart oven with the rack in position 2.

2. Season salmon fillets with pepper and salt.
3. In a small bowl, mix Dijon mustard and brown sugar.
4. Brush salmon fillets with Dijon mustard mixture.
5. Place salmon fillets in the air fryer basket then place an air fryer basket in the baking pan.
6. Place a baking pan on the oven rack. Set to air fry at 350 F for 15 minutes.
7. Serve and enjoy.

Nutritional Value (Amount per Serving):
Calories 190; Fat 7.3 g; Carbohydrates 9.3 g; Sugar 8.9 g; Protein 22.4 g; Cholesterol 50 mg

Old Bay Seasoned Scallops

Preparation Time: 10 minutes; Cooking Time: 4 minutes; Serve: 4
Ingredients:
- 1 lb sea scallops
- 1/2 tsp garlic powder
- 1/2 cup crushed crackers
- 2 tbsp butter, melted
- 1/2 tsp old bay seasoning

Directions:
1. Fit the Cuisinart oven with the rack in position 2.
2. In a shallow dish, mix crushed crackers, garlic powder, and old bay seasoning.
3. Add melted butter in a separate shallow dish.
4. Dip scallops in melted butter and coat with crushed crackers.
5. Place coated scallops in air fryer basket then place air fryer basket in baking pan.
6. Place a baking pan on the oven rack. Set to air fry at 390 F for 4 minutes.
7. Serve and enjoy.

Nutritional Value (Amount per Serving):
Calories 167; Fat 7.4 g; Carbohydrates 4.8 g; Sugar 0.5 g; Protein 19.5 g; Cholesterol 53 mg

Lemon Pepper White Fish Fillets

Preparation Time: 10 minutes; Cooking Time: 12 minutes; Serve: 2
Ingredients:
- 12 oz white fish fillets
- 1/2 tsp lemon pepper seasoning
- Pepper
- Salt

Directions:
1. Fit the Cuisinart oven with the rack in position 2.
2. Spray fish fillets with cooking spray and season with lemon pepper seasoning, pepper, and salt.
3. Place fish fillets in the air fryer basket then place an air fryer basket in the baking pan.
4. Place a baking pan on the oven rack. Set to air fry at 360 F for 12 minutes.
5. Serve and enjoy.

Nutritional Value (Amount per Serving):
Calories 294; Fat 12.8 g; Carbohydrates 0.4 g; Sugar 0 g; Protein 41.7 g; Cholesterol 131 mg

Basil Tomato Salmon

Preparation Time: 10 minutes; Cooking Time: 20 minutes; Serve: 2
Ingredients:
- 2 salmon fillets
- 1 tomato, sliced
- 1 tbsp dried basil
- 2 tbsp parmesan cheese, grated
- 1 tbsp olive oil

Directions:
1. Fit the Cuisinart oven with the rack in position 1.
2. Place salmon fillets in a baking dish.

3. Sprinkle basil on top of salmon fillets.
4. Arrange tomato slices on top of salmon fillets. Drizzle with oil and top with cheese.
5. Set to bake at 375 F for 25 minutes. After 5 minutes place the baking dish in the preheated oven.
6. Serve and enjoy.

Nutritional Value (Amount per Serving):
Calories 324; Fat 19.6 g; Carbohydrates 1.5 g; Sugar 0.8 g; Protein 37.1 g; Cholesterol 83 mg

Greek Cod with Asparagus

Preparation Time: 10 minutes; Cooking Time: 20 minutes; Serve: 2

Ingredients:
- 1 lb cod, cut into 4 pieces
- 8 asparagus spears
- 1 leek, sliced
- 1 onion, quartered
- 2 tomatoes, halved
- 1/2 tsp oregano
- 1/2 tsp red chili flakes
- 1/2 cup olives, chopped
- 2 tbsp olive oil
- 1/4 tsp pepper
- 1/4 tsp salt

Directions:
1. Fit the Cuisinart oven with the rack in position 1.
2. Arrange fish pieces, olives, asparagus, leek, onion, and tomatoes in a baking dish.
3. Season with oregano, chili flakes, pepper, and salt and drizzle with olive oil.
4. Set to bake at 400 F for 25 minutes. After 5 minutes place the baking dish in the preheated oven.
5. Serve and enjoy.

Nutritional Value (Amount per Serving):
Calories 489; Fat 20.2 g; Carbohydrates 22.5 g; Sugar 9.1 g; Protein 56.6 g; Cholesterol 125 mg

Italian Cod

Preparation Time: 10 minutes; Cooking Time: 20 minutes; Serve: 4

Ingredients:
- 1 1/2 lbs cod fillet
- 1/4 cup olives, sliced
- 1 lb cherry tomatoes, halved
- 2 garlic cloves, crushed
- 1 small onion, chopped
- 1 tbsp olive oil
- 1/4 cup of water
- 1 tsp Italian seasoning
- Pepper
- Salt

Directions:
1. Fit the Cuisinart oven with the rack in position 1.
2. Place fish fillets, olives, tomatoes, garlic, and onion in a baking dish. Drizzle with oil.
3. Sprinkle with Italian seasoning, pepper, and salt. Pour water into the dish.
4. Set to bake at 400 F for 25 minutes. After 5 minutes place the baking dish in the preheated oven.
5. Serve and enjoy.

Nutritional Value (Amount per Serving):
Calories 210; Fat 6.5 g; Carbohydrates 7.2 g; Sugar 3.8 g; Protein 31.7 g; Cholesterol 84 mg

Spinach Scallops

Preparation Time: 10 minutes; Cooking Time: 10 minutes; Serve: 2

Ingredients:
- 8 sea scallops
- 1 tbsp fresh basil, chopped
- 1 tbsp tomato paste
- 3/4 cup heavy cream

- 12 oz frozen spinach, thawed and drained
- 1 tsp garlic, minced
- 1/2 tsp pepper
- 1/2 tsp salt

Directions:
1. Fit the Cuisinart oven with the rack in position 1.
2. Layer spinach in the baking dish.
3. Spray scallops with cooking spray and season with pepper and salt.
4. Place scallops on top of spinach.
5. In a small bowl, mix garlic, basil, tomato paste, whipping cream, pepper, and salt and pour over scallops and spinach.
6. Set to bake at 350 F for 15 minutes. After 5 minutes place the baking dish in the preheated oven.
7. Serve and enjoy.

Nutritional Value (Amount per Serving):
Calories 310; Fat 18.3 g; Carbohydrates 12.6 g; Sugar 1.7 g; Protein 26.5 g; Cholesterol 101 mg

Miso White Fish Fillets

Preparation Time: 10 minutes; Cooking Time: 10 minutes; Serve: 2

Ingredients:
- 2 cod fish fillets
- 2 tbsp brown sugar
- 2 tbsp miso
- 1 tbsp garlic, chopped

Directions:
1. Fit the Cuisinart oven with the rack in position 2.
2. Add all ingredients to the zip-lock bag and marinate fish in the refrigerator overnight.
3. Place marinated fish fillets in the air fryer basket then place an air fryer basket in the baking pan.
4. Place a baking pan on the oven rack. Set to air fry at 350 F for 10 minutes.
5. Serve and enjoy.

Nutritional Value (Amount per Serving):
Calories 9; Fat 0.1 g; Carbohydrates 0.5 g; Sugar 0.3 g; Protein 1.5 g; Cholesterol 3 mg

Perfect Crab Cakes

Preparation Time: 10 minutes; Cooking Time: 30 minutes; Serve: 6

Ingredients:
- 16 oz lump crab meat
- 1/4 cup celery, diced
- 1/4 cup onion, diced
- 1 cup crushed crackers
- 1 tsp old bay seasoning
- 1 tsp brown mustard
- 2/3 cup mashed avocado

Directions:
1. Fit the Cuisinart oven with the rack in position 1.
2. Add all ingredients into the bowl and mix until just combined.
3. Make small patties from mixture and place in parchment-lined baking pan.
4. Set to bake at 350 F for 35 minutes. After 5 minutes place the baking dish in the preheated oven.
5. Serve and enjoy.

Nutritional Value (Amount per Serving):
Calories 84; Fat 7.7 g; Carbohydrates 4.6 g; Sugar 0.8 g; Protein 11.5 g; Cholesterol 43 mg

Chapter 6: Vegetables & Side Dishes

Baked Vegetables

Preparation Time: 10 minutes; Cooking Time: 30 minutes; Serve: 6
Ingredients:
- 2 zucchini, sliced
- 2 tomatoes, quartered
- 6 fresh basil leaves, sliced
- 2 tsp Italian seasoning
- 2 tbsp olive oil
- 1 eggplant, sliced
- 1 onion, sliced
- 1 bell pepper, cut into strips
- Pepper
- Salt

Directions:
1. Fit the Cuisinart oven with the rack in position 1.
2. Add all ingredients except basil leaves into the bowl and toss well.
3. Transfer vegetable mixture in parchment-lined baking pan.
4. Set to bake at 400 F for 35 minutes. After 5 minutes place the baking pan in the preheated oven.
5. Garnish with basil and serve.

Nutritional Value (Amount per Serving):
Calories 96; Fat 5.5 g; Carbohydrates 11.7 g; Sugar 6.4 g; Protein 2.3 g; Cholesterol 1 mg

Cheese Herb Zucchini

Preparation Time: 10 minutes; Cooking Time: 15 minutes; Serve: 4
Ingredients:
- 4 zucchini, quartered
- 1/2 tsp dried oregano
- 2 tbsp fresh parsley, chopped
- 2 tbsp olive oil
- 1/2 tsp dried thyme
- 1/2 cup parmesan cheese, grated
- 1/4 tsp garlic powder
- 1/2 tsp dried basil
- Pepper
- Salt

Directions:
1. Fit the Cuisinart oven with the rack in position 1.
2. In a small bowl, mix parmesan cheese, garlic powder, basil, oregano, thyme, pepper, and salt.
3. Arrange zucchini in baking pan and drizzle with oil and sprinkle with parmesan cheese mixture.
4. Set to bake at 350 F for 20 minutes. After 5 minutes place the baking pan in the preheated oven.
5. Garnish with parsley and serve.

Nutritional Value (Amount per Serving):
Calories 130; Fat 9.8 g; Carbohydrates 7.4 g; Sugar 3.5 g; Protein 6.1 g; Cholesterol 8 mg

Healthy Spinach Muffins

Preparation Time: 10 minutes; Cooking Time: 15 minutes; Serve: 12
Ingredients:
- 10 eggs
- 2 cups spinach, chopped
- 1/2 tsp dried basil
- 1 1/2 cups parmesan cheese, grated
- 1/4 tsp garlic powder
- 1/4 tsp onion powder
- Salt

Directions:
1. Fit the Cuisinart oven with the rack in position 1.
2. Spray 12-cups muffin tin with cooking spray and set aside.

3. In a large bowl, whisk eggs with basil, garlic powder, onion powder, and salt.
4. Add cheese and spinach and stir well.
5. Pour egg mixture into the prepared muffin tin.
6. Set to bake at 400 F for 20 minutes. After 5 minutes place muffin tin in the preheated oven.
7. Serve and enjoy.

Nutritional Value (Amount per Serving):
Calories 90; Fat 6.1 g; Carbohydrates 0.9 g; Sugar 0.3 g; Protein 8.4 g; Cholesterol 144 mg

Honey Corn Muffins

Preparation Time: 10 minutes; Cooking Time: 20 minutes; Serve: 8

Ingredients:
- 2 eggs
- 1/2 cup sugar
- 1 1/4 cups self-rising flour
- 3/4 cup yellow cornmeal
- 1/2 cup butter, melted
- 3/4 cup buttermilk
- 1 tbsp honey

Directions:
1. Fit the Cuisinart oven with the rack in position 1.
2. Spray 8-cups muffin tin with cooking spray and set aside.
3. In a large bowl, mix together cornmeal, sugar, and flour.
4. In a separate bowl, whisk the eggs with buttermilk and honey until well combined.
5. Slowly add egg mixture and melted butter to the cornmeal mixture and stir until just mixed.
6. Spoon batter into the prepared muffin tin.
7. Set to bake at 350 F for 25 minutes. After 5 minutes place muffin tin in the preheated oven.
8. Serve and enjoy.

Nutritional Value (Amount per Serving):
Calories 294; Fat 13.4 g; Carbohydrates 39.6 g; Sugar 16 g; Protein 5.2 g; Cholesterol 72 mg

Delicious Mac and Cheese

Preparation Time: 10 minutes; Cooking Time: 30 minutes; Serve: 6

Ingredients:
- 2 1/2 cups pasta, uncooked
- 1/2 cup cream
- 1 cup vegetable broth
- 2 tbsp flour
- 1/2 cup parmesan cheese, grated
- 1/2 cup Velveeta cheese, cut into small cubes
- 2 cups Colby cheese, shredded
- 2 tbsp butter
- 1 tsp salt

Directions:
1. Fit the Cuisinart oven with the rack in position 1.
2. Cook pasta according to the packet instructions. Drain well.
3. Melt butter in a pan over medium heat. Slowly whisk in flour.
4. Whisk constantly and slowly add the broth.
5. Slowly pour the cream and whisk constantly.
6. Slowly add parmesan cheese, Velveeta cheese, and Colby cheese and whisk until smooth.
7. Add cooked pasta to the sauce and stir well to coat.
8. Transfer pasta into the greased casserole dish.
9. Set to bake at 350 F for 35 minutes. After 5 minutes place the casserole dish in the preheated oven.
10. Serve and enjoy.

Nutritional Value (Amount per Serving):
Calories 410; Fat 21.8 g; Carbohydrates 34 g; Sugar 1.3 g; Protein 20 g; Cholesterol 99 mg

Jalapeno Bread

Preparation Time: 10 minutes; Cooking Time: 50 minutes; Serve: 10

Ingredients:
- 3 cups all-purpose flour
- 8 oz cheddar cheese, shredded
- 1/2 tsp ground white pepper
- 1 1/2 tbsp baking powder
- 1/4 cup butter, melted
- 1 1/2 cups buttermilk
- 3 jalapeno peppers, chopped
- 2 tbsp sugar
- 1 1/4 tsp salt

Directions:
1. Fit the Cuisinart oven with the rack in position 1.
2. In a mixing bowl, mix flour, baking powder, sugar, white pepper, and salt.
3. Add jalapenos and cheese and stir to combine.
4. Whisk butter and buttermilk together and add to the flour mixture. Stir until just combined.
5. Pour batter into the greased 9*5-inch loaf pan.
6. Set to bake at 375 F for 55 minutes. After 5 minutes place the loaf pan in the preheated oven.
7. Slice and serve.

Nutritional Value (Amount per Serving):
Calories 297; Fat 12.9 g; Carbohydrates 34.5 g; Sugar 4.5 g; Protein 10.9 g; Cholesterol 37 mg

Healthy Barley Bread

Preparation Time: 10 minutes; Cooking Time: 40 minutes; Serve: 16

Ingredients:
- 2 eggs
- 1/2 tsp baking soda
- 2 tbsp baking powder
- 3 cups barley flour
- 3 tbsp honey
- 1/3 cup olive oil
- 1 1/2 cups buttermilk
- 1 1/4 tsp salt

Directions:
1. Fit the Cuisinart oven with the rack in position 1.
2. In a large bowl, mix together flour, baking powder, baking soda, and salt.
3. In a separate bowl, whisk eggs with honey, oil, and buttermilk.
4. Add egg mixture into the flour mixture and stir until just combined.
5. Pour batter into the greased loaf pan.
6. Set to bake at 350 F for 40 minutes. After 5 minutes place the loaf pan in the preheated oven.
7. Slice and serve.

Nutritional Value (Amount per Serving):
Calories 163; Fat 5.4 g; Carbohydrates 26 g; Sugar 4.6 g; Protein 4.4 g; Cholesterol 21 mg

Rice Broccoli Casserole

Preparation Time: 10 minutes; Cooking Time: 40 minutes; Serve: 8

Ingredients:
- 2 cups brown rice, cooked
- 3 cups broccoli florets
- 1 tbsp olive oil
- 2 garlic cloves, minced
- 1 onion, chopped

For sauce:

- 1 tbsp onion, chopped
- 1/4 cup nutritional yeast flakes
- 1 cup of water
- 1 garlic clove, minced
- 1 tbsp tapioca starch
- 1 cup cashews
- 1 1/2 tsp salt

Directions:
1. Fit the Cuisinart oven with the rack in position 1.
2. For the sauce: add all sauce ingredients into the blender and blend until smooth.
3. Heat oil in a pan over medium-high heat.
4. Add garlic and onion and sauté until onion is softened.
5. Add broccoli and cook for a minute.
6. Add rice and sauce and stir to combine.
7. Transfer broccoli rice mixture into the greased casserole dish.
8. Set to bake at 400 F for 45 minutes. After 5 minutes place the casserole dish in the preheated oven.
9. Serve and enjoy.

Nutritional Value (Amount per Serving):
Calories 327; Fat 11.4 g; Carbohydrates 49.2 g; Sugar 2.1 g; Protein 9.7 g; Cholesterol 0 mg

Cinnamon Sweet Potatoes

Preparation Time: 10 minutes; Cooking Time: 30 minutes; Serve: 4
Ingredients:
- 2 large sweet potatoes, peel and cut into cubes
- 2 tbsp brown sugar
- 1/4 cup maple syrup
- 2 tbsp olive oil
- 1/4 tsp cinnamon
- Salt

Directions:
1. Fit the Cuisinart oven with the rack in position 1.
2. Add sweet potatoes, oil, cinnamon, brown sugar, maple syrup, and salt into the large mixing bowl and toss well.
3. Spread sweet potatoes in a parchment-lined baking pan.
4. Set to bake at 400 F for 35 minutes. After 5 minutes place the baking pan in the preheated oven.
5. Serve and enjoy.

Nutritional Value (Amount per Serving):
Calories 188; Fat 7.1 g; Carbohydrates 31.7 g; Sugar 16.3 g; Protein 0.8 g; Cholesterol 0 mg

Herb Cheese Sweet Potatoes

Preparation Time: 10 minutes; Cooking Time: 30 minutes; Serve: 6
Ingredients:
- 2 lbs sweet potatoes, peeled and cut into 1-inch cubes
- 2 tbsp olive oil
- 1/4 cup parmesan cheese, grated
- 1 tsp dried rosemary
- 1/2 tsp garlic powder
- Pepper
- Salt

Directions:
1. Fit the Cuisinart oven with the rack in position 1.
2. Add sweet potatoes into the mixing bowl along with oil, rosemary, garlic powder, pepper, and salt and toss well.
3. Spread sweet potatoes in baking pan.
4. Set to bake at 425 F for 35 minutes. After 5 minutes place the baking pan in the preheated oven.

5. Toss sweet potatoes with parmesan cheese and serve.

Nutritional Value (Amount per Serving):
Calories 232; Fat 5.8 g; Carbohydrates 42.6 g; Sugar 0.8 g; Protein 3.6 g; Cholesterol 3 mg

Baked Paprika Sweet Potatoes

Preparation Time: 10 minutes; Cooking Time: 20 minutes; Serve: 4

Ingredients:
- 3 sweet potatoes, peel and cut into 1/2-inch pieces
- 2 tbsp olive oil
- 1/2 tsp pepper
- 2 tsp smoked paprika
- 1 tsp garlic salt

Directions:
1. Fit the Cuisinart oven with the rack in position 1.
2. Add sweet potatoes, paprika, oil, pepper, and salt into the mixing bowl and toss well.
3. Spread sweet potatoes in baking pan.
4. Set to bake at 425 F for 25 minutes. After 5 minutes place the baking pan in the preheated oven.
5. Serve and enjoy.

Nutritional Value (Amount per Serving):
Calories 155; Fat 7.3 g; Carbohydrates 22.2 g; Sugar 0.7 g; Protein 1.5 g; Cholesterol 0 mg

Cheesy Broccoli Rice

Preparation Time: 10 minutes; Cooking Time: 20 minutes; Serve: 8

Ingredients:
- 1 1/2 cups cooked brown rice
- 1 garlic clove, chopped
- 16 oz frozen broccoli florets
- 1 large onion, chopped
- 1 tbsp butter
- 3 tbsp parmesan cheese, grated
- 10.5 oz condensed cheddar cheese soup
- 1/3 cup almond milk

Directions:
1. Fit the Cuisinart oven with the rack in position 1.
2. Heat butter in a 10-inch pan over medium heat.
3. Add onion and cook until tender.
4. Add garlic and broccoli in the pan and cook until broccoli is tender.
5. Stir in rice, soup, and milk and cook until hot.
6. Stir in cheese and pour broccoli mixture into the greased baking dish.
7. Set to bake at 350 F for 25 minutes. After 5 minutes place the baking dish in the preheated oven.
8. Serve and enjoy.

Nutritional Value (Amount per Serving):
Calories 244; Fat 8.3 g; Carbohydrates 35.4 g; Sugar 2.7 g; Protein 6 g; Cholesterol 14 mg

Creamy Broccoli Casserole

Preparation Time: 10 minutes; Cooking Time: 30 minutes; Serve: 6

Ingredients:
- 16 oz frozen broccoli florets, defrosted and drained
- 1/2 tsp onion powder
- 10.5 oz can cream of mushroom soup
- 1 cup cheddar cheese, shredded
- 1/3 cup almond milk
- For topping:
- 1 tbsp butter, melted
- 1/2 cup cracker crumbs

Directions:

1. Fit the Cuisinart oven with the rack in position 1.
2. Add all ingredients except topping ingredients into the 1.5-qt casserole dish.
3. In a small bowl, mix together cracker crumbs and melted butter and sprinkle over the casserole dish mixture.
4. Set to bake at 350 F for 35 minutes. After 5 minutes place the casserole dish in the preheated oven.
5. Serve and enjoy.

Nutritional Value (Amount per Serving):
Calories 203; Fat 13.5 g; Carbohydrates 11.9 g; Sugar 3.6 g; Protein 6.9 g; Cholesterol 26 mg

Baked Apple Sweet Potatoes

Preparation Time: 10 minutes; Cooking Time: 30 minutes; Serve: 2

Ingredients:
- 2 large sweet potatoes, diced
- 2 tsp cinnamon
- 2 large green apples, diced
- 2 tbsp maple syrup
- 1 tbsp olive oil

Directions:
1. Fit the Cuisinart oven with the rack in position 1.
2. In a large bowl, add sweet potatoes, oil, cinnamon, and apples and toss well.
3. Spread sweet potatoes mixture in baking pan.
4. Set to bake at 400 F for 35 minutes. After 5 minutes place the baking pan in the preheated oven.
5. Drizzle with maple syrup and serve.

Nutritional Value (Amount per Serving):
Calories 352; Fat 7.6 g; Carbohydrates 74 g; Sugar 35.7 g; Protein 2.2 g; Cholesterol 0 mg

Mac & Cheese

Preparation Time: 10 minutes; Cooking Time: 20 minutes; Serve: 10

Ingredients:
- 1 lb cooked macaroni
- 4 1/2 cups almond milk
- 1/2 cup flour
- 1/2 cup breadcrumbs
- 12 oz cheddar cheese, shredded
- 1/2 cup butter
- Pepper
- Salt

Directions:
1. Fit the Cuisinart oven with the rack in position 1.
2. Melt butter in a pan over medium heat.
3. Remove pan from heat and slowly mix flour salt and pepper in melted butter.
4. Add 1/2 cup milk and stir until well blended.
5. Return to heat and slowly add remaining milk.
6. Add cheese and stir until cheese is melted.
7. Pour over cooked macaroni and mix well.
8. Transfer macaroni in a casserole dish and sprinkle with breadcrumbs.
9. Set to bake at 350 F for 25 minutes. After 5 minutes place the casserole dish in the preheated oven.
10. Serve and enjoy.

Nutritional Value (Amount per Serving):
Calories 679; Fat 47.3 g; Carbohydrates 49 g; Sugar 5.4 g; Protein 18.3 g; Cholesterol 60 mg

Dijon Zucchini Patties

Preparation Time: 10 minutes; Cooking Time: 30 minutes; Serve: 6

Ingredients:
- 1 cup zucchini, shredded and squeeze out all liquid
- 2 tbsp onion, minced
- 1 egg, lightly beaten
- 1/4 tsp red pepper flakes
- 1/4 cup parmesan cheese, grated
- 1/2 tbsp Dijon mustard
- 1/2 tbsp mayonnaise
- 1/2 cup breadcrumbs
- Pepper
- Salt

Directions:
1. Fit the Cuisinart oven with the rack in position 1.
2. Add all ingredients into the bowl and mix until well combined.
3. Make small patties from the zucchini mixture and place it in a parchment-lined baking pan.
4. Set to bake at 400 F for 35 minutes. After 5 minutes place the baking pan in the preheated oven.
5. Serve and enjoy.

Nutritional Value (Amount per Serving):
Calories 69; Fat 2.5 g; Carbohydrates 8 g; Sugar 1.2 g; Protein 3.7 g; Cholesterol 30 mg

Baked Asparagus

Preparation Time: 10 minutes; Cooking Time: 15 minutes; Serve: 4

Ingredients:
- 30 asparagus spears, cut the ends
- 1/2 tsp garlic powder
- 1 tbsp olive oil
- Pepper
- Salt

Directions:
1. Fit the Cuisinart oven with the rack in position 1.
2. Add asparagus into the large bowl. Drizzle with oil.
3. Sprinkle with garlic powder, pepper, and salt. Toss well.
4. Arrange asparagus in baking pan.
5. Set to bake at 400 F for 20 minutes. After 5 minutes place the baking pan in the preheated oven.
6. Serve and enjoy.

Nutritional Value (Amount per Serving):
Calories 67; Fat 3.7 g; Carbohydrates 7.3 g; Sugar 3.5 g; Protein 4 g; Cholesterol 0 mg

Baked Potatoes & Carrots

Preparation Time: 10 minutes; Cooking Time: 40 minutes; Serve: 2

Ingredients:
- 1/2 lb potatoes, cut into 1-inch cubes
- 1/2 onion, diced
- 1/2 tsp Italian seasoning
- 1/4 tsp garlic powder
- 1/2 lb carrots, peeled & cut into chunks
- 1 tbsp olive oil
- Pepper
- Salt

Directions:
1. Fit the Cuisinart oven with the rack in position 1.
2. In a large bowl, toss carrots, potatoes, garlic powder, Italian seasoning, oil, onion, pepper, and salt.
3. Transfer carrot potato in baking pan.
4. Set to bake at 400 F for 45 minutes. After 5 minutes place the baking pan in the preheated oven.

5. Serve and enjoy.

Nutritional Value (Amount per Serving):
   Calories 201; Fat 7.5 g; Carbohydrates 32 g; Sugar 8.2 g; Protein 3.2 g; Cholesterol 1 mg

Spicy Brussels Sprouts

Preparation Time: 10 minutes; Cooking Time: 15 minutes; Serve: 2

Ingredients:
- 1/2 lb Brussels sprouts, trimmed and halved
- 1 tbsp chives, chopped
- 1/4 tsp cayenne
- 1/2 tsp chili powder
- 1/2 tbsp olive oil
- Pepper
- Salt

Directions:
1. Fit the Cuisinart oven with the rack in position 1.
2. Add all ingredients into the large bowl and toss well.
3. Spread Brussels sprouts in baking pan.
4. Set to bake at 370 F for 20 minutes. After 5 minutes place the baking pan in the preheated oven.
5. Serve and enjoy.

Nutritional Value (Amount per Serving):
   Calories 82; Fat 4.1 g; Carbohydrates 10.9 g; Sugar 2.6 g; Protein 4 g; Cholesterol 0 mg

Cheddar Broccoli Fritters

Preparation Time: 10 minutes; Cooking Time: 30 minutes; Serve: 4

Ingredients:
- 3 cups broccoli florets, steam & chopped
- 2 cups cheddar cheese, shredded
- 1/4 cup breadcrumbs
- 2 eggs, lightly beaten
- 2 garlic cloves, minced
- Pepper
- Salt

Directions:
1. Fit the Cuisinart oven with the rack in position 1.
2. Add all ingredients into the large bowl and mix until well combined.
3. Make patties from broccoli mixture and place in baking pan.
4. Set to bake at 375 F for 35 minutes. After 5 minutes place the baking pan in the preheated oven.
5. Serve and enjoy.

Nutritional Value (Amount per Serving):
   Calories 311; Fat 21.5 g; Carbohydrates 10.8 g; Sugar 2.1 g; Protein 19.8 g; Cholesterol 141 mg

Baked Cauliflower & Mushrooms

Preparation Time: 10 minutes; Cooking Time: 20 minutes; Serve: 6

Ingredients:
- 1 lb mushrooms, cleaned
- 8 garlic cloves, peeled
- 2 cups cherry tomatoes
- 2 cups cauliflower florets
- 1 tbsp fresh parsley, chopped
- 1 tbsp Italian seasoning
- 2 tbsp olive oil
- Pepper
- Salt

Directions:
1. Fit the Cuisinart oven with the rack in position 1.
2. Add cauliflower, mushrooms, Italian seasoning, olive oil, garlic, cherry tomatoes, pepper, and salt into the mixing bowl and toss well.

3. Transfer cauliflower and mushroom mixture on a baking pan.
4. Set to bake at 400 F for 25 minutes. After 5 minutes place the baking pan in the preheated oven.
5. Garnish with parsley and serve.

Nutritional Value (Amount per Serving):
Calories 89; Fat 5.8 g; Carbohydrates 8.2 g; Sugar 3.9 g; Protein 3.8 g; Cholesterol 2 mg

Baked Cauliflower & Tomatoes

Preparation Time: 10 minutes; Cooking Time: 20 minutes; Serve: 4
Ingredients:
- 4 cups cauliflower florets
- 1 tbsp capers, drained
- 3 tbsp olive oil
- 1/2 cup cherry tomatoes, halved
- 2 tbsp fresh parsley, chopped
- 2 garlic cloves, sliced
- Pepper
- Salt

Directions:
1. Fit the Cuisinart oven with the rack in position 1.
2. In a bowl, toss together cherry tomatoes, cauliflower, oil, garlic, capers, pepper, and salt and spread in baking pan.
3. Set to bake at 450 F for 25 minutes. After 5 minutes place the baking pan in the preheated oven.
4. Garnish with parsley and serve.

Nutritional Value (Amount per Serving):
Calories 123; Fat 10.7 g; Carbohydrates 6.9 g; Sugar 3 g; Protein 2.4 g; Cholesterol 0 mg

Parmesan Baked Asparagus

Preparation Time: 10 minutes; Cooking Time: 12 minutes; Serve: 4
Ingredients:
- 1 lb asparagus, wash, trimmed, and cut the ends
- 1 tbsp dried parsley
- 2 garlic cloves, minced
- 2 tbsp olive oil
- 3 oz parmesan cheese, shaved
- 1 tsp dried oregano
- Pepper
- Salt

Directions:
1. Fit the Cuisinart oven with the rack in position 1.
2. Arrange asparagus in baking pan. Drizzle with olive oil and season with pepper and salt.
3. Spread cheese, oregano, parsley, and garlic over the asparagus
4. Set to bake at 425 F for 17 minutes. After 5 minutes place the baking pan in the preheated oven.
5. Serve and enjoy.

Nutritional Value (Amount per Serving):
Calories 155; Fat 11.8 g; Carbohydrates 6 g; Sugar 2.2 g; Protein 9.5 g; Cholesterol 15 mg

Baked Cauliflower & Pepper

Preparation Time: 10 minutes; Cooking Time: 30 minutes; Serve: 4
Ingredients:
- 1 cauliflower head, cut into florets
- 1/2 cup fresh dill, chopped
- 12/ onion, sliced
- 1 red bell pepper, cut into 1-inch pieces
- 2 tsp olive oil
- 2 tbsp white wine vinegar
- 3 tbsp balsamic vinegar
- Pepper
- Salt

Directions:
1. Fit the Cuisinart oven with the rack in position 1.
2. Add all ingredients into the zip-lock bag. Seal the bag and shake well and place in the fridge for 1 hour.
3. Pour marinated cauliflower mixture in the baking dish.
4. Set to bake at 450 F for 35 minutes. After 5 minutes place the baking dish in the preheated oven.
5. Serve and enjoy.

Nutritional Value (Amount per Serving):
Calories 86; Fat 2.7 g; Carbohydrates 15.3 g; Sugar 6.2 g; Protein 2.8 g; Cholesterol 0 mg

Baked Broccoli

Preparation Time: 10 minutes; Cooking Time: 20 minutes; Serve: 6
Ingredients:
- 4 cups broccoli florets
- 3 tbsp olive oil
- 1/2 tsp pepper
- 1/2 tsp garlic powder
- 1 tsp Italian seasoning
- 1 tsp salt

Directions:
1. Fit the Cuisinart oven with the rack in position 1.
2. Spread broccoli in baking pan and drizzle with oil and season with garlic powder, Italian seasoning, pepper, and salt.
3. Set to bake at 400 F for 25 minutes. After 5 minutes place the baking pan in the preheated oven.
4. Serve and enjoy.

Nutritional Value (Amount per Serving):
Calories 84; Fat 7.4 g; Carbohydrates 4.4 g; Sugar 1.2 g; Protein 1.8 g; Cholesterol 1 mg

Baked Eggplant Pepper & Mushrooms

Preparation Time: 10 minutes; Cooking Time: 20 minutes; Serve: 4
Ingredients:
- 2 eggplants
- 2 cups mushrooms
- 1/4 tsp black pepper
- 4 bell peppers
- 2 tbsp olive oil
- 1 tsp salt

Directions:
1. Fit the Cuisinart oven with the rack in position 1.
2. Cut all vegetables into the small bite-sized pieces and place in a baking dish.
3. Drizzle vegetables with olive oil and season with pepper and salt.
4. Set to bake at 390 F for 25 minutes. After 5 minutes place the baking dish in the preheated oven.
5. Serve and enjoy.

Nutritional Value (Amount per Serving):
Calories 87; Fat 4 g; Carbohydrates 13.2 g; Sugar 7.4 g; Protein 2.5 g; Cholesterol 0 mg

Baked Garlic Mushrooms

Preparation Time: 10 minutes; Cooking Time: 10 minutes; Serve: 2
Ingredients:
- 1 lb button mushrooms, clean and stems removed
- 2 tbsp olive oil
- 2 tbsp fresh chives, sliced
- 3 garlic cloves, chopped
- 1/2 tsp salt

Directions:

1. Fit the Cuisinart oven with the rack in position 1.
2. Add mushrooms, chives, garlic, olive oil, and salt into the zip-lock bag and shake well.
3. Place mushrooms in baking pan.
4. Set to bake at 400 F for 15 minutes. After 5 minutes place the baking pan in the preheated oven.
5. Serve and enjoy.

Nutritional Value (Amount per Serving):
Calories 176; Fat 14.7 g; Carbohydrates 9.1 g; Sugar 4 g; Protein 7.5 g; Cholesterol 0 mg

Herb Balsamic Mushrooms

Preparation Time: 10 minutes; Cooking Time: 20 minutes; Serve: 6

Ingredients:
- 1 lb button mushrooms, scrubbed and stems trimmed
- 2 tbsp olive oil
- 4 tbsp balsamic vinegar
- 1/2 tsp dried basil
- 1/2 tsp dried oregano
- 3 garlic cloves, crushed
- 1/4 tsp black pepper
- 1 tsp sea salt

Directions:
1. Fit the Cuisinart oven with the rack in position 1.
2. In a large bowl, whisk together vinegar, basil, oregano, garlic, olive oil, pepper, and salt. Stir in mushrooms and let sit for 15 minutes.
3. Spread mushrooms in baking pan.
4. Set to bake at 425 F for 25 minutes. After 5 minutes place the baking pan in the preheated oven.
5. Serve and enjoy.

Nutritional Value (Amount per Serving):
Calories 61; Fat 4.9 g; Carbohydrates 3.2 g; Sugar 1.4 g; Protein 2.5 g; Cholesterol 0 mg

Parmesan Zucchini

Preparation Time: 10 minutes; Cooking Time: 15 minutes; Serve: 4

Ingredients:
- 1 lb zucchini, sliced
- 1 garlic clove, minced
- 2 tbsp olive oil
- 1 oz parmesan cheese, grated
- 1 tsp dried mixed herbs

Directions:
1. Fit the Cuisinart oven with the rack in position 1.
2. Add all ingredients except parmesan cheese into the large bowl and toss well.
3. Transfer the zucchini mixture to the baking dish.
4. Set to bake at 450 F for 20 minutes. After 5 minutes place the baking dish in the preheated oven.
5. Sprinkle parmesan cheese over zucchini and bake for 5 minutes more.

Nutritional Value (Amount per Serving):
Calories 103; Fat 8.7 g; Carbohydrates 4.4 g; Sugar 1.3 g; Protein 3.7 g; Cholesterol 5 mg

Baked Italian Vegetables

Preparation Time: 10 minutes; Cooking Time: 30 minutes; Serve: 6

Ingredients:
- 1 eggplant, sliced
- 1 onion, sliced
- 1 potato, peel & cut into chunks
- 1 bell pepper, cut into strips
- 2 zucchini, sliced
- 2 tomatoes, quartered

- 5 fresh basil leaves, sliced
- 2 tsp Italian seasoning
- 2 tbsp olive oil
- Pepper
- Salt

Directions:
1. Fit the Cuisinart oven with the rack in position 1.
2. Add all ingredients except basil leaves into the mixing bowl and toss well.
3. Transfer vegetable mixture on a prepared baking pan.
4. Set to bake at 400 F for 35 minutes. After 5 minutes place the baking dish in the preheated oven.
5. Garnish with basil leaves and serve.

Nutritional Value (Amount per Serving):
Calories 117; Fat 5.6 g; Carbohydrates 16.6 g; Sugar 6.6 g; Protein 2.9 g; Cholesterol 1 mg

Broccoli Olives Tomatoes

Preparation Time: 10 minutes; Cooking Time: 10 minutes; Serve: 4
Ingredients:
- 4 cups broccoli florets
- 1/2 tsp lemon zest, grated
- 2 garlic cloves, minced
- 1 tbsp olive oil
- 1 tsp dried oregano
- 10 olives, pitted and sliced
- 1 tbsp fresh lemon juice
- 1 cup cherry tomatoes
- 1/4 tsp salt

Directions:
1. Fit the Cuisinart oven with the rack in position 1.
2. Add broccoli, garlic, oil, tomatoes, and salt in a large bowl and toss well.
3. Spread broccoli mixture onto the baking pan.
4. Set to bake at 450 F for 15 minutes. After 5 minutes place the baking pan in the preheated oven.
5. Meanwhile, mix together oregano, olives, lemon juice, and lemon zest in a mixing bowl.
6. Add roasted vegetables to the bowl and toss well.
7. Serve and enjoy.

Nutritional Value (Amount per Serving):
Calories 86; Fat 5.1 g; Carbohydrates 9.4 g; Sugar 2.9 g; Protein 3.2 g; Cholesterol 0 mg

Baked Artichoke Hearts

Preparation Time: 10 minutes; Cooking Time: 25 minutes; Serve: 6
Ingredients:
- 15 oz frozen artichoke hearts, defrosted
- 1 tbsp olive oil
- Pepper
- Salt

Directions:
1. Fit the Cuisinart oven with the rack in position 1.
2. Arrange artichoke hearts in baking pan and drizzle with olive oil. Season with pepper and salt.
3. Set to bake at 400 F for 30 minutes. After 5 minutes place the baking pan in the preheated oven.
4. Serve and enjoy.

Nutritional Value (Amount per Serving):
Calories 53; Fat 2.4 g; Carbohydrates 7.5 g; Sugar 0.7 g; Protein 2.3 g; Cholesterol 0 mg

Healthy Asparagus Potatoes

Preparation Time: 10 minutes; Cooking Time: 35 minutes; Serve: 4
Ingredients:
- 9 oz asparagus, cut into 2-inch pieces
- 2 lbs potatoes, cut into quarters
- 1/4 cup balsamic vinegar
- 2 tbsp olive oil

Directions:
1. Fit the Cuisinart oven with the rack in position 1.
2. In a large bowl, add potatoes, balsamic vinegar, olive oil, and salt and toss well.
3. Spread potatoes in baking pan.
4. Set to bake at 390 F for 25 minutes. After 5 minutes place the baking pan in the preheated oven.
5. Add asparagus and stir well and bake for 15 minutes more.
6. Season with pepper and salt.
7. Serve and enjoy.

Nutritional Value (Amount per Serving):
Calories 232; Fat 7.3 g; Carbohydrates 38.3 g; Sugar 3.9 g; Protein 5.2 g; Cholesterol 0 mg

Easy Broccoli Bread

Preparation Time: 10 minutes; Cooking Time: 30 minutes; Serve: 6
Ingredients:
- 5 eggs, lightly beaten
- 3/4 cup broccoli florets, chopped
- 2 tsp baking powder
- 3 1/1 tbsp coconut flour
- 1 cup cheddar cheese, shredded

Directions:
1. Fit the Cuisinart oven with the rack in position 1.
2. Add all ingredients into the bowl and mix well.
3. Pour egg mixture into the greased loaf pan.
4. Set to bake at 350 F for 35 minutes. After 5 minutes place the loaf pan in the preheated oven.
5. Cut the loaf into the slices and serve.

Nutritional Value (Amount per Serving):
Calories 174; Fat 11.3 g; Carbohydrates 7.4 g; Sugar 1.2 g; Protein 11 g; Cholesterol 156 mg

Baked Lemon Broccoli

Preparation Time: 10 minutes; Cooking Time: 20 minutes; Serve: 4
Ingredients:
- 1 1/2 lbs broccoli florets
- 3 tbsp slivered almonds, toasted
- 2 garlic cloves, sliced
- 3 tbsp olive oil
- 1 tbsp fresh lemon juice

Directions:
1. Fit the Cuisinart oven with the rack in position 1.
2. Add broccoli, pepper, salt, garlic, and oil in a large bowl and toss well.
3. Spread broccoli in baking dish.
4. Set to bake at 425 F for 25 minutes. After 5 minutes place the baking dish in the preheated oven.
5. Add lemon juice and almonds over broccoli and toss well.
6. Serve and enjoy.

Nutritional Value (Amount per Serving):
Calories 177; Fat 13.3 g; Carbohydrates 12.8 g; Sugar 3.2 g; Protein 5.8 g; Cholesterol 0 mg

Baked Root Vegetables

Preparation Time: 10 minutes; Cooking Time: 30 minutes; Serve: 6
Ingredients:
- 1 lb beetroot, cubed
- 3 tsp paprika
- 1/2 lb carrots, cut into chunks
- 1 lb sweet potato, cubed
- 2 tsp olive oil

Directions:
1. Fit the Cuisinart oven with the rack in position 1.
2. Add all ingredients in a large mixing bowl and toss well.
3. Transfer root mixture onto a baking pan.
4. Set to bake at 350 F for 35 minutes. After 5 minutes place the baking pan in the preheated oven.
5. Serve and enjoy.

Nutritional Value (Amount per Serving):
Calories 133; Fat 2 g; Carbohydrates 27.5 g; Sugar 12.9 g; Protein 3.3 g; Cholesterol 0 mg

Cheesy Squash Casserole

Preparation Time: 10 minutes; Cooking Time: 30 minutes; Serve: 6
Ingredients:
- 2 lbs yellow summer squash, cut into chunks
- 1/2 cup liquid egg substitute
- 3/4 cup cheddar cheese, shredded
- 1/4 cup mayonnaise
- 1/4 tsp salt

Directions:
1. Fit the Cuisinart oven with the rack in position 1.
2. Add squash in a saucepan then pour enough water in a saucepan to cover the squash. Bring to boil.
3. Turn heat to medium and cook for 10 minutes or until tender. Drain well.
4. In a large mixing bowl, combine together squash, egg substitute, mayonnaise, 1/2 cup cheese, and salt.
5. Transfer squash mixture into a greased baking dish.
6. Set to bake at 375 F for 35 minutes. After 5 minutes place the baking dish in the preheated oven.
7. Sprinkle remaining cheese on top.
8. Serve and enjoy.

Nutritional Value (Amount per Serving):
Calories 130; Fat 8.2 g; Carbohydrates 7.7 g; Sugar 3.5 g; Protein 8 g; Cholesterol 18 mg

Cheddar Cheese Cauliflower Casserole

Preparation Time: 10 minutes; Cooking Time: 35 minutes; Serve: 8
Ingredients:
- 4 cups cauliflower florets
- 1 1/2 cups cheddar cheese, shredded
- 1 cup sour cream
- 4 bacon slices, cooked and crumbled
- 3 green onions, chopped

Directions:
1. Fit the Cuisinart oven with the rack in position 1.
2. Boil water in a large pot. Add cauliflower in boiling water and cook for 8-10 minutes or until tender. Drain well.
3. Transfer cauliflower in a large bowl.
4. Add half bacon, half green onion, 1 cup cheese, and sour cream in cauliflower bowl and mix well.

5. Transfer mixture into a greased baking dish and sprinkle with remaining cheese.
6. Set to bake at 350 F for 30 minutes. After 5 minutes place the baking dish in the preheated oven.
7. Garnish with remaining green onion and bacon.
8. Serve and enjoy.

Nutritional Value (Amount per Serving):
Calories 213; Fat 17.1 g; Carbohydrates 4.7 g; Sugar 1.5 g; Protein 10.8 g; Cholesterol 45 mg

Baked Honey Carrots

Preparation Time: 10 minutes; Cooking Time: 25 minutes; Serve: 4

Ingredients:
- 1 lb baby carrots
- 2 tbsp butter, melted
- 3 tbsp honey
- 2 tsp fresh parsley, chopped
- 1 tbsp Dijon mustard
- Pepper
- Salt

Directions:
1. Fit the Cuisinart oven with the rack in position 1.
2. In a large bowl, toss carrots with Dijon mustard, honey, butter, pepper, and salt.
3. Transfer carrots in a baking dish and spread evenly.
4. Set to bake at 400 F for 30 minutes. After 5 minutes place the baking dish in the preheated oven.
5. Serve and enjoy.

Nutritional Value (Amount per Serving):
Calories 141; Fat 6.1 g; Carbohydrates 22.6 g; Sugar 18.4 g; Protein 1 g; Cholesterol 15 mg

Paprika Potatoes

Preparation Time: 10 minutes; Cooking Time: 30 minutes; Serve: 4

Ingredients:
- 1 lb baby potatoes, quartered
- 1/4 tsp rosemary, crushed
- 1/2 tsp thyme
- 2 tbsp paprika
- 2 tbsp coconut oil, melted
- 1 tbsp olive oil
- Pepper
- Salt

Directions:
1. Fit the Cuisinart oven with the rack in position 1.
2. Place potatoes in a baking dish and sprinkle with paprika, rosemary, thyme, pepper, and salt.
3. Drizzle with oil and melted coconut oil.
4. Set to bake at 425 F for 35 minutes. After 5 minutes place the baking dish in the preheated oven.
5. Serve and enjoy.

Nutritional Value (Amount per Serving):
Calories 165; Fat 10.9 g; Carbohydrates 16.2 g; Sugar 0.4 g; Protein 3.4 g; Cholesterol 0 mg

Baked Potatoes Eggplant

Preparation Time: 10 minutes; Cooking Time: 40 minutes; Serve: 4

Ingredients:
- 2 medium eggplants, cut into pieces
- 1 tbsp lemon juice
- 1 lb potatoes, cut into cubes
- 1/4 cup olive oil
- Pepper
- Salt

Directions:

1. Fit the Cuisinart oven with the rack in position 1.
2. Add eggplant, potatoes, oil, pepper, and salt in a baking dish and toss well.
3. Set to bake at 400 F for 45 minutes. After 5 minutes place the baking dish in the preheated oven.
4. Drizzle with lemon juice and serve.

Nutritional Value (Amount per Serving):
Calories 244; Fat 13.2 g; Carbohydrates 31.4 g; Sugar 8.3 g; Protein 4.2 g; Cholesterol 0 mg

Baked Sweet Potatoes

Preparation Time: 10 minutes; Cooking Time: 35 minutes; Serve: 6
Ingredients:
- 4 large sweet potatoes, peel and cut into cubes
- 8 sage leaves
- 1 tsp honey
- 2 tsp vinegar
- 1/2 tsp paprika
- 2 tbsp olive oil
- 1/2 tsp sea salt

Directions:
1. Fit the Cuisinart oven with the rack in position 1.
2. Add sweet potato, oil, sage, and salt in a baking dish and mix well.
3. Set to bake at 375 F for 40 minutes. After 5 minutes place the baking dish in the preheated oven.
4. Transfer roasted sweet potatoes into the large bowl and toss with honey, vinegar, and paprika.
5. Serve and enjoy.

Nutritional Value (Amount per Serving):
Calories 92; Fat 5.1 g; Carbohydrates 12 g; Sugar 1.2 g; Protein 0.8 g; Cholesterol 0 mg

Baked Ratatouille

Preparation Time: 10 minutes; Cooking Time: 55 minutes; Serve: 6
Ingredients:
- 1 large eggplant, steamed and sliced
- 1/4 tsp dried thyme
- 2 bell pepper, sliced
- 4 tomatoes, sliced
- 2 tbsp olive oil
- 4 medium zucchini, sliced
- 1 tsp dried basil
- 1/2 tsp dried oregano

Directions:
1. Fit the Cuisinart oven with the rack in position 1.
2. Add all vegetable slices to a large bowl and season with salt and drizzle with oil.
3. Layer vegetable slices into the greased baking dish.
4. Set to bake at 400 F for 60 minutes. After 5 minutes place the baking dish in the preheated oven.
5. Sprinkle with dried herbs.
6. Serve and enjoy.

Nutritional Value (Amount per Serving):
Calories 108; Fat 5.3 g; Carbohydrates 15.2 g; Sugar 8.7 g; Protein 3.5 g; Cholesterol 0 mg

Baked Turnip & Sweet Potato

Preparation Time: 10 minutes; Cooking Time: 30 minutes; Serve: 4
Ingredients:
- 1 1/2 lbs sweet potato, sliced 1/4-inch thick
- 2 tbsp olive oil
- 1 lb turnips, sliced 1/4-inch thick
- 1 tbsp thyme, chopped
- 1 tsp paprika

- 1/4 tsp pepper
- 1/2 tsp sea salt

Directions:
1. Fit the Cuisinart oven with the rack in position 1.
2. Add sliced sweet potatoes and turnips in a bowl and toss with seasoning and olive oil.
3. Arrange sliced sweet potatoes and turnips in baking dish.
4. Set to bake at 425 F for 35 minutes. After 5 minutes place the baking dish in the preheated oven.
5. Garnish with thyme and serve.

Nutritional Value (Amount per Serving):
Calories 250; Fat 7.4 g; Carbohydrates 43.5 g; Sugar 15.8 g; Protein 4.5 g; Cholesterol 0 mg

Scalloped Potatoes

Preparation Time: 10 minutes; Cooking Time: 45 minutes; Serve: 6
Ingredients:
- 4 sweet potatoes, peeled
- 1/4 cup olive oil
- 1/2 tsp paprika
- 1 tbsp maple syrup
- 1/2 cup fresh orange juice
- 1/2 tsp orange zest
- 1 tsp salt

Directions:
1. Fit the Cuisinart oven with the rack in position 1.
2. Slice sweet potatoes 1/16-inch thick using a slicer.
3. Arrange sweet potato slices in a greased 8*8-inch baking dish.
4. In a bowl, whisk together the remaining ingredients and pour over sweet potatoes.
5. Set to bake at 350 F for 50 minutes. After 5 minutes place the baking dish in the preheated oven.
6. Serve and enjoy.

Nutritional Value (Amount per Serving):
Calories 130; Fat 8.5 g; Carbohydrates 13.8 g; Sugar 3.9 g; Protein 0.7 g; Cholesterol 0 mg

Delicious Baked Potatoes

Preparation Time: 10 minutes; Cooking Time: 50 minutes; Serve: 6
Ingredients:
- 3 lbs potatoes, peeled
- 1 tsp pepper
- 3 tbsp olive oil
- 3 tbsp coconut oil, melted
- 2 tsp salt

Directions:
1. Fit the Cuisinart oven with the rack in position 1.
2. Slice potatoes 1/4-inch thick using a slicer.
3. Transfer sliced potatoes to the bowl and toss with olive oil and coconut oil.
4. Arrange potato slices in a baking dish in a circular pattern. Season with pepper and salt.
5. Set to bake at 450 F for 55 minutes. After 5 minutes place the baking dish in the preheated oven.
6. Serve and enjoy.

Nutritional Value (Amount per Serving):
Calories 276; Fat 14 g; Carbohydrates 35.9 g; Sugar 2.6 g; Protein 3.9 g; Cholesterol 0 mg

Simple Baked Potatoes

Preparation Time: 10 minutes; Cooking Time: 55 minutes; Serve: 6
Ingredients:
- 1 1/2 lbs baby potatoes
- 3 tbsp olive oil

- Pepper
- Salt

Directions:
1. Fit the Cuisinart oven with the rack in position 1.
2. Add baby potatoes, salt, and water to a large pot and bring to boil over medium heat.
3. Cook potatoes until tender. Drain well and transfer to the skillet.
4. Gently smash each potato using the back of a spoon.
5. Drizzle potatoes with oil. Season with pepper and salt. Place potatoes in baking pan.
6. Set to bake at 450 F for 45 minutes. After 5 minutes place the baking pan in the preheated oven.
7. Serve and enjoy.

Nutritional Value (Amount per Serving):
Calories 126; Fat 7.1 g; Carbohydrates 14.1 g; Sugar 0 g; Protein 2.9 g; Cholesterol 0 mg

Air Fry Broccoli Florets

Preparation Time: 10 minutes; Cooking Time: 10 minutes; Serve: 2

Ingredients:
- 1 lb broccoli florets
- 1/2 tsp chili powder
- 1/4 tsp turmeric
- 2 tbsp plain yogurt
- 1 tbsp chickpea flour
- 1/2 tsp salt

Directions:
1. Fit the Cuisinart oven with the rack in position 2.
2. Add all ingredients to the bowl and toss well.
3. Place marinated broccoli in a refrigerator for 15 minutes.
4. Place marinated broccoli in an air fryer basket then places an air fryer basket in a baking pan.
5. Place a baking pan on the oven rack. Set to air fry at 390 F for 10 minutes.
6. Serve and enjoy.

Nutritional Value (Amount per Serving):
Calories 114; Fat 1.5 g; Carbohydrates 20.5 g; Sugar 5.7 g; Protein 8.5 g; Cholesterol 1 mg

Air-Fried Herb Mushrooms

Preparation Time: 10 minutes; Cooking Time: 25 minutes; Serve: 2

Ingredients:
- 1 lbs mushrooms, wash, dry, and cut into quarter
- 1 tbsp white vermouth
- 1 tsp herb de Provence
- 1/4 tsp garlic powder
- 1/2 tbsp olive oil

Directions:
1. Fit the Cuisinart oven with the rack in position 2.
2. Add all ingredients to the bowl and toss well.
3. Transfer mushrooms in the air fryer basket then place the air fryer basket in the baking pan.
4. Place a baking pan on the oven rack. Set to air fry at 350 F for 25 minutes.
5. Serve and enjoy.

Nutritional Value (Amount per Serving):
Calories 99; Fat 4.5 g; Carbohydrates 8.1 g; Sugar 4 g; Protein 7.9 g; Cholesterol 0 mg

Lemon Garlic Brussels Sprouts

Preparation Time: 10 minutes; Cooking Time: 12 minutes; Serve: 2

Ingredients:

- 1/2 lb Brussels sprouts, rinse and pat dry with a paper towel
- 1/2 tsp garlic powder
- 1 tbsp lemon juice
- 1/4 tsp black pepper
- 1 tbsp olive oil
- 1/2 tsp salt

Directions:
1. Fit the Cuisinart oven with the rack in position 2.
2. Cut the stem of Brussels sprouts and cut each Brussels sprouts in half.
3. Transfer Brussels sprouts in a bowl and toss with garlic powder, olive oil, pepper, and salt.
4. Transfer Brussels sprouts in air fryer basket then place air fryer basket in baking pan.
5. Place baking pan on the oven rack. Set to air fry at 360 F for 12 minutes.
6. Drizzle with lemon juice and serve.

Nutritional Value (Amount per Serving):
Calories 114; Fat 7.5 g; Carbohydrates 11.2 g; Sugar 2.8 g; Protein 4.1 g; Cholesterol 0 mg

Air Fryer Corn

Preparation Time: 10 minutes; Cooking Time: 10 minutes; Serve: 2

Ingredients:
- 2 fresh ears of corn, remove husks, wash, and pat dry
- 1 tbsp fresh lemon juice
- 2 tsp oil
- Pepper
- Salt

Directions:
1. Fit the Cuisinart oven with the rack in position 2.
2. Cut the corn to fit in the air fryer basket.
3. Drizzle oil over the corn. Season with pepper and salt.
4. Place corn in the air fryer basket then places an air fryer basket in the baking pan.
5. Place a baking pan on the oven rack. Set to air fry at 400 F for 10 minutes.
6. Serve and enjoy.
7. Drizzle lemon juice over corn and serve.

Nutritional Value (Amount per Serving):
Calories 122; Fat 5.6 g; Carbohydrates 18.2 g; Sugar 4.2 g; Protein 3.1 g; Cholesterol 0 mg

Air Fried Eggplant Cubes

Preparation Time: 10 minutes; Cooking Time: 12 minutes; Serve: 2

Ingredients:
- 1 eggplant, cut into cubes
- 1/4 tsp oregano
- 1 tbsp olive oil
- 1/2 tsp garlic powder

Directions:
1. Fit the Cuisinart oven with the rack in position 2.
2. Add all ingredients into the large bowl and toss well.
3. Transfer eggplant into in air fryer basket then places the air fryer basket in the baking pan.
4. Place a baking pan on the oven rack. Set to air fry at 390 F for 12 minutes.
5. Serve and enjoy.

Nutritional Value (Amount per Serving):
Calories 120; Fat 7.4 g; Carbohydrates 14.1 g; Sugar 7.1 g; Protein 2.4 g; Cholesterol 0 mg

Healthy Green Beans

Preparation Time: 10 minutes; Cooking Time: 10 minutes; Serve: 2

Ingredients:
- 8 oz green beans, trimmed and cut in half
- 1 tbsp tamari
- 1 tsp toasted sesame oil

Directions:
1. Fit the Cuisinart oven with the rack in position 2.
2. Add all ingredients into the large bowl and toss well.
3. Transfer green beans in the air fryer basket then place an air fryer basket in the baking pan.
4. Place a baking pan on the oven rack. Set to air fry at 400 F for 10 minutes.
5. Serve and enjoy.

Nutritional Value (Amount per Serving):
Calories 61; Fat 2.4 g; Carbohydrates 8.6 g; Sugar 1.7 g; Protein 3 g; Cholesterol 0 mg

Ranch Potatoes

Preparation Time: 10 minutes; Cooking Time: 20 minutes; Serve: 6
Ingredients:
- 1 1/2 lbs baby potatoes, cut in half
- 1/2 tsp paprika
- 1/2 tsp onion powder
- 1/2 tsp dill
- 1/2 tsp chives
- 1/2 tsp parsley
- 1/2 tsp garlic powder
- 2 tbsp olive oil
- 1/2 tsp salt

Directions:
1. Fit the Cuisinart oven with the rack in position 2.
2. Add baby potatoes and remaining ingredients into the mixing bowl and toss until well coated.
3. Transfer baby potatoes in air fryer basket then place air fryer basket in baking pan.
4. Place a baking pan on the oven rack. Set to air fry at 400 F for 20 minutes.
5. Serve and enjoy.

Nutritional Value (Amount per Serving):
Calories 108; Fat 4.8 g; Carbohydrates 14.6 g; Sugar 0.2 g; Protein 3 g; Cholesterol 0 mg

Air Fry Garlic Baby Potatoes

Preparation Time: 10 minutes; Cooking Time: 20 minutes; Serve: 4
Ingredients:
- 1 lb baby potatoes, cut into quarters
- 1/2 tsp granulated garlic
- 1 tbsp olive oil
- 1/2 tsp dried parsley
- 1/4 tsp salt

Directions:
1. Fit the Cuisinart oven with the rack in position 2.
2. In a mixing bowl, toss baby potatoes with oil, garlic, parsley, and salt.
3. Transfer potatoes in air fryer basket then place air fryer basket in baking pan.
4. Place a baking pan on the oven rack. Set to air fry at 350 F for 20 minutes.
5. Serve and enjoy.

Nutritional Value (Amount per Serving):
Calories 97; Fat 3.6 g; Carbohydrates 14.4 g; Sugar 0.1 g; Protein 3 g; Cholesterol 0 mg

Brussels Sprouts & Sweet Potatoes

Preparation Time: 10 minutes; Cooking Time: 15 minutes; Serve: 6
Ingredients:
- 1 lb sweet potatoes, peeled and diced into 1/2-inch cubes
- 1 lb Brussels sprouts, remove stem & into quartered
- 2 tbsp olive oil
- 1 tsp chili powder
- Pepper
- Salt

Directions:
1. Fit the Cuisinart oven with the rack in position 2.
2. Add Brussels sprouts, sweet potatoes, chili powder, olive oil, pepper, and salt into the mixing bowl and toss well.
3. Transfer Brussels sprouts & sweet potato mixture in air fryer basket then place air fryer basket in baking pan.
4. Place a baking pan on the oven rack. Set to air fry at 380 F for 15 minutes.
5. Serve and enjoy.

Nutritional Value (Amount per Serving):
Calories 163; Fat 5.1 g; Carbohydrates 28.2 g; Sugar 2 g; Protein 3.8 g; Cholesterol 0 mg

Tasty Hassel Back Potatoes

Preparation Time: 10 minutes; Cooking Time: 30 minutes; Serve: 4
Ingredients:
- 4 potatoes, peel & cut potato across the potato to make 1/8-inch slices
- 1/4 cup parmesan cheese, shredded
- 1 tbsp olive oil

Directions:
1. Fit the Cuisinart oven with the rack in position 2.
2. Brush potatoes with olive oil.
3. Place potatoes in the air fryer basket then place an air fryer basket in the baking pan.
4. Place a baking pan on the oven rack. Set to air fry at 350 F for 30 minutes.
5. Sprinkle cheese on top of potatoes and serve.

Nutritional Value (Amount per Serving):
Calories 195; Fat 4.9 g; Carbohydrates 33.7 g; Sugar 2.5 g; Protein 5.4 g; Cholesterol 4 mg

Spicy Brussels Sprouts

Preparation Time: 10 minutes; Cooking Time: 15 minutes; Serve: 4
Ingredients:
- 1 lb Brussels sprouts, cut in half
- 1 1/2 tbsp olive oil
- 1 tbsp gochujang
- 1/2 tsp salt

Directions:
1. Fit the Cuisinart oven with the rack in position 2.
2. In a large mixing bowl, mix together olive oil, gochujang, and salt.
3. Add Brussels sprouts into the bowl and toss until well coated.
4. Transfer Brussels sprouts in air fryer basket then place air fryer basket in baking pan.
5. Place a baking pan on the oven rack. Set to air fry at 360 F for 20 minutes.
6. Serve and enjoy.

Nutritional Value (Amount per Serving):
Calories 98; Fat 5.6 g; Carbohydrates 11.2 g; Sugar 3 g; Protein 4 g; Cholesterol 0 mg

Chili Lime Sweet Potatoes

Preparation Time: 10 minutes; Cooking Time: 15 minutes; Serve: 4
Ingredients:
- 2 large sweet potatoes, peeled & cut into 1-inch pieces
- 1 tbsp chili powder
- 2 tbsp olive oil
- 2 tsp fresh lime juice
- 1 tsp cumin

Directions:
1. Fit the Cuisinart oven with the rack in position 2.
2. In a mixing bowl, add sweet potatoes, lime juice, cumin, chili powder, and olive oil and toss well.

3. Transfer sweet potatoes in air fryer basket then place air fryer basket in baking pan.
4. Place a baking pan on the oven rack. Set to air fry at 380 F for 20 minutes.
5. Serve and enjoy.

Nutritional Value (Amount per Serving):
Calories 132; Fat 1.1 g; Carbohydrates 17.1 g; Sugar 0.8 g; Protein 1.2 g; Cholesterol 0 mg

Tasty Butternut Squash

Preparation Time: 10 minutes; Cooking Time: 15 minutes; Serve: 4

Ingredients:
- 4 cups butternut squash, cut into 1-inch pieces
- 1 tbsp brown sugar
- 2 tbsp olive oil
- 1 tsp Chinese 5 spice powder

Directions:
1. Fit the Cuisinart oven with the rack in position 2.
2. Toss squash into the bowl with remaining ingredients.
3. Transfer squash in the air fryer basket then places the air fryer basket in the baking pan.
4. Place a baking pan on the oven rack. Set to air fry at 400 F for 15 minutes.
5. Serve and enjoy.

Nutritional Value (Amount per Serving):
Calories 132; Fat 7.1 g; Carbohydrates 18.6 g; Sugar 5.3 g; Protein 1.4 g; Cholesterol 0 mg

Chapter 7: Snacks & Appetizers

Jalapeno Spinach Dip

Preparation Time: 10 minutes; Cooking Time: 30 minutes; Serve: 6

Ingredients:
- 10 oz frozen spinach, thawed and drained
- 2 tsp jalapeno pepper, minced
- 1/2 cup cheddar cheese, shredded
- 8 oz cream cheese
- 1/2 cup onion, diced
- 2 tsp garlic, minced
- 1/2 cup mozzarella cheese, shredded
- 1/2 cup Monterey jack cheese, shredded
- 1/2 tsp salt

Directions:
1. Fit the Cuisinart oven with the rack in position 1.
2. Add all ingredients into the mixing bowl and mix until well combined.
3. Pour mixture into the 1-quart casserole dish.
4. Set to bake at 350 F for 35 minutes. After 5 minutes place the casserole dish in the preheated oven.
5. Serve and enjoy.

Nutritional Value (Amount per Serving):
Calories 228; Fat 19.8 g; Carbohydrates 4.2 g; Sugar 0.8 g; Protein 9.7 g; Cholesterol 61 mg

Flavorful Crab Dip

Preparation Time: 10 minutes; Cooking Time: 15 minutes; Serve: 6

Ingredients:
- 6 oz crab lump meat
- 1 tbsp mayonnaise
- 1/8 tsp paprika
- 1/4 cup sour cream
- 4 tsp bell pepper, diced
- 1 tbsp butter, softened
- 1 tsp parsley, chopped
- 1 tbsp green onion, sliced
- 1/4 cup mozzarella cheese, shredded
- 4 tsp onion, chopped
- 2 oz cream cheese, softened
- 1/4 tsp salt

Directions:
1. Fit the Cuisinart oven with the rack in position 1.
2. In a bowl, mix together cream cheese, butter, sour cream, and mayonnaise until smooth.
3. Add remaining ingredients and stir well.
4. Pour mixture into the greased baking dish.
5. Set to bake at 350 F for 20 minutes. After 5 minutes place the baking dish in the preheated oven.
6. Serve and enjoy.

Nutritional Value (Amount per Serving):
Calories 131; Fat 10.8 g; Carbohydrates 8.1 g; Sugar 4.3 g; Protein 6.4 g; Cholesterol 37 mg

Spicy Brussels Sprouts

Preparation Time: 10 minutes; Cooking Time: 35 minutes; Serve: 6

Ingredients:
- 2 cups Brussels sprouts, halved
- 1/4 tsp cayenne pepper
- 1/2 tsp smoked paprika
- 1/4 tsp chili powder
- 1/4 tsp garlic powder
- 1/4 cup olive oil
- 1/4 tsp salt

Directions:
1. Fit the Cuisinart oven with the rack in position 1.

2. Add all ingredients into the large bowl and toss well.
3. Transfer Brussels sprouts on a baking pan.
4. Set to bake at 400 F for 40 minutes. After 5 minutes place the baking pan in the preheated oven.
5. Serve and enjoy.

Nutritional Value (Amount per Serving):
Calories 86; Fat 8.6 g; Carbohydrates 3 g; Sugar 0.7 g; Protein 1.1 g; Cholesterol 0 mg

Baked Almonds

Preparation Time: 10 minutes; Cooking Time: 20 minutes; Serve: 6
Ingredients:
- 1 1/2 cups raw almonds
- 1/2 tsp cayenne
- 1/4 tsp onion powder
- 1/4 tsp dried basil
- 2 tbsp butter, melted
- 1/2 tsp garlic powder
- 1/2 tsp cumin
- 1 1/2 tsp chili powder
- 1/2 tsp sea salt

Directions:
1. Fit the Cuisinart oven with the rack in position 1.
2. Add almonds and remaining ingredients into the mixing bowl and toss well.
3. Spread almonds in baking pan.
4. Set to bake at 350 F for 25 minutes. After 5 minutes place the baking pan in the preheated oven.
5. Serve and enjoy.

Nutritional Value (Amount per Serving):
Calories 176; Fat 15.9 g; Carbohydrates 5.9 g; Sugar 1.2 g; Protein 5.2 g; Cholesterol 10 mg

Cheesy Spinach Dip

Preparation Time: 10 minutes; Cooking Time: 20 minutes; Serve: 12
Ingredients:
- 3 oz frozen spinach, defrosted & chopped
- 1 cup sour cream
- 1 tsp garlic salt
- 2 cups cheddar cheese, shredded
- 8 oz cream cheese

Directions:
1. Fit the Cuisinart oven with the rack in position 1.
2. Add all ingredients into the mixing bowl and mix well.
3. Transfer mixture into the baking dish.
4. Set to bake at 350 F for 25 minutes. After 5 minutes place the baking dish in the preheated oven.
5. Serve and enjoy.

Nutritional Value (Amount per Serving):
Calories 185; Fat 16.9 g; Carbohydrates 2 g; Sugar 0.3 g; Protein 7 g; Cholesterol 49 mg

Cheese Garlic Dip

Preparation Time: 10 minutes; Cooking Time: 20 minutes; Serve: 12
Ingredients:
- 4 garlic cloves, minced
- 5 oz Asiago cheese, shredded
- 1 cup sour cream
- 1 cup mozzarella cheese, shredded
- 8 oz cream cheese, softened

Directions:
1. Fit the Cuisinart oven with the rack in position 1.

2. Add all ingredients into the mixing bowl and mix until well combined.
3. Pour mixture into the baking dish.
4. Set to bake at 350 F for 25 minutes. After 5 minutes place the baking dish in the preheated oven.
5. Serve and enjoy.

Nutritional Value (Amount per Serving):
Calories 157; Fat 14.4 g; Carbohydrates 1.7 g; Sugar 0.1 g; Protein 5.7 g; Cholesterol 41 mg

Tasty Ricotta Dip

Preparation Time: 10 minutes; Cooking Time: 15 minutes; Serve: 6
Ingredients:
- 1 cup ricotta cheese, shredded
- 1 tbsp lemon juice
- 2 tbsp olive oil
- 1/4 cup parmesan cheese, grated
- 1/2 cup mozzarella cheese, shredded
- 1 tbsp rosemary, chopped
- 2 garlic cloves, minced
- Pepper
- Salt

Directions:
1. Fit the Cuisinart oven with the rack in position 1.
2. Add all ingredients into the mixing bowl and mix until well combined.
3. Pour mixture into the prepared baking dish.
4. Set to bake at 400 F for 20 minutes. After 5 minutes place the baking dish in the preheated oven.
5. Serve and enjoy.

Nutritional Value (Amount per Serving):
Calories 120; Fat 9.3 g; Carbohydrates 3.1 g; Sugar 0.2 g; Protein 6.7 g; Cholesterol 17 mg

Cheesy Onion Dip

Preparation Time: 10 minutes; Cooking Time: 40 minutes; Serve: 8
Ingredients:
- 1 1/2 onions, chopped
- 1/2 tsp garlic powder
- 1 1/2 cup Swiss cheese, shredded
- 1 cup mozzarella cheese, shredded
- 1 cup cheddar cheese, shredded
- 1 1/2 cup mayonnaise
- Pepper
- Salt

Directions:
1. Fit the Cuisinart oven with the rack in position 1.
2. Add all ingredients into the mixing bowl and mix until well combined.
3. Pour mixture into the prepared baking dish.
4. Set to bake at 350 F for 45 minutes. After 5 minutes place the baking dish in the preheated oven.
5. Serve and enjoy.

Nutritional Value (Amount per Serving):
Calories 325; Fat 25.7 g; Carbohydrates 14 g; Sugar 4.1 g; Protein 10.6 g; Cholesterol 47 mg

Easy Cheese Dip

Preparation Time: 10 minutes; Cooking Time: 30 minutes; Serve: 12
Ingredients:
- 1/2 cup mayonnaise
- 1 small onion, diced
- 1 1/2 cups mozzarella cheese, shredded
- 4 oz cream cheese, cubed
- 1 1/2 cups cheddar cheese, shredded

Directions:
1. Fit the Cuisinart oven with the rack in position 1.
2. Add all ingredients into the mixing bowl and mix until well combined.
3. Pour mixture into the prepared baking dish.
4. Set to bake at 400 F for 35 minutes. After 5 minutes place the baking dish in the preheated oven.
5. Serve and enjoy.

Nutritional Value (Amount per Serving):
Calories 140; Fat 11.9 g; Carbohydrates 3.4 g; Sugar 1 g; Protein 5.4 g; Cholesterol 30 mg

Spicy Cauliflower Florets

Preparation Time: 10 minutes; Cooking Time: 15 minutes; Serve: 4

Ingredients:
- 1 medium cauliflower head, cut into florets
- 1/2 tsp old bay seasoning
- 1/4 tsp paprika
- 1/4 tsp cayenne
- 1/4 tsp chili powder
- 1 tbsp garlic, minced
- 3 tbsp olive oil
- Pepper
- Salt

Directions:
1. Fit the Cuisinart oven with the rack in position 2.
2. In a bowl, toss cauliflower with remaining ingredients.
3. Add cauliflower florets in air fryer basket then place air fryer basket in baking pan.
4. Place a baking pan on the oven rack. Set to air fry at 400 F for 15 minutes.
5. Serve and enjoy.

Nutritional Value (Amount per Serving):
Calories 130; Fat 10.7 g; Carbohydrates 8.6 g; Sugar 3.5 g; Protein 3 g; Cholesterol 0 mg

Delicious Jalapeno Poppers

Preparation Time: 10 minutes; Cooking Time: 7 minutes; Serve: 10

Ingredients:
- 10 jalapeno peppers, cut in half, remove seeds & membranes
- 1/2 cup cheddar cheese, shredded
- 4 oz cream cheese
- 1/4 tsp paprika
- 1 tsp ground cumin
- 1 tsp salt

Directions:
1. Fit the Cuisinart oven with the rack in position 2.
2. In a small bowl, mix together cream cheese, cheddar cheese, cumin, paprika, and salt.
3. Stuff cream cheese mixture into each jalapeno half.
4. Place stuffed jalapeno peppers in air fryer basket then place air fryer basket in baking pan.
5. Place a baking pan on the oven rack. Set to air fry at 350 F for 7 minutes.
6. Serve and enjoy.

Nutritional Value (Amount per Serving):
Calories 69; Fat 6.1 g; Carbohydrates 1.5 g; Sugar 0.5 g; Protein 2.5 g; Cholesterol 18 mg

Air Fryer Walnuts

Preparation Time: 10 minutes; Cooking Time: 5 minutes; Serve: 6

Ingredients:
- 2 cups walnuts
- 1 tsp olive oil
- Pepper
- Salt

Directions:

1. Fit the Cuisinart oven with the rack in position 2.
2. Add walnuts, oil, pepper, and salt into the bowl and toss well.
3. Add walnuts to the air fryer basket then place an air fryer basket in baking pan.
4. Place a baking pan on the oven rack. Set to air fry at 350 F for 5 minutes.
5. Serve and enjoy.

Nutritional Value (Amount per Serving):
Calories 264; Fat 25.4 g; Carbohydrates 4.1 g; Sugar 0.5 g; Protein 10 g; Cholesterol 0 mg

Garlic Cauliflower Florets

Preparation Time: 10 minutes; Cooking Time: 20 minutes; Serve: 4
Ingredients:
- 5 cups cauliflower florets
- 6 garlic cloves, chopped
- 4 tablespoons olive oil
- 1/2 tsp cumin powder
- 1/2 tsp salt

Directions:
1. Fit the Cuisinart oven with the rack in position 2.
2. Add all ingredients into the large bowl and toss well.
3. Add cauliflower florets in air fryer basket then place air fryer basket in baking pan.
4. Place a baking pan on the oven rack. Set to air fry at 400 F for 20 minutes.
5. Serve and enjoy.

Nutritional Value (Amount per Serving):
Calories 159; Fat 14.2 g; Carbohydrates 8.2 g; Sugar 3.1 g; Protein 2.8 g; Cholesterol 0 mg

Cheesy Brussels Sprouts

Preparation Time: 10 minutes; Cooking Time: 12 minutes; Serve: 4
Ingredients:
- 1 lb Brussels sprouts, cut stems and halved
- 1/4 cup parmesan cheese, grated
- 1 tbsp olive oil
- 1/4 tsp paprika
- 1/4 tsp chili powder
- 1/2 tsp garlic powder
- Pepper
- Salt

Directions:
1. Fit the Cuisinart oven with the rack in position 2.
2. Toss Brussels sprouts with remaining ingredients except for cheese and place in air fryer basket then place air fryer basket in baking pan.
3. Place a baking pan on the oven rack. Set to air fry at 350 F for 12 minutes.
4. Top with parmesan cheese and serve.

Nutritional Value (Amount per Serving):
Calories 100; Fat 5.2 g; Carbohydrates 11 g; Sugar 2.6 g; Protein 5.8 g; Cholesterol 4 mg

Air Fryer Spicy Chickpeas

Preparation Time: 10 minutes; Cooking Time: 12 minutes; Serve: 4
Ingredients:
- 14 oz can chickpeas, rinsed, drained and pat dry
- 1/2 tsp smoked paprika
- 1/4 tsp cayenne
- 1/2 tsp chili powder
- 1 tbsp olive oil
- Pepper
- Salt

Directions:
1. Fit the Cuisinart oven with the rack in position 2.

2. Add chickpeas, chili powder, cayenne, paprika, oil, pepper, and salt into the bowl and toss well.
3. Spread chickpeas in the air fryer basket then place the air fryer basket in the baking pan.
4. Place a baking pan on the oven rack. Set to air fry at 375 F for 12 minutes.
5. Serve and enjoy.

Nutritional Value (Amount per Serving):
Calories 150; Fat 4.7 g; Carbohydrates 22.8 g; Sugar 0.1 g; Protein 5 g; Cholesterol 0 mg

Sweet Cinnamon Chickpeas

Preparation Time: 10 minutes; Cooking Time: 12 minutes; Serve: 4
Ingredients:
- 15 oz can chickpeas, rinsed, drained and pat dry
- 1 tbsp olive oil
- 1/2 tsp ground cinnamon
- 1 tbsp honey
- Pepper
- Salt

Directions:
1. Fit the Cuisinart oven with the rack in position 2.
2. Spread chickpeas in the air fryer basket then place an air fryer basket in the baking pan.
3. Place a baking pan on the oven rack. Set to air fry at 375 F for 12 minutes.
4. In a large bowl, mix cinnamon, honey, oil, pepper, and salt. Add chickpeas and toss well.
5. Serve and enjoy.

Nutritional Value (Amount per Serving):
Calories 173; Fat 4.7 g; Carbohydrates 28.6 g; Sugar 4.3 g; Protein 5.3 g; Cholesterol 0 mg

Easy Sweet Potato Fries

Preparation Time: 10 minutes; Cooking Time: 16 minutes; Serve: 2
Ingredients:
- 2 sweet potatoes, peeled and cut into fries shape
- 1 tbsp olive oil
- Salt

Directions:
1. Fit the Cuisinart oven with the rack in position 2.
2. Toss sweet potato fries with oil and salt and place in the air fryer basket then place the air fryer basket in the baking pan.
3. Place a baking pan on the oven rack. Set to air fry at 375 F for 16 minutes.
4. Serve and enjoy.

Nutritional Value (Amount per Serving):
Calories 178; Fat 7.2 g; Carbohydrates 27.9 g; Sugar 0.5 g; Protein 1.5 g; Cholesterol 0 mg

Salsa Cheese Dip

Preparation Time: 10 minutes; Cooking Time: 30 minutes; Serve: 10
Ingredients:
- 16 oz cream cheese, softened
- 3 cups cheddar cheese, shredded
- 1 cup sour cream
- 1/2 cup hot salsa

Directions:
1. Fit the Cuisinart oven with the rack in position 1.
2. In a bowl, mix all ingredients until just combined and pour into the baking dish.
3. Set to bake at 350 F for 35 minutes. After 5 minutes place the baking dish in the preheated oven.
4. Serve and enjoy.

Nutritional Value (Amount per Serving):

Calories 348; Fat 31.9 g; Carbohydrates 3.4 g; Sugar 0.7 g; Protein 12.8 g; Cholesterol 96 mg

Perfect Ranch Potatoes

Preparation Time: 10 minutes; Cooking Time: 20 minutes; Serve: 2

Ingredients:
- 1/2 lb baby potatoes, wash and cut in half
- 1/4 tsp parsley
- 1/2 tbsp olive oil
- 1/4 tsp dill
- 1/4 tsp paprika
- 1/4 tsp onion powder
- 1/4 tsp garlic powder
- 1/4 tsp chives
- Salt

Directions:
1. Fit the Cuisinart oven with the rack in position 2.
2. Add all ingredients into the bowl and toss well.
3. Spread potatoes in the air fryer basket then place an air fryer basket in the baking pan.
4. Place a baking pan on the oven rack. Set to air fry at 400 F for 20 minutes.
5. Serve and enjoy.

Nutritional Value (Amount per Serving):
Calories 99; Fat 3.7 g; Carbohydrates 14.8 g; Sugar 0.2 g; Protein 3.1 g; Cholesterol 0 mg

Tasty Potato Wedges

Preparation Time: 10 minutes; Cooking Time: 15 minutes; Serve: 4

Ingredients:
- 2 medium potatoes, cut into wedges
- 1/4 tsp garlic powder
- 1/4 tsp pepper
- 1/2 tsp paprika
- 1 1/2 tbsp olive oil
- 1/8 tsp cayenne
- 1 tsp sea salt

Directions:
1. Fit the Cuisinart oven with the rack in position 2.
2. Soak potato wedges into the water for 30 minutes.
3. Drain well and pat dry with a paper towel.
4. In a bowl, toss potato wedges with remaining ingredients.
5. Place potato wedges in the air fryer basket then place an air fryer basket in the baking pan.
6. Place a baking pan on the oven rack. Set to air fry at 400 F for 15 minutes.
7. Serve and enjoy.

Nutritional Value (Amount per Serving):
Calories 120; Fat 5.4 g; Carbohydrates 17.1 g; Sugar 1.3 g; Protein 1.9 g; Cholesterol 0 mg

Delicious Cauliflower Hummus

Preparation Time: 10 minutes; Cooking Time: 35 minutes; Serve: 8

Ingredients:
- 1 cauliflower head, cut into florets
- 3 tbsp olive oil
- 1/2 tsp ground cumin
- 2 tbsp fresh lemon juice
- 1/3 cup tahini
- 1 tsp garlic, chopped
- Pepper
- Salt

Directions:
1. Fit the Cuisinart oven with the rack in position 1.
2. Spread cauliflower florets in baking pan.
3. Set to bake at 400 F for 40 minutes. After 5 minutes place the baking dish in the preheated oven.

4. Transfer roasted cauliflower into the food processor along with remaining ingredients and process until smooth.
5. Serve and enjoy.

Nutritional Value (Amount per Serving):
Calories 115; Fat 10.7 g; Carbohydrates 4.2 g; Sugar 0.9 g; Protein 2.4 g; Cholesterol 0 mg

Air Fryer Mixed Nuts

Preparation Time: 10 minutes; Cooking Time: 4 minutes; Serve: 2

Ingredients:
- 2 cup mixed nuts
- 1 tbsp olive oil
- 1 tsp ground cumin
- 1 tsp pepper
- 1/4 tsp cayenne
- 1 tsp salt

Directions:
1. Fit the Cuisinart oven with the rack in position 2.
2. In a bowl, add all ingredients and toss well.
3. Add the nuts mixture to the air fryer basket then place an air fryer basket in the baking pan.
4. Place a baking pan on the oven rack. Set to air fry at 350 F for 4 minutes.
5. Serve and enjoy.

Nutritional Value (Amount per Serving):
Calories 953; Fat 88.2 g; Carbohydrates 33.3 g; Sugar 6.4 g; Protein 22.7 g; Cholesterol 0 mg

Air Fry Olives

Preparation Time: 10 minutes; Cooking Time: 5 minutes; Serve: 4

Ingredients:
- 2 cups olives
- 2 tsp garlic, minced
- 2 tbsp olive oil
- 1/2 tsp dried oregano
- Pepper
- Salt

Directions:
1. Fit the Cuisinart oven with the rack in position 2.
2. Add olives and remaining ingredients into the large bowl and toss well.
3. Add olives to the air fryer basket then place an air fryer basket in baking pan.
4. Place a baking pan on the oven rack. Set to air fry at 300 F for 5 minutes.
5. Serve and enjoy.

Nutritional Value (Amount per Serving):
Calories 140; Fat 14.2 g; Carbohydrates 4.8 g; Sugar 0 g; Protein 0.7 g; Cholesterol 0 mg

Sweet Potato Croquettes

Preparation Time: 10 minutes; Cooking Time: 55 minutes; Serve: 6

Ingredients:
- 2 cups cooked quinoa
- 1/4 cup parsley, chopped
- 1/4 cup flour
- 2 cups sweet potatoes, mashed
- 2 tsp Italian seasoning
- 1 garlic clove, minced
- 1/4 cup celery, diced
- 1/4 cup scallions, chopped
- Pepper
- Salt

Directions:
1. Fit the Cuisinart oven with the rack in position 1.
2. Add all ingredients into the mixing bowl and mix until well combined.
3. Make 1-inch round croquettes from mixture and place in baking pan.

4. Set to bake at 375 F for 60 minutes. After 5 minutes place the baking pan in the preheated oven.
5. Serve and enjoy.

Nutritional Value (Amount per Serving):
Calories 295; Fat 4.1 g; Carbohydrates 55.2 g; Sugar 0.6 g; Protein 9.5 g; Cholesterol 1 mg

Healthy Carrot Fries

Preparation Time: 10 minutes; Cooking Time: 25 minutes; Serve: 4

Ingredients:
- 4 medium carrots, peel and cut into fries shape
- 1/2 tbsp paprika
- 1 1/2 tbsp olive oil
- 1/2 tsp salt

Directions:
1. Fit the Cuisinart oven with the rack in position 1.
2. Add carrots, paprika, oil, and salt into the mixing bowl and toss well.
3. Transfer carrot fries in baking pan.
4. Set to bake at 450 F for 30 minutes. After 5 minutes place the baking pan in the preheated oven.
5. Serve and enjoy.

Nutritional Value (Amount per Serving):
Calories 73; Fat 5.4 g; Carbohydrates 6.5 g; Sugar 3.1 g; Protein 0.6 g; Cholesterol 0 mg

Artichoke Cashews Spinach Dip

Preparation Time: 10 minutes; Cooking Time: 20 minutes; Serve: 10

Ingredients:
- 28 oz can artichokes, drained and rinsed
- 1 small onion, diced
- 4 garlic cloves
- 1 1/2 cups cashews
- 1 tsp olive oil
- 4 cups fresh spinach
- 2 tbsp fresh lemon juice
- 1/4 cup nutritional yeast
- 1 1/2 cups milk
- 1 1/2 tsp salt

Directions:
1. Fit the Cuisinart oven with the rack in position 2.
2. Soak cashews in boiling water for 5 minutes. Drain well.
3. Heat oil in a pan over medium heat. Add onion and garlic and sauté for 2-3 minutes.
4. Remove pan from heat and set aside.
5. Add soaked cashews, milk, nutritional yeast, lemon juice, and salt into the blender and blend until smooth.
6. Add sautéed garlic onion, artichokes, and spinach and blend for few minutes until getting chunky texture.
7. Transfer blended mixture into the baking dish.
8. Set to bake at 425 F for 25 minutes. After 5 minutes place the baking dish in the preheated oven.
9. Serve and enjoy.

Nutritional Value (Amount per Serving):
Calories 205; Fat 11.3 g; Carbohydrates 21.4 g; Sugar 3.9 g; Protein 9 g; Cholesterol 3 mg

Easy Air Fryer Tofu

Preparation Time: 10 minutes; Cooking Time: 15 minutes; Serve: 4

Ingredients:

- 16 oz extra firm tofu, cut into bite-sized pieces
- 1 tbsp olive oil
- 1 garlic clove, minced

Directions:
1. Fit the Cuisinart oven with the rack in position 2.
2. Add tofu, garlic, and oil in a mixing bowl and toss well. Let it sit for 15 minutes.
3. Arrange tofu in the air fryer basket then place an air fryer basket in the baking pan.
4. Place a baking pan on the oven rack. Set to air fry at 370 F for 15 minutes.
5. Serve and enjoy.

Nutritional Value (Amount per Serving):
Calories 111; Fat 8.2 g; Carbohydrates 2.2 g; Sugar 0.7 g; Protein 9.3 g; Cholesterol 0 mg

Tasty Broccoli Fritters

Preparation Time: 10 minutes; Cooking Time: 30 minutes; Serve: 4
Ingredients:
- 3 cups broccoli florets, steam & chopped
- 2 eggs, lightly beaten
- 2 garlic cloves, minced
- 2 cups cheddar cheese, shredded
- 1/4 cup breadcrumbs
- 1/2 tsp Italian seasoning
- Pepper
- Salt

Directions:
1. Fit the Cuisinart oven with the rack in position 1.
2. Add all ingredients into the large bowl and mix until well combined.
3. Make patties from broccoli mixture and place in baking pan.
4. Set to bake at 375 F for 35 minutes. After 5 minutes place the baking pan in the preheated oven.
5. Serve and enjoy.

Nutritional Value (Amount per Serving):
Calories 313; Fat 21.7 g; Carbohydrates 10.9 g; Sugar 2.1 g; Protein 19.8 g; Cholesterol 142 mg

Healthy Baked Pecans

Preparation Time: 10 minutes; Cooking Time: 15 minutes; Serve: 8
Ingredients:
- 4 cups pecans
- 1/4 tsp onion powder
- 1/4 tsp garlic powder
- 4 tbsp fresh rosemary, chopped
- 1/4 cup olive oil
- 2 tsp lemon zest
- 1/4 tsp paprika
- 2 tsp Himalayan salt

Directions:
1. Fit the Cuisinart oven with the rack in position 1.
2. Add all ingredients except lemon zest into the large bowl and toss well.
3. Transfer pecans in baking pan.
4. Set to bake at 350 F for 20 minutes. After 5 minutes place the baking pan in the preheated oven.
5. Add lemon zest on top of roasted pecans and stir well.
6. Serve and enjoy.

Nutritional Value (Amount per Serving):
Calories 269; Fat 28 g; Carbohydrates 5.6 g; Sugar 1.2 g; Protein 3.3 g; Cholesterol 0 mg

Vegetables Balls

Preparation Time: 10 minutes; Cooking Time: 10 minutes; Serve: 6
Ingredients:

- 2 cups cauliflower florets
- 1 tsp paprika
- 1 tsp chives
- 2 tsp garlic
- 1 medium Parsnip
- 1 medium carrot
- 1 cup breadcrumbs
- 1/2 cup desiccated coconut
- 2 tsp oregano
- 1 tsp mixed spice
- 1/2 cup sweet potato
- Pepper
- Salt

Directions:
1. Fit the Cuisinart oven with the rack in position 1.
2. Add all vegetables into the food processor and process until resemble breadcrumbs.
3. Add process vegetables into the mixing bowl.
4. Add all remaining ingredients into the bowl and mix well until combine.
5. Make small balls from the mixture and place in the air fryer basket then place an air fryer basket in the baking pan.
6. Place a baking pan on the oven rack. Set to air fry at 400 F for 10 minutes.
7. Serve and enjoy.

Nutritional Value (Amount per Serving):
Calories 131; Fat 2.7 g; Carbohydrates 23.6 g; Sugar 4.5 g; Protein 4 g; Cholesterol 0 mg

Margherita Pizza

Preparation Time: 10 minutes; Cooking Time: 18 minutes; Serve: 4

Ingredients:
- 1 whole-wheat pizza crust
- 1/2 cup mozzarella cheese, grated
- 1/2 cup can tomatoes
- 2 tbsp olive oil
- 3 Roma tomatoes, sliced
- 10 basil leaves

Directions:
1. Fit the Cuisinart oven with the rack in position 1.
2. Roll out whole wheat pizza crust using a rolling pin. Make sure the crust is ½-inch thick.
3. Sprinkle olive oil on top of pizza crust.
4. Spread can tomatoes over pizza crust.
5. Arrange sliced tomatoes and basil on pizza crust. Sprinkle grated cheese on top.
6. Place pizza on top of the oven rack and set to bake at 425 F for 23 minutes.
7. Slice and serve.

Nutritional Value (Amount per Serving):
Calories 126; Fat 7.9 g; Carbohydrates 11.3 g; Sugar 4.2 g; Protein 3.6 g; Cholesterol 2 mg

Rosemary Roasted Almonds

Preparation Time: 10 minutes; Cooking Time: 20 minutes; Serve: 12

Ingredients:
- 2 1/2 cups almonds
- 1 tbsp fresh rosemary, chopped
- 1 tbsp olive oil
- 2 ½ tbsp maple syrup
- 1/4 tsp cayenne
- 1/4 tsp ground coriander
- 1/4 tsp cumin
- 1/4 tsp chili powder
- Pinch of salt

Directions:
1. Fit the Cuisinart oven with the rack in position 1.
2. Spray a baking tray with cooking spray and set aside.
3. In a mixing bowl, whisk together oil, cayenne, coriander, cumin, chili powder, rosemary, maple syrup, and salt.
4. Add almond and stir to coat.

5. Spread almonds in baking pan.
6. Set to bake at 325 F for 20 minutes. After 5 minutes place the baking pan in the preheated oven.
7. Serve and enjoy.

Nutritional Value (Amount per Serving):
Calories 137; Fat 11.2 g; Carbohydrates 7.3 g; Sugar 3.3 g; Protein 4.2 g; Cholesterol 0 mg

Parmesan Green Beans

Preparation Time: 10 minutes; Cooking Time: 15 minutes; Serve: 4
Ingredients:
- 1 lb green beans
- 4 tbsp parmesan cheese
- 2 tbsp olive oil
- Pinch of salt

Directions:
1. Fit the Cuisinart oven with the rack in position 1.
2. Add green beans in a large bowl.
3. Add remaining ingredients on top of green beans and toss to coat.
4. Spread green beans in baking pan.
5. Set to bake at 400 F for 20 minutes. After 5 minutes place the baking pan in the preheated oven.
6. Serve and enjoy.

Nutritional Value (Amount per Serving):
Calories 114; Fat 8.4 g; Carbohydrates 8.3 g; Sugar 1.6 g; Protein 4 g; Cholesterol 4 mg

Tasty Cauliflower Tots

Preparation Time: 10 minutes; Cooking Time: 18 minutes; Serve: 16
Ingredients:
- 2 cups cauliflower, steamed and shredded
- 1 tbsp butter
- 1/2 cup parmesan cheese, shredded
- 1/4 tsp onion powder
- 1 large egg
- Pepper
- Salt

Directions:
1. Fit the Cuisinart oven with the rack in position 1.
2. Add all ingredients to the bowl and mix well to combine.
3. Using a tablespoon make small tots from cauliflower mixture and arrange in baking pan.
4. Set to bake at 425 F for 23 minutes. After 5 minutes place the baking pan in the preheated oven.
5. Serve and enjoy.

Nutritional Value (Amount per Serving):
Calories 23; Fat 1.6 g; Carbohydrates 0.8 g; Sugar 0.3 g; Protein 1.6 g; Cholesterol 16 mg

Cheesy Sweet Pepper Poppers

Preparation Time: 10 minutes; Cooking Time: 15 minutes; Serve: 10
Ingredients:
- 2 tbsp cilantro, chopped
- 8 oz cream cheese
- 8 oz gouda cheese, grated
- 1 lb mini sweet peppers, halved
- 2 garlic cloves, minced
- 1/4 cup onion, grated
- 1/2 cup feta cheese, crumbled

Directions:
1. Fit the Cuisinart oven with the rack in position 1.
2. Add all ingredients except peppers into the bowl and mix well to combine.

3. Stuff each pepper halves with cheese mixture and place in baking pan.
4. Set to bake at 425 F for 20 minutes. After 5 minutes place the baking pan in the preheated oven.
5. Serve and enjoy.

Nutritional Value (Amount per Serving):
Calories 186; Fat 15.8 g; Carbohydrates 2.8 g; Sugar 1.6 g; Protein 8.6 g; Cholesterol 57 mg

Easy Bacon Bites

Preparation Time: 10 minutes; Cooking Time: 10 minutes; Serve: 4
Ingredients:
- 4 bacon strips, cut into small pieces
- 1/4 cup hot sauce
- 1/2 cup pork rinds, crushed

Directions:
1. Fit the Cuisinart oven with the rack in position 2.
2. Add bacon pieces in a bowl.
3. Add hot sauce and toss well.
4. Add crushed pork rinds and toss until bacon pieces are well coated.
5. Transfer bacon pieces in the air fryer basket then place an air fryer basket in the baking pan.
6. Place a baking pan on the oven rack. Set to air fry at 350 F for 10 minutes.
7. Serve and enjoy.

Nutritional Value (Amount per Serving):
Calories 123; Fat 10.4 g; Carbohydrates 0.3 g; Sugar 0.2 g; Protein 6.5 g; Cholesterol 5 mg

Tasty Jalapeno Poppers

Preparation Time: 10 minutes; Cooking Time: 13 minutes; Serve: 4
Ingredients:
- 4 jalapeno peppers, slice in half and deseeded
- 4 oz goat cheese, crumbled
- 1/4 tsp chili powder
- 2 tbsp chunky salsa
- Pepper
- Salt

Directions:
1. Fit the Cuisinart oven with the rack in position 2.
2. In a small bowl, mix together cheese, chunky salsa, chili powder, pepper, and salt.
3. Stuff cheese mixture into each jalapeno half and place in the air fryer basket then place the air fryer basket in the baking pan.
4. Place a baking pan on the oven rack. Set to air fry at 350 F for 13 minutes.
5. Serve and enjoy.

Nutritional Value (Amount per Serving):
Calories 68; Fat 5.1 g; Carbohydrates 2.5 g; Sugar 1.6 g; Protein 3.6 g; Cholesterol 20 mg

Spicy Crab Dip

Preparation Time: 10 minutes; Cooking Time: 10 minutes; Serve: 4
Ingredients:
- 1 cup crabmeat
- 2 cups cheese, grated
- 1/4 cup mayonnaise
- 2 tbsp parsley, chopped
- 2 tbsp fresh lemon juice
- 2 tbsp hot sauce
- 1/2 cup green onion, sliced
- 1/4 tsp pepper
- 1/2 tsp salt

Directions:

1. Fit the Cuisinart oven with the rack in position 1.
2. Add all ingredients into the mixing bowl and mix well.
3. Pour mixture into the greased baking dish.
4. Set to bake at 400 F for 15 minutes. After 5 minutes place the baking dish in the preheated oven.
5. Serve and enjoy.

Nutritional Value (Amount per Serving):
Calories 313; Fat 23.9 g; Carbohydrates 8.8 g; Sugar 3.1 g; Protein 16.2 g; Cholesterol 67 mg

Chestnuts Spinach Dip

Preparation Time: 10 minutes; Cooking Time: 40 minutes; Serve: 8

Ingredients:
- 8 oz cream cheese, softened
- 1 cup mayonnaise
- 1 cup parmesan cheese, grated
- 1 cup frozen spinach, thawed and squeeze out all liquid
- 1/4 tsp garlic powder
- 1/2 cup onion, minced
- 1/3 cup water chestnuts, drained and chopped
- 1/2 tsp pepper

Directions:
1. Fit the Cuisinart oven with the rack in position 1.
2. Spray air fryer baking dish with cooking spray.
3. Add all ingredients into the bowl and mix until well combined.
4. Transfer bowl mixture into the baking dish.
5. Set to bake at 300 F for 45 minutes. After 5 minutes place the baking dish in the preheated oven.
6. Serve and enjoy.

Nutritional Value (Amount per Serving):
Calories 220; Fat 19.8 g; Carbohydrates 9.1 g; Sugar 2.3 g; Protein 2.7 g; Cholesterol 39 mg

Cheesy Beef Dip

Preparation Time: 10 minutes; Cooking Time: 25 minutes; Serve: 12

Ingredients:
- 1 lb corned beef, diced
- ¾ cup mayonnaise
- 14 oz can sauerkraut, drained
- 8 oz Swiss cheese, shredded
- Pepper
- Salt

Directions:
1. Fit the Cuisinart oven with the rack in position 1.
2. Add all ingredients into the bowl and mix well and pour into the greased baking dish.
3. Set to bake at 400 F for 30 minutes. After 5 minutes place the baking dish in the preheated oven.
4. Serve and enjoy.

Nutritional Value (Amount per Serving):
Calories 283; Fat 25 g; Carbohydrates 3 g; Sugar 1 g; Protein 12 g; Cholesterol 62 mg

Cajun Sweet Potato Tots

Preparation Time: 10 minutes; Cooking Time: 8 minutes; Serve: 24

Ingredients:
- 1/2 tsp Cajun seasoning
- 2 sweet potatoes, peeled
- Salt

Directions:
1. Fit the Cuisinart oven with the rack in position 2.

2. Add water in a large pot and bring to boil.
3. Add sweet potatoes to the pot and boil for 15 minutes. Drain well.
4. Grated boil sweet potatoes into a large bowl using a grated.
5. Add Cajun seasoning and salt in grated sweet potatoes and mix until well combined.
6. Make a small tot of sweet potato mixture and place in the air fryer basket then place an air fryer basket in the baking pan.
7. Place a baking pan on the oven rack. Set to air fry at 400 F for 8 minutes.
8. Serve and enjoy.

Nutritional Value (Amount per Serving):
Calories 10; Fat 0 g; Carbohydrates 2.3 g; Sugar 0 g; Protein 0.1 g; Cholesterol 0 mg

Crack Dip

Preparation Time: 10 minutes; Cooking Time: 15 minutes; Serve: 15
Ingredients:
- 8 oz cream cheese
- 1/8 tsp cayenne
- 1/3 cup green onion, chopped
- 1/3 cup bacon bits, cooked
- 1/3 cup sour cream
- ¾ cup ranch dressing

Directions:
1. Fit the Cuisinart oven with the rack in position 2.
2. Add all ingredients into the bowl and mix well and pour into the greased baking dish.
3. Set to bake at 350 F for 20 minutes. After 5 minutes place the baking dish in the preheated oven.
4. Serve and enjoy.

Nutritional Value (Amount per Serving):
Calories 168; Fat 16 g; Carbohydrates 1 g; Sugar 0 g; Protein 3 g; Cholesterol 8 mg

Tasty Sweet Potato Fries

Preparation Time: 10 minutes; Cooking Time: 20 minutes; Serve: 2
Ingredients:
- 2 small sweet potatoes, peel and cut into fries shape
- 2 tbsp olive oil
- 1/4 tsp sea salt
- 1/4 tsp coriander
- 1/2 tsp curry powder

Directions:
1. Fit the Cuisinart oven with the rack in position 2.
2. Add all ingredients into the large mixing bowl and toss well.
3. Spray air fryer basket with cooking spray.
4. Transfer sweet potato fries in the air fryer basket then place the air fryer basket in the baking pan.
5. Place a baking pan on the oven rack. Set to air fry at 370 F for 20 minutes.
6. Serve and enjoy.

Nutritional Value (Amount per Serving):
Calories 240; Fat 14.2 g; Carbohydrates 28.3 g; Sugar 0.5 g; Protein 1.6 g; Cholesterol 0 mg

Parmesan Zucchini Fries

Preparation Time: 10 minutes; Cooking Time: 10 minutes; Serve: 4
Ingredients:
- 2 medium zucchini, cut into fries shape
- 1/2 cup breadcrumbs
- 1 egg, lightly beaten
- 1/2 tsp garlic powder
- 1 tsp Italian seasoning
- 1/2 cup parmesan cheese, grated
- Pepper

- Salt

Directions:
1. Fit the Cuisinart oven with the rack in position 2.
2. Add egg in a bowl and whisk well.
3. In a shallow bowl, mix together breadcrumbs, spices, parmesan cheese, pepper, and salt.
4. Dip zucchini in egg then coat with breadcrumb mixture and place in air fryer basket then place air fryer basket in baking pan.
5. Place a baking pan on the oven rack. Set to air fry at 400 F for 10 minutes.
6. Serve and enjoy.

Nutritional Value (Amount per Serving):
Calories 126; Fat 4.8 g; Carbohydrates 13.9 g; Sugar 2.8 g; Protein 8.1 g; Cholesterol 50 mg

Air Fryer Pepperoni Chips

Preparation Time: 10 minutes; Cooking Time: 8 minutes; Serve: 6
Ingredients:
- 6 oz pepperoni slices

Directions:
1. Fit the Cuisinart oven with the rack in position 2.
2. Place pepperoni slices in an air fryer basket then place an air fryer basket in baking pan.
3. Place a baking pan on the oven rack. Set to air fry at 360 F for 8 minutes.
4. Serve and enjoy.

Nutritional Value (Amount per Serving):
Calories 51; Fat 1 g; Carbohydrates 2 g; Sugar 0 g; Protein 9.1 g; Cholesterol 0 mg

Crispy Eggplant Bites

Preparation Time: 10 minutes; Cooking Time: 20 minutes; Serve: 4
Ingredients:
- 1 eggplant, cut into 1-inch pieces
- 1 tsp garlic powder
- 2 tbsp olive oil
- 1/2 tsp Italian seasoning
- 1 tsp paprika
- 1/2 tsp red pepper

Directions:
1. Fit the Cuisinart oven with the rack in position 2.
2. Add all ingredients into the large mixing bowl and toss well.
3. Transfer eggplant mixture in air fryer basket then places air fryer basket in baking pan.
4. Place a baking pan on the oven rack. Set to air fry at 375 F for 20 minutes.
5. Serve and enjoy.

Nutritional Value (Amount per Serving):
Calories 99; Fat 7.5 g; Carbohydrates 8.7 g; Sugar 4.5 g; Protein 1.5 g; Cholesterol 0 mg

Bacon Cheese Jalapeno Poppers

Preparation Time: 10 minutes; Cooking Time: 5 minutes; Serve: 5
Ingredients:
- 10 fresh jalapeno peppers, cut in half and remove seeds
- 1/4 cup cheddar cheese, shredded
- 5 oz cream cheese, softened
- 1/4 tsp paprika
- 2 bacon slices, cooked and crumbled

Directions:
1. Fit the Cuisinart oven with the rack in position 2.
2. In a bowl, mix bacon, cream cheese, paprika and cheddar cheese.
3. Stuff cheese mixture into each jalapeno.
4. Place stuffed jalapeno halved in air fryer basket then place air fryer basket in baking pan.

    5. Place a baking pan on the oven rack. Set to air fry at 370 F for 5 minutes.
    6. Serve and enjoy.

Nutritional Value (Amount per Serving):
Calories 176; Fat 15.7 g; Carbohydrates 3.2 g; Sugar 1 g; Protein 6.2 g; Cholesterol 47 mg

Air Fryer Cabbage Chips

Preparation Time: 10 minutes; Cooking Time: 25 minutes; Serve: 6
Ingredients:
- 1 large cabbage head, tear cabbage leaves into pieces
- 2 tbsp olive oil
- 1/4 cup parmesan cheese, grated
- Pepper
- Salt

Directions:
1. Fit the Cuisinart oven with the rack in position 2.
2. Add all ingredients into the large mixing bowl and toss well.
3. Add cabbage pieces to the air fryer basket then place an air fryer basket in the baking pan.
4. Place a baking pan on the oven rack. Set to air fry at 300 F for 25 minutes.
5. Serve and enjoy.

Nutritional Value (Amount per Serving):
Calories 104; Fat 5.7 g; Carbohydrates 12.2 g; Sugar 6.7 g; Protein 3.9 g; Cholesterol 3 mg

Healthy Broccoli Tots

Preparation Time: 10 minutes; Cooking Time: 12 minutes; Serve: 4
Ingredients:
- 1 lb broccoli, cooked & chopped
- 1/2 tsp garlic powder
- 1/2 cup almond flour
- 1/4 cup ground flaxseed
- 1 tsp salt

Directions:
1. Fit the Cuisinart oven with the rack in position 2.
2. Add broccoli into the food processor and process until it looks like rice.
3. Transfer broccoli to a large mixing bowl.
4. Add remaining ingredients into the bowl and mix until well combined.
5. Make tots from broccoli mixture and place in the air fryer basket then place an air fryer basket in the baking pan.
6. Place a baking pan on the oven rack. Set to air fry at 375 F for 12 minutes.
7. Serve and enjoy.

Nutritional Value (Amount per Serving):
Calories 97; Fat 4.3 g; Carbohydrates 10.5 g; Sugar 2.3 g; Protein 5.3 g; Cholesterol 0 mg

Kale Chips

Preparation Time: 10 minutes; Cooking Time: 5 minutes; Serve: 2
Ingredients:
- 1 bunch of kale, remove stem and cut into pieces
- 1 tsp olive oil
- 1/2 tsp salt

Directions:
1. Fit the Cuisinart oven with the rack in position 2.
2. Add all ingredients into the large bowl and toss well.
3. Transfer kale mixture in air fryer basket then places air fryer basket in baking pan.
4. Place a baking pan on the oven rack. Set to air fry at 370 F for 5 minutes.
5. Serve and enjoy.

Nutritional Value (Amount per Serving):

Calories 41; Fat 2.3 g; Carbohydrates 4.4 g; Sugar 0 g; Protein 1.3 g; Cholesterol 0 mg

Easy Bacon Jalapeno Poppers

Preparation Time: 10 minutes; Cooking Time: 8 minutes; Serve: 10

Ingredients:
- 10 jalapeno peppers, cut in half and remove seeds
- 1/3 cup cream cheese, softened
- 1/4 tsp paprika
- 1/4 tsp chili powder
- 5 bacon strips, cut in half

Directions:
1. Fit the Cuisinart oven with the rack in position 2.
2. In a small bowl, mix cream cheese, paprika, chili powder, and bacon and stuff in each jalapeno half.
3. Place jalapeno half in the air fryer basket then place an air fryer basket in the baking pan.
4. Place a baking pan on the oven rack. Set to air fry at 370 F for 8 minutes.
5. Serve and enjoy.

Nutritional Value (Amount per Serving):
Calories 83; Fat 7.4 g; Carbohydrates 1.3 g; Sugar 0.5 g; Protein 2.8 g; Cholesterol 9 mg

BBQ Chicken Wings

Preparation Time: 10 minutes; Cooking Time: 15 minutes; Serve: 4

Ingredients:
- 1 lb chicken wings
- 1/4 tsp garlic powder
- 1/2 cup BBQ sauce, sugar-free
- Pepper

Directions:
1. Fit the Cuisinart oven with the rack in position 2.
2. Season chicken wings with garlic powder and pepper and place in the air fryer basket then place the air fryer basket in the baking pan.
3. Place a baking pan on the oven rack. Set to air fry at 400 F for 15 minutes.
4. Transfer cooked chicken wings in a large bowl.
5. Pour BBQ sauce over chicken wings and toss to coat.
6. Serve and enjoy.

Nutritional Value (Amount per Serving):
Calories 263; Fat 8.5 g; Carbohydrates 11.5 g; Sugar 8.2 g; Protein 32.8 g; Cholesterol 101 mg

Vegetable Kebabs

Preparation Time: 10 minutes; Cooking Time: 10 minutes; Serve: 3

Ingredients:
- 1/2 onion, cut into 1-inch pieces
- 2 bell peppers, cut into 1-inch pieces
- 1 zucchini, cut into 1-inch pieces
- 1 eggplant, cut into 1-inch pieces
- Pepper
- Salt

Directions:
1. Fit the Cuisinart oven with the rack in position 2.
2. Thread veggie onto the skewers and season with pepper and salt.
3. Place skewers in the air fryer basket then place an air fryer basket in the baking pan.
4. Place a baking pan on the oven rack. Set to air fry at 390 F for 10 minutes.
5. Serve and enjoy.

Nutritional Value (Amount per Serving):
Calories 81; Fat 0.6 g; Carbohydrates 18.9 g; Sugar 10.5 g; Protein 3.3 g; Cholesterol 0 mg

Shrimp Kebabs

Preparation Time: 10 minutes; Cooking Time: 8 minutes; Serve: 2
Ingredients:
- 1 cup shrimp
- 1/4 tsp pepper
- 1/8 tsp salt
- 1 lime juice
- 1 garlic clove, minced

Directions:
1. Fit the Cuisinart oven with the rack in position 2.
2. Add shrimp and remaining ingredients into the bowl and toss well.
3. Thread shrimp onto the skewers and place in the air fryer basket then place an air fryer basket in the baking pan.
4. Place a baking pan on the oven rack. Set to air fry at 350 F for 8 minutes.
5. Serve and enjoy.

Nutritional Value (Amount per Serving):
Calories 59; Fat 0.8 g; Carbohydrates 3.2 g; Sugar 0.4 g; Protein 9.9 g; Cholesterol 90 mg

Tofu Steaks

Preparation Time: 10 minutes; Cooking Time: 35 minutes; Serve: 4
Ingredients:
- 1 package tofu, press and remove excess liquid
- 2 tbsp lemon zest
- 3 garlic cloves, minced
- 1/4 cup olive oil
- 1/4 tsp dried thyme
- 1/4 cup lemon juice
- Pepper
- Salt

Directions:
1. Fit the Cuisinart oven with the rack in position 2.
2. Cut tofu into eight pieces.
3. In a bowl, mix together olive oil, thyme, lemon juice, lemon zest, garlic, pepper, and salt.
4. Add tofu into the bowl and coat well and place it in the refrigerator overnight.
5. Place marinated tofu in an air fryer basket then places an air fryer basket in the baking pan.
6. Place a baking pan on the oven rack. Set to air fry at 350 F for 35 minutes.
7. Serve and enjoy.

Nutritional Value (Amount per Serving):
Calories 139; Fat 14.1 g; Carbohydrates 2.3 g; Sugar 0.7 g; Protein 2.9 g; Cholesterol 0 mg

Healthy Lemon Tofu

Preparation Time: 10 minutes; Cooking Time: 15 minutes; Serve: 4
Ingredients:
- 1 lb tofu, drained and pressed
- 1 tbsp tamari
- 1 tbsp arrowroot powder
- For sauce:
- 2 tsp arrowroot powder
- 1/3 cup lemon juice
- 1 tsp lemon zest
- 2 tbsp erythritol
- 1/2 cup water

Directions:
1. Fit the Cuisinart oven with the rack in position 2.
2. Cut tofu into cubes. Add tofu and tamari into the zip-lock bag and shake well.
3. Add 1 tbsp arrowroot into the bag and shake well to coat the tofu. Set aside for 15 minutes.
4. Meanwhile, in a bowl, mix together all sauce ingredients and set aside.

5. Add tofu to the air fryer basket then place an air fryer basket in the baking pan.
6. Place a baking pan on the oven rack. Set to air fry at 390 F for 15 minutes.
7. Serve and enjoy.

Nutritional Value (Amount per Serving):
Calories 102; Fat 4.9 g; Carbohydrates 6 g; Sugar 1.2 g; Protein 9.9 g; Cholesterol 0 mg

Broccoli Nuggets

Preparation Time: 10 minutes; Cooking Time: 15 minutes; Serve: 4

Ingredients:
- 2 cups broccoli florets, cooked & mashed
- 1 cup mozzarella cheese, shredded
- 1/4 cup almond flour
- 2 egg whites
- 1/8 tsp salt

Directions:
1. Fit the Cuisinart oven with the rack in position 2.
2. Add all ingredients to the bowl and mix well to combine.
3. Make nuggets from broccoli mixture and place in the air fryer basket then place an air fryer basket in the baking pan.
4. Place a baking pan on the oven rack. Set to air fry at 325 F for 15 minutes.
5. Serve and enjoy.

Nutritional Value (Amount per Serving):
Calories 165; Fat 9.9 g; Carbohydrates 8.4 g; Sugar 1.5 g; Protein 11 g; Cholesterol 30 mg

Yummy Turkey Jalapeno Poppers

Preparation Time: 10 minutes; Cooking Time: 20 minutes; Serve: 12

Ingredients:
- 1/2 cup turkey, cooked and shredded
- 4 oz cream cheese
- 1/4 tsp dried basil
- 6 jalapenos, halved and seed removed
- 1/4 cup mozzarella cheese, shredded
- 1/4 tsp salt

Directions:
1. Fit the Cuisinart oven with the rack in position 2.
2. Mix all ingredients in a bowl except jalapenos.
3. Stuff cheese mixture into each jalapeno half and place in the air fryer basket then place the air fryer basket in the baking pan.
4. Place a baking pan on the oven rack. Set to air fry at 370 F for 20 minutes.
5. Serve and enjoy.

Nutritional Value (Amount per Serving):
Calories 54; Fat 4.2 g; Carbohydrates 0.9 g; Sugar 0.3 g; Protein 3.1 g; Cholesterol 17 mg

Arugula Artichoke Dip

Preparation Time: 10 minutes; Cooking Time: 25 minutes; Serve: 6

Ingredients:
- 15 oz artichoke hearts, drained
- 1 cup cheddar cheese, shredded
- 1 tbsp onion, minced
- 1/2 cup mayonnaise
- 1 tsp Worcestershire sauce
- 3 cups arugula, chopped

Directions:
1. Fit the Cuisinart oven with the rack in position 1.
2. Add all ingredients into the blender and blend until smooth.
3. Pour artichoke mixture into air fryer baking dish.
4. Set to bake at 400 F for 30 minutes. After 5 minutes place the baking dish in the preheated oven.

5. Serve and enjoy.

Nutritional Value (Amount per Serving):
Calories 190; Fat 13 g; Carbohydrates 13.1 g; Sugar 2.5 g; Protein 7.5 g; Cholesterol 25 mg

Crab Stuffed Mushrooms

Preparation Time: 10 minutes; Cooking Time: 8 minutes; Serve: 16

Ingredients:
- 16 mushrooms, clean and chop stems
- 2 oz crab meat, chopped
- 8 oz cream cheese, softened
- 1/4 tsp chili powder
- 1/4 cup mozzarella cheese, shredded

Directions:
1. Fit the Cuisinart oven with the rack in position 2.
2. In a bowl, mix chopped stems, chili powder, cheese, crabmeat, and cream cheese.
3. Stuff cheese mixture in mushrooms and place in air fryer basket then place air fryer basket in baking pan.
4. Place a baking pan on the oven rack. Set to air fry at 370 F for 8 minutes.
5. Serve and enjoy.

Nutritional Value (Amount per Serving):
Calories 59; Fat 5.1 g; Carbohydrates 1.2 g; Sugar 0.4 g; Protein 2.2 g; Cholesterol 18 mg

Creamy Chicken Dip

Preparation Time: 10 minutes; Cooking Time: 20 minutes; Serve: 6

Ingredients:
- 2 cups chicken, cooked and shredded
- 8 oz cream cheese, softened
- 3 tbsp hot sauce
- 1/4 tsp garlic powder
- 3/4 cup sour cream
- 1/4 tsp onion powder

Directions:
1. Fit the Cuisinart oven with the rack in position 2.
2. Add all ingredients in a large bowl and mix until well combined.
3. Transfer mixture in air fryer baking dish.
4. Set to bake at 325 F for 25 minutes. After 5 minutes place the baking dish in the preheated oven.
5. Serve and enjoy.

Nutritional Value (Amount per Serving):
Calories 265; Fat 20.7 g; Carbohydrates 2.5 g; Sugar 0.3 g; Protein 17.4 g; Cholesterol 90 mg

Air Fryer Paprika Almonds

Preparation Time: 5 minutes; Cooking Time: 6 minutes; Serve: 6

Ingredients:
- 1 cup almonds
- 1/4 tsp smoked paprika
- 2 tsp olive oil
- 1/4 tsp cumin
- 1 tsp chili powder

Directions:
1. Fit the Cuisinart oven with the rack in position 2.
2. Add almond into the bowl and remaining ingredients and toss to coat.
3. Transfer almonds in the air fryer basket then place an air fryer basket in the baking pan.
4. Place a baking pan on the oven rack. Set to air fry at 320 F for 6 minutes.
5. Serve and enjoy.

Nutritional Value (Amount per Serving):
Calories 107; Fat 9.6 g; Carbohydrates 3.7 g; Sugar 0.7 g; Protein 3.4 g; Cholesterol 0 mg

Zucchini Coconut Bites

Preparation Time: 10 minutes; Cooking Time: 10 minutes; Serve: 6
Ingredients:
- 4 zucchini, grated and squeeze out all liquid
- 1 cup shredded coconut
- 1 egg, lightly beaten
- 1 tsp Italian seasoning
- 1/2 cup parmesan cheese, grated

Directions:
1. Fit the Cuisinart oven with the rack in position 2.
2. Add all ingredients into the bowl and mix until well combined.
3. Make small balls from the zucchini mixture and place in the air fryer basket then place the air fryer basket in the baking pan.
4. Place a baking pan on the oven rack. Set to air fry at 400 F for 10 minutes.
5. Serve and enjoy.

Nutritional Value (Amount per Serving):
Calories 105; Fat 7.3 g; Carbohydrates 6.8 g; Sugar 3.2 g; Protein 5.4 g; Cholesterol 33 mg

Coconut Broccoli Pop-Corn

Preparation Time: 10 minutes; Cooking Time: 6 minutes; Serve: 4
Ingredients:
- 2 cups broccoli florets
- 4 eggs yolks
- 2 cups coconut flour
- 1/4 cup butter, melted
- Pepper
- Salt

Directions:
1. Fit the Cuisinart oven with the rack in position 2.
2. In a bowl whisk egg yolks with melted butter, pepper, and salt. Add coconut flour and stir to combine.
3. Coat each broccoli floret with egg mixture and place in the air fryer basket then place an air fryer basket in the baking pan.
4. Place a baking pan on the oven rack. Set to air fry at 400 F for 6 minutes.
5. Serve and enjoy.

Nutritional Value (Amount per Serving):
Calories 201; Fat 17.2 g; Carbohydrates 7.7 g; Sugar 1.4 g; Protein 5.1 g; Cholesterol 240 mg

Cheese Artichoke Spinach Dip

Preparation Time: 10 minutes; Cooking Time: 17 minutes; Serve: 10
Ingredients:
- 1/2 cup mozzarella cheese, shredded
- 3 cups spinach, chopped
- 2 garlic cloves, minced
- 1/3 cup sour cream
- 1/3 can artichoke hearts, drained and chopped
- 1/2 cup mayonnaise
- 7 oz brie cheese
- 1/3 tsp dried basil
- 1/3 tsp pepper
- 1 tsp sea salt

Directions:
1. Fit the Cuisinart oven with the rack in position 2.
2. Add all ingredients except mozzarella cheese into the air fryer baking dish and mix until well combined.
3. Spread mozzarella cheese on top.
4. Set to bake at 325 F for 22 minutes. After 5 minutes place the baking dish in the preheated oven.
5. Serve and enjoy.

Nutritional Value (Amount per Serving):
Calories 138; Fat 11.3 g; Carbohydrates 4.3 g; Sugar 0.9 g; Protein 5.3 g; Cholesterol 27 mg

Spicy Chicken Wings

Preparation Time: 10 minutes; Cooking Time: 16 minutes; Serve: 6
Ingredients:
- 1/2 lb chicken wings
- 2 tsp ginger powder
- 1 tsp paprika
- 1/3 cup hot sauce
- 2 tsp garlic powder
- Pepper
- Salt

Directions:
1. Fit the Cuisinart oven with the rack in position 2.
2. Toss chicken wings with paprika, garlic powder, pepper, ginger powder, and salt.
3. Add chicken wings to the air fryer basket then place an air fryer basket in the baking pan.
4. Place a baking pan on the oven rack. Set to air fry at 360 F for 16 minutes.
5. Serve with hot sauce.

Nutritional Value (Amount per Serving):
Calories 104; Fat 2.9 g; Carbohydrates 5.8 g; Sugar 3.9 g; Protein 11.2 g; Cholesterol 34 mg

Habanero Chicken Wings

Preparation Time: 10 minutes; Cooking Time: 16 minutes; Serve: 6
Ingredients:
- 1 1/2 lbs chicken wings
- 2 tbsp habanero hot sauce
- 2 garlic cloves, chopped
- 1 tsp pepper
- 1 tsp garlic salt
- 1 tsp cayenne pepper
- 1/2 tbsp soy sauce

Directions:
1. Fit the Cuisinart oven with the rack in position 2.
2. Add chicken wings into the large bowl and toss with remaining ingredients.
3. Transfer chicken wings in air fryer basket then place air fryer basket in baking pan.
4. Place a baking pan on the oven rack. Set to air fry at 360 F for 16 minutes.
5. Serve and enjoy.

Nutritional Value (Amount per Serving):
Calories 226; Fat 8.5 g; Carbohydrates 2.2 g; Sugar 0.2 g; Protein 33.1 g; Cholesterol 101 mg

Cheddar Dill Mushrooms

Preparation Time: 10 minutes; Cooking Time: 5 minutes; Serve: 6
Ingredients:
- 9 oz mushrooms, cut stems
- 6 oz mozzarella cheese, shredded
- 1 tbsp butter
- 1 tsp dried parsley
- 1/2 tsp salt

Directions:
1. Fit the Cuisinart oven with the rack in position 2.
2. Add parsley, cheese, butter, and salt into the bowl and mix until well combined.
3. Stuff cheese mixture into the mushroom caps and place in the air fryer basket then place an air fryer basket in the baking pan.
4. Place a baking pan on the oven rack. Set to air fry at 400 F for 5 minutes.
5. Serve and enjoy.

Nutritional Value (Amount per Serving):
Calories 141; Fat 11.5 g; Carbohydrates 1.9 g; Sugar 0.9 g; Protein 8.5 g; Cholesterol 35 mg

Air Fryer Nuts

Preparation Time: 10 minutes; Cooking Time: 9 minutes; Serve: 4

Ingredients:
- 1/2 cup macadamia nuts
- 1/4 cup walnuts
- 1/4 cup hazelnuts
- 1/2 cup pecans
- 1 tbsp olive oil
- 1 tsp salt

Directions:
1. Fit the Cuisinart oven with the rack in position 2.
2. Add all nuts to the air fryer basket then place an air fryer basket in the baking pan.
3. Place a baking pan on the oven rack. Set to air fry at 320 F for 9 minutes.
4. Drizzle nuts with olive oil and season with salt and toss well.
5. Serve and enjoy.

Nutritional Value (Amount per Serving):
Calories 280; Fat 29 g; Carbohydrates 4.9 g; Sugar 1.3 g; Protein 4.7 g; Cholesterol 0 mg

Air Fryer Radish Chips

Preparation Time: 10 minutes; Cooking Time: 15 minutes; Serve: 12

Ingredients:
- 1 lb radish, wash and slice into chips
- 1/4 tsp pepper
- 2 tbsp olive oil
- 1 tsp salt

Directions:
1. Fit the Cuisinart oven with the rack in position 2.
2. Add all ingredients into the large bowl and toss well.
3. Add radish slices to the air fryer basket then place an air fryer basket in baking pan.
4. Place a baking pan on the oven rack. Set to air fry at 375 F for 15 minutes.
5. Serve and enjoy.

Nutritional Value (Amount per Serving):
Calories 26; Fat 2.4 g; Carbohydrates 1.3 g; Sugar 0.7 g; Protein 0.3 g; Cholesterol 0 mg

Chapter 8: Desserts

Delicious Raspberry Cobbler

Preparation Time: 10 minutes; Cooking Time: 10 minutes; Serve: 6
Ingredients:
- 1 egg, lightly beaten
- 1 cup raspberries, sliced
- 2 tsp swerve
- 1/2 tsp vanilla
- 1 tbsp butter, melted
- 1 cup almond flour

Directions:
1. Fit the Cuisinart oven with the rack in position 1.
2. Add raspberries into the baking dish.
3. Sprinkle sweetener over raspberries.
4. Mix together almond flour, vanilla, and butter in the bowl.
5. Add egg in almond flour mixture and stir well to combine.
6. Spread almond flour mixture over sliced raspberries.
7. Set to bake at 350 F for 15 minutes. After 5 minutes place the baking dish in the preheated oven.
8. Serve and enjoy.

Nutritional Value (Amount per Serving):
Calories 66; Fat 5 g; Carbohydrates 3 g; Sugar 1 g; Protein 2 g; Cholesterol 32 mg

Orange Almond Muffins

Preparation Time: 10 minutes; Cooking Time: 20 minutes; Serve: 12
Ingredients:
- 4 eggs
- 1 tsp baking soda
- 1 orange zest
- 1 orange juice
- 1/2 cup butter, melted
- 3 cups almond flour

Directions:
1. Fit the Cuisinart oven with the rack in position 1.
2. Line 12-cups muffin tin with cupcake liners and set aside.
3. Add all ingredients into the large bowl and mix until well combined.
4. Pour mixture into the prepared muffin tin.
5. Set to bake at 350 F for 25 minutes. After 5 minutes place muffin tin in the preheated oven.
6. Serve and enjoy.

Nutritional Value (Amount per Serving):
Calories 273; Fat 24 g; Carbohydrates 6 g; Sugar 1 g; Protein 2 g; Cholesterol 75 mg

Easy Almond Butter Pumpkin Spice Cookies

Preparation Time: 10 minutes; Cooking Time: 18 minutes; Serve: 6
Ingredients:
- 1/4 tsp pumpkin pie spice
- 1 tsp liquid Stevie
- 6 oz almond butter
- 1/3 cup pumpkin puree

Directions:
1. Fit the Cuisinart oven with the rack in position 1.
2. Add all ingredients into the food processor and process until just combined.
3. Drop spoonfuls of mixture onto the parchment-lined baking pan.
4. Set to bake at 350 F for 23 minutes. After 5 minutes place the baking pan in the preheated oven.
5. Serve and enjoy.

Nutritional Value (Amount per Serving):
Calories 85; Fat 7 g; Carbohydrates 3 g; Sugar 1 g; Protein 3 g; Cholesterol 0 mg

Moist Pound Cake

Preparation Time: 10 minutes; Cooking Time: 55 minutes; Serve: 10
Ingredients:
- 4 eggs
- 1 cup almond flour
- 1/2 cup sour cream
- 1 tsp vanilla
- 1 cup monk fruit sweetener
- 1/4 cup cream cheese
- 1/4 cup butter
- 1 tsp baking powder
- 1 tbsp coconut flour

Directions:
1. Fit the Cuisinart oven with the rack in position 1.
2. In a large bowl, mix together almond flour, baking powder, and coconut flour.
3. In a separate bowl, add cream cheese and butter and microwave for 30 seconds. Stir well and microwave for 30 seconds more.
4. Stir in sour cream, vanilla, and sweetener. Stir well.
5. Pour cream cheese mixture into the almond flour mixture and stir until just combined.
6. Add eggs in batter one by one and stir until well combined.
7. Pour batter into the prepared grease cake pan.
8. Set to bake at 350 F for 60 minutes. After 5 minutes place the cake pan in the preheated oven.
9. Slice and serve.

Nutritional Value (Amount per Serving):
Calories 210; Fat 17 g; Carbohydrates 8 g; Sugar 5 g; Protein 3 g; Cholesterol 89 mg

Banana Butter Brownie

Preparation Time: 10 minutes; Cooking Time: 16 minutes; Serve: 4
Ingredients:
- 1 scoop protein powder
- 2 tbsp cocoa powder
- 1 cup bananas, overripe
- 1/2 cup almond butter, melted

Directions:
1. Fit the Cuisinart oven with the rack in position 1.
2. Add all ingredients into the blender and blend until smooth.
3. Pour batter into the greased cake pan.
4. Set to bake at 325 F for 21 minutes. After 5 minutes place the cake pan in the preheated oven.
5. Serve and enjoy.

Nutritional Value (Amount per Serving):
Calories 83; Fat 2 g; Carbohydrates 10 g; Sugar 5 g; Protein 7 g; Cholesterol 16 mg

Peanut Butter Muffins

Preparation Time: 10 minutes; Cooking Time: 20 minutes; Serve: 12
Ingredients:
- 1 cup peanut butter
- 1/2 cup maple syrup
- 1/2 cup of cocoa powder
- 1 cup applesauce
- 1 tsp baking soda
- 1 tsp vanilla

Directions:
1. Fit the Cuisinart oven with the rack in position 1.
2. Line 12-cups muffin tin with cupcake liners and set aside.

3. Add all ingredients into the blender and blend until smooth.
4. Pour blended mixture into the prepared muffin tin.
5. Set to bake at 350 F for 25 minutes. After 5 minutes place muffin tin in the preheated oven.
6. Serve and enjoy.

Nutritional Value (Amount per Serving):
Calories 178; Fat 11.3 g; Carbohydrates 17.3 g; Sugar 12 g; Protein 6.1 g; Cholesterol 0 mg

Baked Apple Slices

Preparation Time: 10 minutes; Cooking Time: 30 minutes; Serve: 6
Ingredients:
- 2 apples, peel, core, and slice
- 1 tsp cinnamon
- 2 tbsp butter
- 1/4 cup of sugar
- 1/4 cup brown sugar
- 1/4 tsp salt

Directions:
1. Fit the Cuisinart oven with the rack in position 1.
2. Add cinnamon, sugar, brown sugar, and salt into the zip-lock bag and mix well.
3. Add apple slices into the bag and shake until well coated.
4. Add apple slices into the 9-inch greased baking dish.
5. Set to bake at 350 F for 35 minutes. After 5 minutes place the baking dish in the preheated oven.
6. Serve and enjoy.

Nutritional Value (Amount per Serving):
Calories 128; Fat 4 g; Carbohydrates 24.8 g; Sugar 21.9 g; Protein 0.3 g; Cholesterol 10 mg

Vanilla Peanut Butter Cake

Preparation Time: 10 minutes; Cooking Time: 30 minutes; Serve: 8
Ingredients:
- 1 1/2 cups all-purpose flour
- 1/3 cup vegetable oil
- 1 tsp baking soda
- 1/2 cup peanut butter powder
- 1 tsp vanilla
- 1 tbsp apple cider vinegar
- 1 cup of water
- 1 cup of sugar
- 1/2 tsp salt

Directions:
1. Fit the Cuisinart oven with the rack in position 1.
2. In a large mixing bowl, mix together flour, baking soda, peanut butter powder, sugar, and salt.
3. In a small bowl, whisk together oil, vanilla, vinegar, and water.
4. Pour oil mixture into the flour mixture and stir until well combined.
5. Pour batter into the greased cake pan.
6. Set to bake at 350 F for 35 minutes. After 5 minutes place the cake pan in the preheated oven.
7. Slice and serve.

Nutritional Value (Amount per Serving):
Calories 264; Fat 1.8 g; Carbohydrates 43.2 g; Sugar 25.3 g; Protein 2.6 g; Cholesterol 0 mg

Strawberry Cobbler

Preparation Time: 10 minutes; Cooking Time: 45 minutes; Serve: 6
Ingredients:
- 2 cups strawberries, diced
- 1 cup milk

- 1 cup self-rising flour
- 1 1/4 cup sugar
- 1 tsp vanilla
- 1/2 cup butter, melted

Directions:
1. Fit the Cuisinart oven with the rack in position 1.
2. In a bowl, mix together flour and 1 cup sugar.
3. Add milk and whisk until smooth.
4. Add vanilla and butter and mix well.
5. Pour mixture into the greased baking dish and sprinkle with strawberries and top with remaining sugar.
6. Set to bake at 350 F for 50 minutes. After 5 minutes place the baking dish in the preheated oven.
7. Serve and enjoy.

Nutritional Value (Amount per Serving):
Calories 405; Fat 16.5 g; Carbohydrates 63.4 g; Sugar 46 g; Protein 4 g; Cholesterol 44 mg

Moist Chocolate Brownies

Preparation Time: 10 minutes; Cooking Time: 20 minutes; Serve: 16
Ingredients:
- 1 1/3 cups all-purpose flour
- 1/2 tsp baking powder
- 1/3 cup cocoa powder
- 1 cup of sugar
- 1/2 tsp vanilla
- 1/2 cup vegetable oil
- 1/2 cup water
- 1/2 tsp salt

Directions:
1. Fit the Cuisinart oven with the rack in position 1.
2. In a large mixing bowl, mix together flour, baking powder, cocoa powder, sugar, and salt.
3. In a small bowl, whisk together oil, water, and vanilla.
4. Pour oil mixture into the flour mixture and mix until well combined.
5. Pour batter into the greased baking dish.
6. Set to bake at 350 F for 25 minutes. After 5 minutes place the baking dish in the preheated oven.
7. Slice and serve.

Nutritional Value (Amount per Serving):
Calories 150; Fat 7.1 g; Carbohydrates 21.5 g; Sugar 12.6 g; Protein 1.4 g; Cholesterol 0 mg

Yummy Scalloped Pineapple

Preparation Time: 10 minutes; Cooking Time: 35 minutes; Serve: 6
Ingredients:
- 3 eggs, lightly beaten
- 8 oz can crushed pineapple, undrained
- 2 cups of sugar
- 4 cups of bread cubes
- 1/4 cup milk
- 1/2 cup butter, melted

Directions:
1. Fit the Cuisinart oven with the rack in position 1.
2. In a mixing bowl, whisk eggs with milk, butter, crushed pineapple, and sugar.
3. Add bread cubes and stir well to coat.
4. Transfer mixture to the greased baking dish.
5. Set to bake at 350 F for 40 minutes. After 5 minutes place the baking dish in the preheated oven.
6. Serve and enjoy.

Nutritional Value (Amount per Serving):

Calories 510; Fat 17 g; Carbohydrates 85 g; Sugar 71 g; Protein 3.4 g; Cholesterol 123 mg

Vanilla Lemon Cupcakes

Preparation Time: 10 minutes; Cooking Time: 15 minutes; Serve: 6

Ingredients:
- 1 egg
- 1/2 cup milk
- 2 tbsp canola oil
- 1/4 tsp baking soda
- 3/4 tsp baking powder
- 1 tsp lemon zest, grated
- 1/2 cup sugar
- 1 cup flour
- 1/2 tsp vanilla
- 1/2 tsp salt

Directions:
1. Fit the Cuisinart oven with the rack in position 1.
2. Line 12-cups muffin tin with cupcake liners and set aside.
3. In a bowl, whisk egg, vanilla, milk, oil, and sugar until creamy.
4. Add remaining ingredients and stir until just combined.
5. Pour batter into the prepared muffin tin.
6. Set to bake at 350 F for 20 minutes. After 5 minutes place muffin tin in the preheated oven.
7. Serve and enjoy.

Nutritional Value (Amount per Serving):
Calories 200; Fat 6 g; Carbohydrates 35 g; Sugar 17 g; Protein 3 g; Cholesterol 30 mg

Walnut Carrot Cake

Preparation Time: 10 minutes; Cooking Time: 25 minutes; Serve: 4

Ingredients:
- 1 egg
- 1/2 cup sugar
- 1/4 cup canola oil
- 1/4 cup walnuts, chopped
- 1/2 tsp baking powder
- 1/2 cup flour
- 1/4 cup grated carrot
- 1/2 tsp vanilla
- 1/2 tsp cinnamon

Directions:
1. Fit the Cuisinart oven with the rack in position 1.
2. In a medium bowl, beat sugar and oil for 1 minute. Add vanilla, cinnamon, and egg and beat for 30 seconds.
3. Add remaining ingredients and stir everything well until just combined.
4. Pour batter into the greased baking dish.
5. Set to bake at 350 F for 30 minutes. After 5 minutes place the baking dish in the preheated oven.
6. Serve and enjoy.

Nutritional Value (Amount per Serving):
Calories 340; Fat 20 g; Carbohydrates 40 g; Sugar 25 g; Protein 5 g; Cholesterol 41 mg

Baked Peaches

Preparation Time: 10 minutes; Cooking Time: 30 minutes; Serve: 4

Ingredients:
- 4 freestone peaches, cut in half and remove stones
- 2 tbsp sugar
- 8 tsp brown sugar
- 1 tsp cinnamon
- 4 tbsp butter, cut into pieces

Directions:
1. Fit the Cuisinart oven with the rack in position 1.

2. Place peach halves in a baking dish and fill each half with 1 tsp brown sugar.
3. Place butter pieces on top of each peach halves.
4. Mix together cinnamon and sugar and sprinkle over peaches.
5. Set to bake at 375 F for 30 minutes. After 5 minutes place the baking dish in the preheated oven.
6. Serve and enjoy.

Nutritional Value (Amount per Serving):
Calories 200; Fat 12 g; Carbohydrates 25 g; Sugar 22 g; Protein 1 g; Cholesterol 31 mg

Cinnamon Apple Crisp

Preparation Time: 10 minutes; Cooking Time: 35 minutes; Serve: 4

Ingredients:
- 1/8 tsp ground clove
- 1/8 tsp ground nutmeg
- 2 tbsp honey
- 4 1/2 cups apples, diced
- 1 tsp ground cinnamon
- 1 tbsp cornstarch
- 1 tsp vanilla
- 1/2 lemon juice

For topping:
- 1 cup rolled oats
- 1/3 cup coconut oil, melted
- 1 tsp cinnamon
- 1/3 cup honey
- 1/2 cup almond flour

Directions:
1. Fit the Cuisinart oven with the rack in position 1.
2. In a medium bowl, mix apples, vanilla, lemon juice, and honey. Sprinkle spices and cornstarch on top and stir well.
3. Pour apple mixture into the greased baking dish.
4. In a small bowl, mix together coconut oil, cinnamon, almond flour, oats, and honey and spread on top of apple mixture.
5. Set to bake at 350 F for 40 minutes. After 5 minutes place the baking dish in the preheated oven.
6. Serve and enjoy.

Nutritional Value (Amount per Serving):
Calories 450; Fat 21 g; Carbohydrates 65 g; Sugar 40 g; Protein 4 g; Cholesterol 0 mg

Apple Cake

Preparation Time: 10 minutes; Cooking Time: 45 minutes; Serve: 12

Ingredients:
- 2 cups apples, peeled and chopped
- 1/4 cup sugar
- 1/4 cup butter, melted
- 12 oz apple juice
- 3 cups all-purpose flour
- 3 tsp baking powder
- 1 1/2 tbsp ground cinnamon
- 1 tsp Salt

Directions:
1. Fit the Cuisinart oven with the rack in position 1.
2. In a large bowl, mix together flour, salt, sugar, cinnamon, and baking powder.
3. Add melted butter and apple juice and mix until well combined.
4. Add apples and fold well.
5. Pour batter into the greased baking dish.
6. Set to bake at 350 F for 45 minutes. After 5 minutes place the baking dish in the preheated oven.
7. Serve and enjoy.

Nutritional Value (Amount per Serving):

Calories 200; Fat 4 g; Carbohydrates 38 g; Sugar 11 g; Protein 3 g; Cholesterol 10 mg

Almond Cranberry Muffins

Preparation Time: 10 minutes; Cooking Time: 30 minutes; Serve: 6
Ingredients:
- 2 eggs
- 1 tsp vanilla
- 1/4 cup sour cream
- 1/2 cup cranberries
- 1 1/2 cups almond flour
- 1/4 tsp cinnamon
- 1 tsp baking powder
- 1/4 cup Swerve
- Pinch of salt

Directions:
1. Fit the Cuisinart oven with the rack in position 1.
2. Line 6-cups muffin tin with cupcake liners and set aside.
3. In a bowl, beat sour cream, vanilla, and eggs.
4. Add remaining ingredients except for cranberries and beat until smooth.
5. Add cranberries and fold well.
6. Pour batter into the prepared muffin tin.
7. Set to bake at 325 F for 30 minutes. After 5 minutes place muffin tin in the preheated oven.
8. Serve and enjoy.

Nutritional Value (Amount per Serving):
Calories 218; Fat 16 g; Carbohydrates 18 g; Sugar 10 g; Protein 8 g; Cholesterol 59 mg

Vanilla Butter Cake

Preparation Time: 10 minutes; Cooking Time: 30 minutes; Serve: 8
Ingredients:
- 1 egg, beaten
- 1/2 tsp vanilla
- 3/4 cup sugar
- 1 cup all-purpose flour
- 1/2 cup butter, softened

Directions:
1. Fit the Cuisinart oven with the rack in position 1.
2. In a mixing bowl, mix together sugar and butter.
3. Add egg, flour, and vanilla and mix until combined.
4. Pour batter into the greased baking dish.
5. Set to bake at 350 F for 35 minutes. After 5 minutes place the baking dish in the preheated oven.
6. Slice and serve.

Nutritional Value (Amount per Serving):
Calories 211; Fat 11 g; Carbohydrates 27 g; Sugar 16 g; Protein 2 g; Cholesterol 45 mg

Coconut Butter Apple Bars

Preparation Time: 10 minutes; Cooking Time: 45 minutes; Serve: 8
Ingredients:
- 1 tbsp ground flax seed
- 1/4 cup coconut butter, softened
- 1 cup pecans
- 1 cup of water
- 1/4 cup dried apples
- 1 1/2 tsp baking powder
- 1 1/2 tsp cinnamon
- 1 tsp vanilla
- 2 tbsp swerve

Directions:
1. Fit the Cuisinart oven with the rack in position 1.

2. Add all ingredients into the blender and blend until smooth.
3. Pour blended mixture into the greased baking dish.
4. Set to bake at 350 F for 50 minutes. After 5 minutes place the baking dish in the preheated oven.
5. Slice and serve.

Nutritional Value (Amount per Serving):
Calories 161; Fat 15 g; Carbohydrates 6 g; Sugar 2 g; Protein 2 g; Cholesterol 0 mg

Easy Blueberry Muffins

Preparation Time: 10 minutes; Cooking Time: 30 minutes; Serve: 12

Ingredients:
- 5.5 oz plain yogurt
- ½ cup fresh blueberries
- 2 tsp baking powder, gluten-free
- ¼ cup Swerve
- 2 ½ cups almond flour
- ½ tsp vanilla
- 3 eggs
- Pinch of salt

Directions:
1. Fit the Cuisinart oven with the rack in position 1.
2. Line 6-cups muffin tin with cupcake liners and set aside.
3. In a bowl, whisk egg, yogurt, vanilla, and salt until smooth.
4. Add flour, swerve and baking powder and blend again until smooth.
5. Add blueberries and stir well.
6. Pour batter into the prepared muffin tin.
7. Set to bake at 325 F for 35 minutes. After 5 minutes place muffin tin in the preheated oven.
8. Serve and enjoy.

Nutritional Value (Amount per Serving):
Calories 63; Fat 4.2 g; Carbohydrates 3.6 g; Sugar 1.8 g; Protein 3.4 g; Cholesterol 42 mg

Tasty Almond Macaroons

Preparation Time: 10 minutes; Cooking Time: 10 minutes; Serve: 36

Ingredients:
- 2 egg whites
- 10 oz almonds, sliced
- 1/2 tsp vanilla extract
- 3/4 cup Splenda

Directions:
1. Fit the Cuisinart oven with the rack in position 1.
2. In a bowl, beat egg whites until foamy then add Splenda and vanilla and blend on low.
3. Add almonds in the egg mixture and fold gently.
4. Using a scoop drop out the mixture onto the parchment-lined baking pan.
5. Set to bake at 350 F for 15 minutes. After 5 minutes place the baking pan in the preheated oven.
6. Serve and enjoy.

Nutritional Value (Amount per Serving):
Calories 67; Fat 3.9 g; Carbohydrates 5.7 g; Sugar 4.4 g; Protein 1.9 g; Cholesterol 0 mg

Moist Baked Donuts

Preparation Time: 10 minutes; Cooking Time: 15 minutes; Serve: 12

Ingredients:
- 2 eggs
- 3/4 cup sugar
- 1/2 cup buttermilk
- 1/4 cup vegetable oil
- 1 cup all-purpose flour
- 1/2 tsp vanilla

- 1 tsp baking powder
- 1/2 tsp salt

Directions:
1. Fit the Cuisinart oven with the rack in position 1.
2. Spray donut pan with cooking spray and set aside.
3. In a bowl, mix together oil, vanilla, baking powder, sugar, eggs, buttermilk, and salt until well combined.
4. Stir in flour and mix until smooth.
5. Pour batter into the prepared donut pan.
6. Set to bake at 350 F for 20 minutes. After 5 minutes place the donut pan in the preheated oven.
7. Serve and enjoy.

Nutritional Value (Amount per Serving):
Calories 140; Fat 5.5 g; Carbohydrates 21.2 g; Sugar 13.1 g; Protein 2.3 g; Cholesterol 28 mg

Eggless Brownies

Preparation Time: 10 minutes; Cooking Time: 40 minutes; Serve: 8

Ingredients:
- 1/4 cup walnuts, chopped
- 1/3 cup cocoa powder
- 2 tsp baking powder
- 1 cup of sugar
- 1 cup all-purpose flour
- 1/2 cup chocolate chips
- 2 tsp vanilla
- 1 tbsp milk
- 3/4 cup yogurt
- 1/2 cup butter, melted
- 1/4 tsp salt

Directions:
1. Fit the Cuisinart oven with the rack in position 1.
2. In a large mixing bowl, sift flour, cocoa powder, baking powder, and salt. Mix well and set aside.
3. In another bowl, add butter, vanilla, milk, and yogurt and whisk until well combined.
4. Add flour mixture into the butter mixture and mix until just combined.
5. Fold in walnuts and chocolate chips.
6. Pour batter into the prepared baking dish.
7. Set to bake at 350 F for 45 minutes. After 5 minutes place the baking dish in the preheated oven.
8. Slice and serve.

Nutritional Value (Amount per Serving):
Calories 363; Fat 18 g; Carbohydrates 48 g; Sugar 32.4 g; Protein 5.5 g; Cholesterol 34 mg

Vanilla Banana Brownies

Preparation Time: 10 minutes; Cooking Time: 20 minutes; Serve: 12

Ingredients:
- 1 egg
- 1 cup all-purpose flour
- 4 oz white chocolate
- 1/4 cup butter
- 1 tsp vanilla extract
- 1/2 cup granulated sugar
- 2 medium bananas, mashed
- 1/4 tsp salt

Directions:
1. Fit the Cuisinart oven with the rack in position 1.
2. Add white chocolate and butter in a microwave-safe bowl and microwave for 30 seconds. Stir until melted.
3. Stir in sugar. Add mashed bananas, eggs, vanilla, and salt and mix until combined.
4. Add flour and mix until just combined.

5. Pour batter into the greased baking dish.
6. Set to bake at 350 F for 25 minutes. After 5 minutes place the baking dish in the preheated oven.
7. Slice and serve.

Nutritional Value (Amount per Serving):
Calories 178; Fat 7.4 g; Carbohydrates 26.4 g; Sugar 16.4 g; Protein 2.3 g; Cholesterol 26 mg

Choco Cookies

Preparation Time: 10 minutes; Cooking Time: 8 minutes; Serve: 8
Ingredients:
- 3 egg whites
- 3/4 cup cocoa powder, unsweetened
- 1 3/4 cup confectioner sugar
- 1 1/2 tsp vanilla

Directions:
1. Fit the Cuisinart oven with the rack in position 1.
2. In a mixing bowl, whip egg whites until fluffy soft peaks. Slowly add in cocoa, sugar, and vanilla.
3. Drop teaspoonful onto parchment-lined baking pan into 32 small cookies.
4. Set to bake at 350 F for 8 minutes. After 5 minutes place the baking pan in the preheated oven.
5. Serve and enjoy.

Nutritional Value (Amount per Serving):
Calories 132; Fat 1.1 g; Carbohydrates 31 g; Sugar 0.3 g; Protein 2 g; Cholesterol 0 mg

Chocolate Chip Cookies

Preparation Time: 10 minutes; Cooking Time: 10 minutes; Serve: 30
Ingredients:
- 1 egg
- 2/3 cup sugar
- 1 tsp vanilla
- 1 cup butter, softened
- 12 oz chocolate chips
- 2 cups self-rising flour
- 1/2 cup brown sugar

Directions:
1. Fit the Cuisinart oven with the rack in position 1.
2. Add butter, vanilla, and egg in a large mixing bowl and beat until combined.
3. Add brown sugar and sugar and beat until creamy consistency.
4. Slowly add flour and mix until just combined.
5. Fold in chocolate chips.
6. Spoon out cookie dough balls onto a parchment-lined baking pan.
7. Set to bake at 375 F for 15 minutes. After 5 minutes place the baking pan in the preheated oven.
8. Serve and enjoy.

Nutritional Value (Amount per Serving):
Calories 174; Fat 9.7 g; Carbohydrates 20 g; Sugar 12.7 g; Protein 2 g; Cholesterol 24 mg

Oatmeal Cake

Preparation Time: 10 minutes; Cooking Time: 40 minutes; Serve: 8
Ingredients:
- 2 eggs, beaten
- 1 tbsp cocoa powder
- 1/2 tsp salt
- 1 tsp baking soda
- 1/2 cup butter, softened
- 1 cup granulated sugar
- 1 cup brown sugar
- 1 3/4 cups flour

- 1 cup quick oats
- 3/4 cup mix nuts, chopped
- 2 cups chocolate chips
- 1 3/4 cup boiling water

Directions:
1. Fit the Cuisinart oven with the rack in position 1.
2. Combine together boiling water and oats in a large bowl.
3. Add butter and sugar stir until butter melted.
4. Add flour, baking soda, salt, cocoa powder, 1 cup chocolate chips, half chopped nuts, and egg. Mix until combine.
5. Pour batter into the greased cake pan and sprinkle remaining nuts and chocolate chips over the top of cake batter.
6. Set to bake at 350 F for 45 minutes. After 5 minutes place the baking dish in the preheated oven.
7. Slice and serve.

Nutritional Value (Amount per Serving):
Calories 699; Fat 30.6 g; Carbohydrates 97.9 g; Sugar 4.1 g; Protein 64.8 g; Cholesterol 81 mg

Delicious Banana Cake

Preparation Time: 10 minutes; Cooking Time: 40 minutes; Serve: 8
Ingredients:
- 2 large eggs, beaten
- 1 tsp baking powder
- 1 1/2 cup sugar, granulated
- 1 tsp vanilla extract
- 1/2 cup butter
- 1 cup milk
- 2 cups all-purpose flour
- 2 bananas, mashed
- 1 tsp baking soda

Directions:
1. Fit the Cuisinart oven with the rack in position 1.
2. In a mixing bowl, beat together sugar and butter until creamy. Add beaten eggs and mix well.
3. Add milk, vanilla extract, baking soda, baking powder, flour, and mashed bananas into the mixture and beat for 2 minutes. Mix well.
4. Pour batter into the greased baking dish.
5. Set to bake at 350 F for 45 minutes. After 5 minutes place the baking dish in the preheated oven.
6. Slices and serve.

Nutritional Value (Amount per Serving):
Calories 418; Fat 13.8 g; Carbohydrates 80 g; Sugar 42.7 g; Protein 6.2 g; Cholesterol 80 mg

Chocolate Cake

Preparation Time: 10 minutes; Cooking Time: 30 minutes; Serve: 8
Ingredients:
- 1/2 cup warm water
- 2 3/4 cups flour
- 1 cup buttermilk
- 1 cup shortening
- 1 cup sugar, granulated
- 1 cup brown sugar
- 2 large eggs
- 1/2 cup cocoa powder
- 1 tsp baking soda

Directions:
1. Fit the Cuisinart oven with the rack in position 1.
2. In a large mixing bowl, beat together brown sugar, granulated sugar, and shortening until creamy.
3. Add eggs, cocoa powder, flour, and buttermilk mix well until combine.

4. Dissolve soda in warm water and stir into batter.
5. Pour batter into the greased baking dish.
6. Set to bake at 350 F for 35 minutes. After 5 minutes place the baking dish in the preheated oven.
7. Slices and serve.

Nutritional Value (Amount per Serving):
Calories 588; Fat 28.3 g; Carbohydrates 80.1 g; Sugar 44.4 g; Protein 8 g; Cholesterol 48 mg

Almond Blueberry Bars

Preparation Time: 10 minutes; Cooking Time: 50 minutes; Serve: 4
Ingredients:
- 1/4 cup blueberries
- 3 tbsp coconut oil
- 2 tbsp coconut flour
- 1/2 cup almond flour
- 3 tbsp water
- 1 tbsp chia seeds
- 1 tsp vanilla
- 1 tsp fresh lemon juice
- 2 tbsp erythritol
- 1/4 cup almonds, sliced
- 1/4 cup coconut flakes

Directions:
1. Fit the Cuisinart oven with the rack in position 1.
2. Line baking dish with parchment paper and set aside.
3. In a small bowl, mix together water and chia seeds. Set aside.
4. In a bowl, combine together all ingredients. Add chia mixture and stir well.
5. Pour mixture into the prepared baking dish and spread evenly.
6. Set to bake at 300 F for 55 minutes. After 5 minutes place the baking dish in the preheated oven.
7. Slice and serve.

Nutritional Value (Amount per Serving):
Calories 208; Fat 18.2 g; Carbohydrates 9.1 g; Sugar 2.3 g; Protein 3.6 g; Cholesterol 0 mg

Healthy Sesame Bars

Preparation Time: 10 minutes; Cooking Time: 15 minutes; Serve: 16
Ingredients:
- 1 1/4 cups sesame seeds
- 1/4 cup applesauce
- 3/4 cup coconut butter
- 10 drops liquid stevia
- 1/2 tsp vanilla
- Pinch of salt

Directions:
1. Fit the Cuisinart oven with the rack in position 1.
2. In a large bowl, add applesauce, coconut butter, vanilla, liquid stevia, and sea salt and stir until well combined.
3. Add sesame seeds and stir to coat.
4. Pour mixture into a greased baking dish.
5. Set to bake at 350 F for 20 minutes. After 5 minutes place the baking dish in the preheated oven.
6. Cut into pieces and serve.

Nutritional Value (Amount per Serving):
Calories 136; Fat 12.4 g; Carbohydrates 5.7 g; Sugar 1.2 g; Protein 2.8 g; Cholesterol 0 mg

Coconut Pumpkin Bars

Preparation Time: 10 minutes; Cooking Time: 28 minutes; Serve: 16
Ingredients:

- 2 eggs
- 1/4 cup coconut flour
- 8 oz pumpkin puree
- 1/2 cup coconut oil, melted
- 1/3 cup Swerve
- 1 1/2 tsp pumpkin pie spice
- 1/2 tsp baking soda
- 1 tsp baking powder
- Pinch of salt

Directions:
1. Fit the Cuisinart oven with the rack in position 1.
2. In a bowl, beat eggs, sweetener, coconut oil, pumpkin pie spice, and pumpkin puree until well combined.
3. In another bowl, mix together baking powder, coconut flour, salt, and baking soda.
4. Add coconut flour mixture to the egg mixture and mix well.
5. Pour the bar mixture into the prepared baking pan and spread evenly.
6. Set to bake at 350 F for 33 minutes. After 5 minutes place the baking dish in the preheated oven.
7. Slice and serve.

Nutritional Value (Amount per Serving):
Calories 73; Fat 7.5 g; Carbohydrates 1.6 g; Sugar 0.5 g; Protein 0.9 g; Cholesterol 20 mg

Almond Peanut Butter Bars

Preparation Time: 10 minutes; Cooking Time: 30 minutes; Serve: 8
Ingredients:
- 2 eggs
- 1/2 cup erythritol
- 1/2 cup butter softened
- 1/2 cup peanut butter
- 1 tbsp coconut flour
- 1/2 cup almond flour

Directions:
1. Fit the Cuisinart oven with the rack in position 1.
2. In a bowl, beat together butter, eggs, and peanut butter until well combined.
3. Add dry ingredients and mix until a smooth batter is formed.
4. Spread batter evenly in greased baking pan.
5. Set to bake at 350 F for 35 minutes. After 5 minutes place the baking pan in the preheated oven.
6. Slice and serve.

Nutritional Value (Amount per Serving):
Calories 168; Fat 12.5 g; Carbohydrates 9.7 g; Sugar 1.8 g; Protein 6.5 g; Cholesterol 41 mg

Delicious Lemon Bars

Preparation Time: 10 minutes; Cooking Time: 40 minutes; Serve: 8
Ingredients:
- 4 eggs
- 1 lemon zest
- 1/4 cup fresh lemon juice
- 1/2 cup butter softened
- 1/2 cup sour cream
- 1/3 cup erythritol
- 2 tsp baking powder
- 2 cups almond flour

Directions:
1. Fit the Cuisinart oven with the rack in position 1.
2. In a bowl, beat eggs until frothy.
3. Add butter and sour cream and beat until well combined.
4. Add sweetener, lemon zest, and lemon juice and blend well.
5. Add baking powder and almond flour and mix until well combined.
6. Transfer batter in a greased baking pan and spread evenly.

7. Set to bake at 350 F for 45 minutes. After 5 minutes place the baking pan in the preheated oven.
   8. Slice and serve.

Nutritional Value (Amount per Serving):
Calories 147; Fat 10.9 g; Carbohydrates 8.8 g; Sugar 0.8 g; Protein 5.3 g; Cholesterol 88 mg

Easy Egg Custard

Preparation Time: 10 minutes; Cooking Time: 40 minutes; Serve: 6
Ingredients:
- 2 egg yolks
- 1 tsp nutmeg
- 1/2 cup erythritol
- 2 cups heavy whipping cream
- 3 eggs
- 1/2 tsp vanilla

Directions:
1. Fit the Cuisinart oven with the rack in position 1.
2. Add all ingredients into the large mixing bowl and beat until just well combined.
3. Pour custard mixture into the greased pie dish.
4. Set to bake at 350 F for 40 minutes. After 5 minutes place the pie dish in the preheated oven.
5. Serve.

Nutritional Value (Amount per Serving):
Calories 190; Fat 18.6 g; Carbohydrates 1.7 g; Sugar 0.4 g; Protein 4.5 g; Cholesterol 207 mg

Flavors Pumpkin Custard

Preparation Time: 10 minutes; Cooking Time: 40 minutes; Serve: 6
Ingredients:
- 4 egg yolks
- 1/2 tsp cinnamon
- 1 tsp liquid stevia
- 15 oz pumpkin puree
- 3/4 cup coconut cream
- 1/8 tsp cloves
- 1/8 tsp ginger

Directions:
1. Fit the Cuisinart oven with the rack in position 1.
2. In a large bowl, mix together pumpkin puree, cloves, ginger, cinnamon, and swerve.
3. Add egg yolks and beat until well combined.
4. Add coconut cream and stir well.
5. Pour mixture into the six ramekins.
6. Set to bake at 350 F for 45 minutes. After 5 minutes place ramekins in the preheated oven.
7. Serve chilled and enjoy.

Nutritional Value (Amount per Serving):
Calories 130; Fat 10.4 g; Carbohydrates 8 g; Sugar 3.4 g; Protein 3.3 g; Cholesterol 140 mg

Almond Butter Cookies

Preparation Time: 10 minutes; Cooking Time: 15 minutes; Serve: 15
Ingredients:
- 1 egg
- 1/2 cup erythritol
- 1 cup almond butter
- 1 tsp vanilla
- Pinch of salt

Directions:
1. Fit the Cuisinart oven with the rack in position 1.
2. Add all ingredients into the large bowl and mix until well combined.

3. Make cookies from bowl mixture and place on a parchment-lined baking pan.
4. Set to bake at 350 F for 20 minutes. After 5 minutes place the baking pan in the preheated oven.
5. Serve.

Nutritional Value (Amount per Serving):
Calories 12; Fat 0.9 g; Carbohydrates 0.3 g; Sugar 0.1 g; Protein 0.6 g; Cholesterol 11 mg

Tasty Pumpkin Cookies

Preparation Time: 10 minutes; Cooking Time: 25 minutes; Serve: 27
Ingredients:
- 1 egg
- 2 cups almond flour
- 1/2 tsp baking powder
- 1 tsp vanilla
- 1/2 cup butter
- 1 tsp liquid stevia
- 1/2 tsp pumpkin pie spice
- 1/2 cup pumpkin puree

Directions:
1. Fit the Cuisinart oven with the rack in position 1.
2. In a large bowl, add all ingredients and mix until well combined.
3. Make cookies from mixture and place onto a parchment-lined baking pan.
4. Set to bake at 300 F for 30 minutes. After 5 minutes place the baking dish in the preheated oven.
5. Serve and enjoy.

Nutritional Value (Amount per Serving):
Calories 46; Fat 4.6 g; Carbohydrates 0.9 g; Sugar 0.3 g; Protein 0.7 g; Cholesterol 15 mg

Almond Pecan Cookies

Preparation Time: 10 minutes; Cooking Time: 20 minutes; Serve: 16
Ingredients:
- 1/2 cup butter
- 1 tsp vanilla
- 2 tsp gelatin
- 2/3 cup Swerve
- 1 cup pecans
- 1/3 cup coconut flour
- 1 cup almond flour

Directions:
1. Fit the Cuisinart oven with the rack in position 1.
2. Add butter, vanilla, gelatin, swerve, coconut flour, and almond flour into the food processor and process until crumbs form.
3. Add pecans and process until chopped.
4. Make cookies from prepared mixture and place onto a parchment-lined baking pan.
5. Set to bake at 350 F for 25 minutes. After 5 minutes place the baking pan in the preheated oven.
6. Serve and enjoy.

Nutritional Value (Amount per Serving):
Calories 101; Fat 10.2 g; Carbohydrates 1.4 g; Sugar 0.3 g; Protein 1.8 g; Cholesterol 15 mg

Butter Cookies

Preparation Time: 10 minutes; Cooking Time: 15 minutes; Serve: 24
Ingredients:
- 1 egg, lightly beaten
- 1 tsp vanilla
- 3/4 cup Swerve
- 1 1/4 cups almond flour
- 1 tsp baking powder
- 1 stick butter
- Pinch of salt

Directions:
1. Fit the Cuisinart oven with the rack in position 1.
2. In a bowl, beat butter and sweetener until creamy.
3. In a separate bowl, mix together almond flour and baking powder.
4. Add egg and vanilla in butter mixture and beat until smooth.
5. Add dry ingredients to the wet ingredients and mix until well combined.
6. Wrap dough in plastic wrap and place in the fridge for 1 hour.
7. Make cookies from dough and place onto a parchment-lined baking pan.
8. Set to bake at 325 F for 20 minutes. After 5 minutes place the baking pan in the preheated oven.
9. Serve and enjoy.

Nutritional Value (Amount per Serving):
Calories 46; Fat 4.7 g; Carbohydrates 0.5 g; Sugar 0.1 g; Protein 0.6 g; Cholesterol 17 mg

Tasty Brownie Cookies

Preparation Time: 10 minutes; Cooking Time: 10 minutes; Serve: 14
Ingredients:
- 1 egg
- 1/2 cup erythritol
- 1/4 cup cocoa powder
- 1 cup almond butter
- 3 tbsp milk
- 1/4 cup chocolate chips

Directions:
1. Fit the Cuisinart oven with the rack in position 1.
2. In a bowl, mix together almond butter, egg, sweetener, almond milk, and cocoa powder until well combined.
3. Stir in Chocó chips.
4. Make cookies from dough and place onto a parchment-lined baking pan.
5. Set to bake at 350 F for 15 minutes. After 5 minutes place the baking pan in the preheated oven.
6. Serve and enjoy.

Nutritional Value (Amount per Serving):
Calories 33; Fat 2.1 g; Carbohydrates 11.6 g; Sugar 10.6 g; Protein 1.3 g; Cholesterol 13 mg

Tasty Gingersnap Cookies

Preparation Time: 10 minutes; Cooking Time: 10 minutes; Serve: 8
Ingredients:
- 1 egg
- 1/2 tsp ground cinnamon
- 1/2 tsp ground ginger
- 1 tsp baking powder
- 3/4 cup erythritol
- 1/2 tsp vanilla
- 1/8 tsp ground cloves
- 1/4 tsp ground nutmeg
- 2/4 cup butter, melted
- 1 1/2 cups almond flour
- Pinch of salt

Directions:
1. Fit the Cuisinart oven with the rack in position 1.
2. In a mixing bowl, mix together all dry ingredients.
3. In another bowl, mix together all wet ingredients.
4. Add dry ingredients to the wet ingredients and mix until a dough-like mixture is formed.
5. Cover and place in the refrigerator for 30 minutes.
6. Make cookies from dough and place onto a parchment-lined baking pan.
7. Set to bake at 350 F for 15 minutes. After 5 minutes place the baking pan in the preheated oven.

8. Serve and enjoy.

Nutritional Value (Amount per Serving):
Calories 142; Fat 14.7 g; Carbohydrates 1.8 g; Sugar 0.3 g; Protein 2 g; Cholesterol 51 mg

Simple Lemon Pie

Preparation Time: 10 minutes; Cooking Time: 45 minutes; Serve: 8

Ingredients:
- 3 eggs
- 3.5 oz butter, melted
- 3 lemon juice
- 1 lemon zest, grated
- 4 oz erythritol
- 5.5 oz almond flour
- Salt

Directions:
1. Fit the Cuisinart oven with the rack in position 1.
2. In a bowl, mix together butter, 1 oz sweetener, 3 oz almond flour, and salt.
3. Transfer the dough in a pie dish and spread evenly and bake for 20 minutes.
4. In a separate bowl, mix together eggs, lemon juice, lemon zest, remaining flour, sweetener, and salt.
5. Pour egg mixture on prepared crust.
6. Set to bake at 350 F for 35 minutes. After 5 minutes place the pie dish in the preheated oven.
7. Slice and serve.

Nutritional Value (Amount per Serving):
Calories 229; Fat 21.5 g; Carbohydrates 5.3 g; Sugar 1.4 g; Protein 6.5 g; Cholesterol 88 mg

Flavorful Coconut Cake

Preparation Time: 10 minutes; Cooking Time: 20 minutes; Serve: 8

Ingredients:
- 5 eggs, separated
- 1/2 cup erythritol
- 1/4 cup coconut milk
- 1/2 cup coconut flour
- 1/2 tsp baking powder
- 1/2 tsp vanilla
- 1/2 cup butter softened
- Pinch of salt

Directions:
1. Fit the Cuisinart oven with the rack in position 1.
2. Grease cake pan with butter and set aside.
3. In a bowl, beat sweetener and butter until combined.
4. Add egg yolks, coconut milk, and vanilla and mix well.
5. Add baking powder, coconut flour, and salt and stir well.
6. In another bowl, beat egg whites until stiff peak forms.
7. Gently fold egg whites into the cake mixture.
8. Pour batter in a prepared cake pan.
9. Set to bake at 400 F for 25 minutes. After 5 minutes place the cake pan in the preheated oven.
10. Slice and serve.

Nutritional Value (Amount per Serving):
Calories 84; Fat 5.9 g; Carbohydrates 4.2 g; Sugar 0.6 g; Protein 4 g; Cholesterol 102 mg

Easy Lemon Cheesecake

Preparation Time: 10 minutes; Cooking Time: 55 minutes; Serve: 8

Ingredients:
- 4 eggs
- 2 tbsp swerve

- 1 fresh lemon juice
- 18 oz ricotta cheese
- 1 fresh lemon zest

Directions:
1. Fit the Cuisinart oven with the rack in position 1.
2. In a large bowl, beat ricotta cheese until smooth.
3. Add egg one by one and whisk well.
4. Add lemon juice, lemon zest, and swerve and mix well.
5. Transfer mixture into the greased cake pan.
6. Set to bake at 350 F for 60 minutes. After 5 minutes place the cake pan in the preheated oven.
7. Slice and serve.

Nutritional Value (Amount per Serving):
Calories 122; Fat 7.3 g; Carbohydrates 4.2 g; Sugar 0.5 g; Protein 10.1 g; Cholesterol 102 mg

Lemon Butter Cake

Preparation Time: 10 minutes; Cooking Time: 55 minutes; Serve: 10
Ingredients:
- 4 eggs
- 1/2 cup butter softened
- 2 tsp baking powder
- 1/4 cup coconut flour
- 2 cups almond flour
- 2 tbsp lemon zest
- 1/2 cup fresh lemon juice
- 1/4 cup erythritol
- 1 tbsp vanilla

Directions:
1. Fit the Cuisinart oven with the rack in position 1.
2. In a large bowl, whisk all ingredients until a smooth batter is formed.
3. Pour batter into the loaf pan.
4. Set to bake at 300 F for 60 minutes. After 5 minutes place the loaf pan in the preheated oven.
5. Slice and serve.

Nutritional Value (Amount per Serving):
Calories 85; Fat 5.7 g; Carbohydrates 5 g; Sugar 0.9 g; Protein 3.8 g; Cholesterol 65 mg

Cream Cheese Butter Cake

Preparation Time: 10 minutes; Cooking Time: 35 minutes; Serve: 8
Ingredients:
- 5 eggs
- 1 cup Swerve
- 4 oz cream cheese, softened
- 1 tsp vanilla
- 1 tsp orange extract
- 1 tsp baking powder
- 6.5 oz almond flour
- 1/2 cup butter, softened

Directions:
1. Fit the Cuisinart oven with the rack in position 1.
2. Add all ingredients into the mixing bowl and whisk until batter is fluffy.
3. Pour batter into the prepared cake pan.
4. Set to bake at 350 F for 40 minutes. After 5 minutes place the cake pan in the preheated oven.
5. Slices and serve.

Nutritional Value (Amount per Serving):
Calories 325; Fat 30.6 g; Carbohydrates 6.2 g; Sugar 1.2 g; Protein 9.5 g; Cholesterol 148 mg

Easy Ricotta Cake

Preparation Time: 10 minutes; Cooking Time: 45 minutes; Serve: 8
Ingredients:
- 2 eggs
- 1/2 cup erythritol
- 1/4 cup coconut flour
- 15 oz ricotta
- Pinch of salt

Directions:
1. Fit the Cuisinart oven with the rack in position 1.
2. In a bowl whisk eggs.
3. Add remaining ingredients and mix until well combined.
4. Transfer batter in greased cake pan.
5. Set to bake at 350 F for 50 minutes. After 5 minutes place the cake pan in the preheated oven.
6. Slice and serve.

Nutritional Value (Amount per Serving):
Calories 91; Fat 5.4 g; Carbohydrates 3.1 g; Sugar 0.3 g; Protein 7.5 g; Cholesterol 57 mg

Strawberry Muffins

Preparation Time: 10 minutes; Cooking Time: 20 minutes; Serve: 12
Ingredients:
- 4 eggs
- 1/4 cup water
- 1/2 cup butter, melted
- 2 tsp baking powder
- 2 cups almond flour
- 2/3 cup strawberries, chopped
- 2 tsp vanilla
- 1/4 cup erythritol
- Pinch of salt

Directions:
1. Fit the Cuisinart oven with the rack in position 1.
2. Line 12-cups muffin tin with cupcake liners and set aside.
3. In a medium bowl, mix together almond flour, baking powder, and salt.
4. In a separate bowl, whisk eggs, sweetener, vanilla, water, and butter.
5. Add almond flour mixture into the egg mixture and mix until well combined.
6. Add strawberries and stir well.
7. Pour batter into the prepared muffin tin.
8. Set to bake at 350 F for 25 minutes. After 5 minutes place muffin tin in the preheated oven.
9. Serve and enjoy.

Nutritional Value (Amount per Serving):
Calories 201; Fat 18.5 g; Carbohydrates 5.2 g; Sugar 1.3 g; Protein 6 g; Cholesterol 75 mg

Mini Brownie Muffins

Preparation Time: 10 minutes; Cooking Time: 15 minutes; Serve: 6
Ingredients:
- 3 eggs
- 1/2 cup Swerve
- 1 cup almond flour
- 1 tbsp gelatin
- 1/3 cup butter, melted
- 1/3 cup cocoa powder

Directions:
1. Fit the Cuisinart oven with the rack in position 1.
2. Line 6-cups muffin tin with cupcake liners and set aside.
3. Add all ingredients into the mixing bowl and stir until well combined.
4. Pour mixture into the prepared muffin tin.

5. Set to bake at 350 F for 20 minutes. After 5 minutes place muffin tin in the preheated oven.
6. Serve and enjoy.

Nutritional Value (Amount per Serving):
Calories 163; Fat 15.4 g; Carbohydrates 4 g; Sugar 0.4 g; Protein 5.8 g; Cholesterol 109 mg

Chapter 9: 30-Day Meal Plan

Day 1
Breakfast- Breakfast Oatmeal Cake
Lunch- Juicy Baked Chicken Breast
Dinner- Perfect Beef Hashbrown Bake

Day 2
Breakfast- Easy Cheese Egg Casserole
Lunch- Tender & Juicy Cajun Cod
Dinner- Juicy & Tender Pork Chops

Day 3
Breakfast- Delicious Baked Eggs
Lunch- Baked Spinach Cheese Chicken
Dinner- Ranch Pork Chops

Day 4
Breakfast- Healthy Baked Oatmeal
Lunch- Spicy Lemon Garlic Tilapia
Dinner- Pesto Pork Chops

Day 5
Breakfast- Easy Apple Pie Baked Oatmeal
Lunch- Green chili Chicken Noodle Casserole
Dinner- Pork Chops with Potatoes

Day 6
Breakfast- Delicious Broccoli Quiche
Lunch- Cajun Red Snapper
Dinner- Curried Beef Patties

Day 7
Breakfast- Tator Tots Casserole
Lunch- Baked Chicken Noodle Casserole
Dinner- Crunchy Parmesan Pork Chops

Day 8
Breakfast- Cheesy Hash Brown Casserole
Lunch- Perfect Baked Cod
Dinner- Cheesy Pork Chops

Day 9
Breakfast- Egg Ham Casserole
Lunch- Simple & Healthy Baked Chicken Breasts
Dinner- Baked Pork Ribs

Day 10
Breakfast- Hashbrown Breakfast Casserole
Lunch- Flavorful Baked Halibut
Dinner- Herb Beef Tips

Day 11
Breakfast- Flavorful Zucchini Frittata
Lunch- Flavorful Lemon Pepper Chicken
Dinner- Curried Beef Patties

Day 12
Breakfast- Mushroom Sausage Breakfast Bake
Lunch- Healthy Haddock
Dinner- Delicious Lamb Patties

Day 13
Breakfast- Delicious Baked Omelet
Lunch- Delicious Tender Chicken Breasts
Dinner- Tender Pork Tenderloin

Day 14
Breakfast- Spicy Egg Casserole
Lunch- Delicious Baked Basa
Dinner- Baked Sweet & Tangy Pork Chops

Day 15
Breakfast- Mediterranean Spinach Frittata
Lunch- Potato Garlic Chicken
Dinner- Curried Beef Patties

Day 16
Breakfast- Breakfast Oatmeal Cake
Lunch- Juicy Baked Chicken Breast
Dinner- Perfect Beef Hashbrown Bake

Day 17
Breakfast- Easy Cheese Egg Casserole
Lunch- Tender & Juicy Cajun Cod
Dinner- Juicy & Tender Pork Chops

Day 18
Breakfast- Delicious Baked Eggs
Lunch- Baked Spinach Cheese Chicken
Dinner- Ranch Pork Chops
Day 19
Breakfast- Healthy Baked Oatmeal
Lunch- Spicy Lemon Garlic Tilapia
Dinner- Pesto Pork Chops
Day 20
Breakfast- Easy Apple Pie Baked Oatmeal
Lunch- Green chili Chicken Noodle Casserole
Dinner- Pork Chops with Potatoes
Day 21
Breakfast- Delicious Broccoli Quiche
Lunch- Cajun Red Snapper
Dinner- Delicious Lamb Patties
Day 22
Breakfast- Tator Tots Casserole
Lunch- Baked Chicken Noodle Casserole
Dinner- Crunchy Parmesan Pork Chops
Day 23
Breakfast- Cheesy Hash Brown Casserole
Lunch- Perfect Baked Cod
Dinner- Cheesy Pork Chops
Day 24
Breakfast- Egg Ham Casserole
Lunch- Simple & Healthy Baked Chicken Breasts
Dinner- Baked Pork Ribs
Day 25
Breakfast- Hashbrown Breakfast Casserole
Lunch- Flavorful Baked Halibut
Dinner- Herb Beef Tips
Day 26
Breakfast- Flavorful Zucchini Frittata
Lunch- Flavorful Lemon Pepper Chicken
Dinner- Curried Beef Patties
Day 27
Breakfast- Mushroom Sausage Breakfast Bake
Lunch- Healthy Haddock
Dinner- Delicious Lamb Patties
Day 28
Breakfast- Delicious Baked Omelet
Lunch- Delicious Tender Chicken Breasts
Dinner- Tender Pork Tenderloin
Day 29
Breakfast- Spicy Egg Casserole
Lunch- Delicious Baked Basa
Dinner- Baked Sweet & Tangy Pork Chops
Day 30
Breakfast- Mediterranean Spinach Frittata
Lunch- Potato Garlic Chicken
Dinner- Curried Beef Patties

Conclusion

The Cuisinart air fryer toaster oven has a versatile cooking appliance which broils, air fry, toast, bake, and reheat your foods. The oven circulates hot air into the cooking chamber to cook food faster and evenly without any cold spot. The Cuisinart oven comes with large enough space which is capable to handle a large number of foods like chicken, small size pizzas, and more.

The Cuisinart air fryer toaster oven book includes healthy and delicious recipes range from breakfast to desserts. The recipes written in this cookbook are easily understandable form and written with their perfect preparation and cooking time. All the recipes are unique and at end of each recipe written with their nutritional value information.